Drunk
the
Night Before

Drunk
the
Night Before

An Anatomy of Intoxication

MARTY ROTH

UNIVERSITY OF MINNESOTA PRESS

MINNEAPOLIS • LONDON

The publication of this book was assisted by a bequest from Josiah H. Chase to honor his parents, Ellen Rankin Chase and Josiah Hook Chase, Minnesota territorial pioneers.

Published by the University of Minnesota Press
111 Third Avenue South, Suite 290
Minneapolis, MN 55401-2520
http://www.upress.umn.edu

Library of Congress Cataloging-in-Publication Data

Roth, Marty, 1934-
    Drunk the night before : an anatomy of intoxication / Marty Roth.
       p. cm.
    Includes bibliographical references and index.
    ISBN 0-8166-4397-0 (hc/j : alk. paper)
    1. Drinking of alcoholic beverages in literature. I. Title.

PN56.D8R68 2005
809'.933556—dc22

                                                              2005002022

Printed in the United States of America on acid-free paper

The University of Minnesota is an equal-opportunity educator and employer.

12 11 10 09 08 07 06 05   10 9 8 7 6 5 4 3 2 1

For Martha, Elinor, Grey, and Profirio

Crowned with clusters of the Vine;
Come let us sit and quaff our wine.
Call on Bacchus; chaunt his praise;
Shake the Thyrse, and bite the Bayes:
Rouse Anacreon from the dead;
And return him drunk to bed:
Sing o'er Horace; for ere long
Death will come and mar the song.

—ROBERT HERRICK

Truly, this thirst for a kind of liquid round which nature wrapped so many veils, this strange desire that assails the whole race of men, in every zone and climate of the world, is most worthy to be taken note of by philosophers.

—JEAN ANTHELME BRILLAT-SAVARIN

Historians wish to avoid naively falling into the traps laid by the words that appear in the sources, and to show themselves better able to interpret the silences and perceive what is implicit. Nowhere is this more important than in the history of time and of desire.

—ALAIN CORBIN

Contents

Acknowledgments

This work would not have taken the shape it has without the examples of Roger Forseth and Tom Gilmore in the field of addiction and culture studies, and Roy Porter, Marcel Détienne, and Alain Corbin in cultural history.

Closer to home, I am grateful to Tom Augst, Roger Forseth, Kurt Heinselman, Catherine Liu, John Mowitt, John Watkins, and the late George Wedge for careful readings of parts of this book.

Martha Roth read every word, several times, and, as always, offered affection, support, and expert advice.

Introduction

For the purposes of this study, the great event in the history of the West was a shift in the valence of alcohol in the mid-nineteenth century from a register of intoxication to one of addiction.[1] Drinking and its effects came to be talked of in ways that were so different from previous discourse—as a substance that enslaved, for example, rather than one that elevated and released—that it's hard to believe they referred to the same object. It was as radical a change as one could imagine, from convivial to miserable, sociable to antisocial, healthy to diseased.

In his essay on the bacchanal paintings of Titian and Velázquez, José Ortega y Gasset bemoaned this sociological change:

> Once, long before wine became an administrative problem, Bacchus was a god, wine was divine. . . . Yet our solution is symptomatic of the dullness of our age, its administrative hypertrophy, its morbidly cautious preoccupation with today's trivia and tomorrow's problems, its total lack of the heroic spirit. Who has now a gaze penetrating enough to see beyond alcoholism—a mountain of printed papers loaded with statistics—to the simple image of twining vine-tendrils and broad clusters of grapes pierced by the golden arrows of the sun. (15)

To some extent, this shift may be imaginary. It may be that addictive drinking was nothing new in fact but a new configuration of the social record.[2] Certainly there is an ample record of miserable drinking that stretches back as far as documents go. On the other hand, this change may be as well founded as historical generalizations can be, the result of some mixture of distillation, industrialization, urbanization, medicalization, secularization, any number of causes that are necessary but not sufficient. With the entrance of distilled liquors onto the social scene, Michael Marrus writes, "even the quality of drunkenness was held to be different. With wine there was an 'ivresse gaie et bon enfant; l'ivresse gauloise.' With spirits, on the other hand, there was an unsavory kind of drunkenness . . . leading to alcoholism and all forms of social disorder" (120). Wolfgang Schivelbusch connects such a reevaluation of heavy drinking—from jolly to grotesque and disgusting—with Reformation sensibility as represented by Martin Luther (31).

The same story could be told of drugs in the West. In his recent study of the "psychoactive revolution," David Courtwright narrativizes this radical shift in modality as industrial societies turning against their own pleasure and profit, shutting down or constraining widespread drug enterprises that had been in active operation since the Renaissance. Ironically, the regime of splendor corresponded to a scarcity of substances, the regime of misery to unimaginable abundance. Courtwright begins his book by describing the habits of an exemplary individual, a petty bootlegger who led a life "of such continuous and varied stimulation and psychoactive pleasure that no emperor, no despot, no potentate of the ancient world, however wealthy, determined or decadent, could have matched" (2).

To complicate matters, intoxication itself is dual: intoxication was not only convivial but was divided into zones of pleasure and pain. How should one relate the pain of intoxication to the pain of addiction? It may be that they are the same, the former signaling the "always already" of addiction at the core of pleasure. But I imagine them to be different, the pain of intoxication being a fierce pleasure like the *jouissance* of Roland Barthes, that second "pleasure" that he needed to "distinguish euphoria, fulfillment, comfort (the feeling of repletion when culture penetrates freely), from shock, disruption, even loss, which are proper to ecstasy" (Culler 98). If Dionysus is drink, then drink in *The Bacchae* is divine but very bad for you. While the Anacreontic text speaks of intoxication as salutory, the Euripidean text expresses it as demonic. At the beginning of a book, which I've implied would be devoted to happy drinking, intoxication also appears as rage and madness. But the truth of drink has always been a continuous dualism; intoxication, however defined, carries along with its bliss a heavy charge of violence, madness, and pain.

The present volume is a study only of the first of these two registers, intoxication. This is not a book about addiction, even though several of the chapters inevitably slide into that later moment in the history of drinking, particularly the treatment of Robert Louis Stevenson's *Strange Case of Dr. Jekyll and Mr. Hyde* in the chapter on potions and elixirs. Addiction will be the province of a separate volume. This book tries to end when intoxication is no longer fun, even though such a move is not always possible. Conversely, the conviviality of heavy drinking, like the Newtonian universe, often persists into the present in a state of forced innocence, disavowing any shadow of addiction—and sometimes seems truly reborn, as in Hollywood comedies of the 1930s and 1940s and the psychedelic scene of the 1960s.

The opposition between intoxication and addiction takes a variety of forms: popular stereotypes about southern (Latin) versus northern drinking, for example, or William Hogarth's matched pair of engravings, "Beer Street" and "Gin Lane." High and popular culture were read by twentieth-century commentary as intoxicatory, as opposed to addictive, art. The café of French Impressionist painting was located somewhere between a genial utopia of the senses and the dreary monotony of everyday life—the café of Toulouse-Lautrec as opposed to that of Degas. In a 1981 dissertation, D. M. Thomas presents a decisive shift in the portrayal of drunkenness in English fiction from the harmless comic drinkers of Charles Dickens to the grim and sodden alcoholics in Thomas Hardy's novels. In the present study, this opposition appears as several sets of conflicts: Dionysus and Pentheus in *The Bacchae;* Shakespeare's comedies and tragedies (André Simon divides the Shakespearean canon into Elizabethan and Jacobean, plays "of the poet's happy wine-drinking days, and those of his morbid spirit-drinking nights"); Romantic light verse and major Romantic poetry; the two categories of fictional elixirs—the elixir of youth as opposed to the love potion; and the difference between Mikhail Bakhtin's two great exemplary artists, Rabelais and Dostoyevsky (Simon 1964, 15).

There is a moment in Billy Wilder's *Lost Weekend* when the alcoholic Don Birnam finds himself trapped in the audience during a performance of *La Traviata*. Birnam has been without liquor for the space of the opera: the bottle he always carries with him is now hanging in the cloakroom. As a result, he is plagued by his craving as it is fed by both the matter and style of the musical representation. What he sees is a dream of an old happy drinking, far different from his present sickness: the Brindisi scene. The tenor holds a full glass of champagne in the center of the film frame, much like the sixteenth-century paintings of merry drinkers by Jan Steen, Frans Hals, or Judith Leyster. The chorus raise their glasses in turn and all drink. A footman with a full bottle refills the glasses, tilting his head with the tilt of the bottle. The lead singers entwine their arms with their glasses and drink to one another. We see the chorus in close-up swaying back and forth. The footman stands by an ice container filled with cooling bottles.

As a consequence of this book's commitment to intoxication, I should refuse entrance to drugs as a separate category of psychoactive experience, although not to drugs as a subcategory of alcohol (they are helplessly thought of in both ways).[3] In the first case, professional opinion repeatedly claims that drugs are not intoxicating, just addicting. Nineteenth-century medical men, according to Virginia Berridge, were agreed that "moderation [in opium use] was impossible, addiction inevitable and moral and physical decline the result"(198): "The smallest use leads infallibly to an intemperate use," as one expert involved in the anti-opium side of the British Opium Wars debate put it (Harding 31). Drink and drugs thus exemplify the distinction between intoxication and addiction.

A review of recent publications on alcohol and culture by Tom Gilmore, Tom Dardis, John Crowley, Nicholas Warner, Anya Taylor, and Jane Lilienfeld shows clearly that the subject of drinking practices has no critical purchase on cultural studies except as it is inflected by addiction. Addiction also has an extensive medical discourse devoted to it, occupying, as it does, a strategic place in the organization of mental disease. While there are many individual studies of drinking practices, drink production, and drunkenness as a public issue, only addiction and temperance engage our historical narratives, and intoxication is lost as so much white noise. The cultural archives may be filled with the records of intoxication, but the corresponding commentary and theory are sparse.[4]

Intoxication is a "lost object" of social and cultural history in several senses. For one thing, a salient feature of addiction is the loss of intoxication (i.e., the difficulty or impossibility for an addict to experience drinking pleasure). Conversely, until the very late stages of the disease, the alcoholic is the person who looks and acts least like a drunk: the mark of alcoholism is tolerance, which is a *drunken performance of sobriety,* as the following dialogue by the nineteenth-century Scots writer John Wilson (a.k.a. "Christopher North") indicates:

TICKLER: I never saw you the worse o' liquor in my life, James.
SHEPHERD: Nor me you.
NORTH: None but your sober men ever get drunk.
(Daiches 49)

But intoxication is also a lost object because it is untheorized. Writing of French drinking songs, Walter Besant said:

These songs, so natural, so gay and lighthearted, want no critic's talk. . . . They are only drinking songs; there is very little humor in them; there are no tears, but there is fun in them; a dance in the measure, and a clashing of rhymes and words that goes well to the clashing of the glasses on the table as the singer trolls out his thirsty strains. (96–97)

Intoxication is visible and untheorized; addiction is invisible (alcoholics can hide within the folds of social drinking so as not to be identifiable) and overtheorized.[5] Ray Oldenburg notes that intoxication was literally lost in the modern study of drinking practices:

No such myopia [overlooking the delights of sociable drinking] was intended fifty years ago when the Yale Center of Alcohol Studies was initiated. Unfortunately, its "broad focus" which was to include drinking in everyday life as distinct from alcoholism was "lost on the mainstream of American sociology, which has tended to regard the subject matter as alcoholism and to treat it as a narrow subfield of social problems." (30–31)

One condition of alcohol's enduring presence in the work of art and the life of the artist has been that it may not signify itself or its proper effects. In this, as in so many other areas of culture, Western thought expresses a terror of the literal. In a story like Ernest Hemingway's "Hills Like White Elephants" or a painting like Jan Steen's *Wedding at Cana,* the drinking and intoxication lurk below the threshold of signification. The Hemingway story is much more about drinking than it is about abortion or a tenuous, failing relationship, but given how signification operates, it may not be understood to be about drinking. As signifiers, alcohol and intoxication are culturally inhibited, both presemantic and presymbolic: they cannot enter a field of metaphoric reflection or cogent relationship. In both the Hemingway tale and the Steen painting there is a constant hum of alcoholic reference that should dominate all other indicators of meaning and yet can be apprehended only as cultural white noise. The wild behavior of Euripides' maenads keeps engaging three vague, abstract, and undefined causes (ecstasy, possession, and madness) and one material cause (drunkenness), but culture keeps advancing the former and eliding the latter.

Drinking tends to recede into the background against which meaning figures itself. Edmund Husserl called such data *hyle:* content that is perceived but dismissed as not being meant (Buck-Morss 1992, 28). Following Raymond Williams, we might categorize the history of intoxication as unvoiced history, the history of "what hadn't quite been said" (Gallagher 2000, 62). Williams distinguished between "signifying systems that announce signification as their primary function" and systems (like food and money) that "dissolve" signification in other processes. "Food and money, therefore," Catherine Gallagher adds, "are not manifestly cultural because as signifying systems they are too much 'in solution'" (1995, 313).

The two most salient texts I look at are Euripides' *Bacchae* and Plato's *Symposium.* Intoxication is not present in the first; in the second, intoxication is everywhere present but denied to be operative. In the chapters on spiritual intoxication and artistic inspiration, intoxication is hidden in plain sight. Like the cultural history of any state or process mantled in shame, the history of intoxication is also a secret, or underground, history in which the object of study is hidden from the epistemological gaze in figures that suppress or displace it. Europe, according to Max Horkheimer and Theodor Adorno, has two histories: "A well-known, written history and an underground history. The latter consists in the fate of the human instincts and passions which are displaced and distorted by civilization," largely, the history of the senses and sensibilities (231).

Alain Corbin opens his history of smell thus: "But how many historians have given us the smell of previous societies. Researchers have been all too silent, repelled, it seems, by modern hygienic sensibilities from even contemplating the stench of the past. Smell—both as an emanation of material culture and as part of the empire of the senses—though fundamental to experience has been neglected by scholars" (v). The history of intoxication is also a "history from below," but not in E. P. Thompson's sense of that phrase. If it is an underground history, it is so in the sense practiced by Mikhail Bakhtin in his study of Rabelais or Dominique Laporte in *Histoire de la merde*.

When intoxication gains a voice, it is all too often transformed into something rich and rare, emptied of all its proper content through oxymoron or allegory. Criticism declares drinking in poetry and painting to be a drinking without drunkenness, a pure aesthetic or philosophical drinking hardly to be conceived, much less credited: "Although he was certainly capable of getting thoroughly drunk on occasion, drunkenness for T'ao [Ch'ien] means, as it generally does in Chinese poetry after him, drinking just enough wine to achieve that serene clarity of attention which he calls idleness" (Hinton 7); or

> to suggest further, as has been done, that his [Li Po's] notorious drunkenness was an inherited "barbarian" trait is certainly beside the point in an age when, among specially talented people, drunkenness was universally recognized as a state of perfect, untrammelled receptivity to divine inspiration. (Cooper 25)

In commentary on Persian poetry, intoxication is vaporized into allegory, transformed into religious ecstasy before it can even wet its lips. Drink and intoxication are made to mean something else, something higher, as in *The Bacchae*, where drink leads only to madness, possession, or ecstasy, but never intoxication.

Art history has been one of the worst offenders in this regard, insisting until quite recently that artists only use drink signifiers allegorically. No one has been free from this evaporation process, not even a documented drinker like Jan Steen or a confessed opium eater like Thomas De Quincey. Referring to Steen's painting of the wedding at Cana, Stephen Bann declares that "no one is supposed to be 'thinking of the grape' in this scene. We are supposed to insert the reading of 'divinely blessed fruitfulness' as a perfect semantic substitution for the neatly tailored bunch. Yet the brush runs away with itself, and we are confronted with an excess of *signifier* over *signified*" (55). For De Quincey, "opium proves to be but a signpost, a metaphor for uncharted ranges of experience" (26), Michael G. Cooke writes; Harry Cockerham says of Théophile Gautier that it is "impossible to see in the mention of intoxication anything other than a literary device used, once again, to justify or perhaps even to underline the strange and the unreal" (45).

Intoxication, then, is both unvoiced and voiced, subject not merely to denial but to alternations of denial and display—invisibility and splendor—as Corbin says, "a maze of fascinating taboos and mysterious attractions" (8). The two chapters on spiritual intoxication and artistic inspiration indicate how important it is to culture that the history of intoxication also be a history of transcendental awareness and individual creativity. Given this terror of the literal, why then, as I ask in chapter 7, should a despised materiality like drunkenness be appropriated as an indispensable index of religious truth in the first place? This unstable alternation between under- and overvoicing resembles most the psychological mechanism of disavowal. How do you write a history of substances and behaviors that are usually considered too trivial or shameful to be mentioned but, at the same or slightly other times, held to be glorious, the source of our ecstasy and inspiration?[6] Similar oscillations are to be found in the subject of Laporte's history: "We dare not speak about shit. But, since the beginning of time, no other subject—not even sex—has caused us to speak so much. The unnameable is enfolded by strange rumor, which combines the most immaculate silence with the most prolix chatter" (112).

While not submitting wholeheartedly to historical discipline, this volume hopes to take its place with other recent studies of objects and processes previously seen as below the radar of history: histories of crying, dust, shit, menstruation, breastfeeding, the penis.

This is also intended to be a book about the reading of cultural texts and, as such, is invested in the materiality of the text. Over the past two decades, the artist and the work of art have been factored by a number of social imperatives resulting in new aesthetics that insist that the principle of aesthetic disruption, whether gender, race, class, or sexual preference, is not merely anecdotal but crucial to a proper understanding of the work. In a similar light, I want to look at intoxication as part of the deep structure of culture, standing in a powerful relationship to the production of art. More than most of the indexes listed above, mine (along with sexual preference) has a long-standing intimacy with creativity. Many artistic periods exhibit a tantalizing connection to intoxication: Romantic writers with opium, later-nineteenth-century French poets and painters with absinthe, and twentieth-century American novelists and painters with whiskey or the gin martini.

The shadow of reductive criticism inevitably hangs over such a project because of a persistent strain of idealism that still controls the production of literary meaning. For a fable like Tristan and Isolde to fully participate in a cultural heritage, the potion that transforms the lovers must symbolize an essence like romantic passion or secret sin. Even better, the liquid should be ideally ideal, standing indeterminately for any number of abstractions. The Monty Python comedy group, Robert Stam writes, reduces the history of philosophy to the "mouthings of an interminable series of drunks":

> Emmanuel Kant was a real pissant
> Who was very rarely stable.
> Heidegger, Heidegger was a boozy beggar
> Who would drink you under the table.
> David Hume could out-consume
> Schopenhauer and Hegel
> and Wittgenstein was a beery swine
> and just as sloshed as Schlegel.
> (111–12)

Stam suggests that this is good comedy but not very good philosophy and implies that it is good comedy precisely because it is such very bad philosophy. My fourth chapter argues that philosophy—in the imaginary of Plato's *Symposium* at least—begins in intoxication. And Plato's *Symposium* has a crucial place in this book. Totally given over to past drunkenness, drunkenness painfully recovered and renewed, it is nonetheless one of the foundation texts of Western culture, founding, among other things, that antiliteral tendency in Western thought that has been so recently reversed in the history of culture.

This book is a study of attitudes and beliefs, and I am neither capable of nor interested in sifting the mythology of intoxication from its truth. In this late stage of seemingly endless commentary, the learned voices have been in contention for far too long for me to pretend to determine any bedrock of truth or falsity. As Laporte says of his subject matter, "In the final analysis, its veracity is less important than its participation in a discursive fabric that incorporates both fiction and fact" (107–8). What I have done is to try to seize this evanescent discourse as I found it, follow it through the twists and turns of individual texts, and get the several texts talking to one another. As in my previous work, this study cares deeply about the dramatics of reception, and I try to let the voices of the historical players emerge and breathe for a space.

Drunk the Night Before is more than a series of studies but less than an argument. It takes up the obvious call of three major "texts" (*The Bacchae, The Symposium,* and the pseudo-Anacreontic canon [and the subsequent traditions of drink poetry]) and three great cultural formations (philosophy, religion, and art) that have a decisive connection to intoxication. The poetry of "Anacreon" (chapter 2) is single-mindedly devoted to the pleasures of intoxication; *The Bacchae* (chapter 3) is quite free of drink or drugs even though Dionysus is most noted for his connection to wine; and *The Symposium* (chapter 4) floats on alcoholic excess and hangover while the text itself and later commentary pretend that, far from being enabling, such a condition is beneath notice. The chapter on *The Symposium* makes radical and subversive claims about the nature of philosophy.

The subject of chapter 6 is religion, particularly Christianity, where intoxication is condemned but regularly used as a figure for the highest and most holy states of the soul. Chapters 7 and 8 are the arts chapters, the first reexamining in some detail the familiar and currently dismissed connection between intoxication and artistic creativity, the second looking hard at the carnival constructions of Friedrich Nietzsche and Mikhail Bakhtin to see their motor in intoxication. Finally, the theme and imagery of magical potions and elixirs recommended themselves as a satisfactory if not logical complement to the above, and that is the subject of chapter 5.

chapter 1

The Mysteries of Intoxication

Wine is the best gift of gods to men, sparkling wine; every song, every dance, every passionate love, goes with wine.

—ATHENAEUS, *The Deipnosophists*

O ye men, how exceedingly strong is wine! it causeth all men to err that drink it: it maketh the mind of the king and of the fatherless child, to be all one: of the bondman and of the freeman, of the poor man and of the rich: it turneth also every thought unto jollity and mirth, so that a man remembereth neither sorrow nor debt: and it maketh every heart rich, so that a man remembereth neither king nor governor; and it maketh to speak all things by their talents; and when they are in their cups, they forget their love both to friends and brethren, and a little after draw out swords: but when they are from the wine, they remember not what they have done.

—FIRST ESDRAS

Until quite recently alcoholic beverages were such elemental signifiers that they had taken over the word "drink"—as in the threshold statement of social encounters, "What will you have to drink?" Alcoholic drink has been so important to human society that it is said to constitute it: drink, Keith Thomas writes in *Religion and the Decline of Magic*, "was built into the fabric of social life. It played a part in nearly every public and private ceremony, every commercial bargain, every craft ritual, every private occasion of mourning or rejoicing" (17). In his biography of Alexander the Great, John M. O'Brien further states that

it is clear that alcohol had become society's grand elixir, the medium through which communion with the god is achieved, grief alleviated, friendship developed, strength renewed, work rewarded, dead men honored, confidence acquired, hospitality provided, and sleep guaranteed. Above all, alcohol

I

proved capable of providing a warm sense of fellowship and escape from the uncertainty and powerlessness of the human condition. (1980, 100)

Drink and drugs even appear on the short list of items said to constitute the human: Rabelais's Bacbuc, the high priestess of the Temple of the Holy Bottle, proclaimed that "not laughter but drinking is the proper lot of man" (705).[1]

What Dionysus brought in his train that has proved so all-absorbing was not so much the drink as an "intoxication," with strangely manic and eccentric effects. Intoxication, or drunkenness, is an altered state of consciousness that takes its place on the periphery of psychology along with dreaming, visionary states, possession trances, and delirium. Walter Benjamin called it a "loosening of the self" (129). Much of the world's poetry and some of its prose has been devoted to the praise of these wondrous effects.

As commonly conceived, intoxication is the excess of strong drink, although, perhaps, a decreed excess, which delighted Charles Lamb:

> It is an observation of a wise man that "moderation is best in all things." I cannot agree with him "in liquor." There is a smoothness and oiliness in wine that makes it go down by a natural channel, which I am positive was made for that descending. Why does not wine choke us? (Bett 86)

It is an excess uniquely human according to a conventional trope whereby "beasts never exceed in such kind of excesse or superfluitie but . . . they measure their appetites by the rule of necessitie" (Phillip Stubbes in Williams 1969, 174).[2] For Friedrich Nietzsche, Dionysus stands for excess: the clamors of the Dionysiac revels "voiced all the *excess* of nature in delight, suffering and knowledge, and even in the most piercing cry" (26).

Despite its excessive nature, intoxication is imagined as a center and circumference, a "just right" and an "everything." As a center it is a "high," a "hit," a "kick" (the exaggerated reaction of someone taking a drink for the first time or a drink of extrastrong, of "savage," spirits). The high of alcohol, however, expands to suffuse the universe, to dissolve the boundary between subject and object and to produce a totality into which the center is absorbed—what Sigmund Freud called an "oceanic" feeling (11). There is a heaven on earth because intoxication is paradisal: Omar Khayyám exhorts his listener to make his paradise here, with ruby wine; and so does Ned Ward for a different religion:

Then still let the bumper round Christendom pass,
For Paradise lost may be found in a glass.[3]

William James declared, "Sobriety diminishes, discriminates and says no; drunkenness expands, unites and says yes" (38). In *Roland Barthes,* Roland Barthes quotes the fourteenth-century Dutch mystic Jan van Ruusbroec: "I call intoxication of the mind that state in which pleasure exceeds the possibilities which desire had entertained" (112). After the narrator of James Mangan's "Extraordinary Adventure in the Shade" has finished his second bottle of wine, he exclaims:

And oh, what a change! Cleverly, indeed, had I calculated upon a glorious reaction. Words I have none to reveal the quiescence of spirit that succeeded the interior balminess that steeped my faculty in blessed sweetness. . . . I had undergone an apotheosis; I wore the cumbrous habiliments of flesh and blood no longer; the shell, hitherto the circumscriber of my soul, was shivered; I stood out in front of the universe a visible and tangible intellect, and beheld, with giant grasp, the key that had power to unlock the deep prison which enclosed the secrets of antiquity and futurity! (60)

Intoxication is also excessive in its miraculous polarity: from earliest antiquity, alcoholic drink had been spoken of as both wonderful and terrible. "Wine," Theognis sang in the seventh century BC, "I both praise you and blame you; I cannot ever hate you or love you completely. You are blessing and curse" (Campbell 1983, 41). Marcel Detienne describes it thus:

Born "of a savage mother," wine is a substance in which death is mixed with life magnified tenfold, in which burning fire alternates with a moistness that quenches thirst. It is as much a remedy as a poison, a drug that either enables man to outdo himself or turns him into a brute, that introduces him to ecstasy or plunges him into bestiality. (35)

As a result of its duality, intoxication is often described as a combination of opposites or a conversion into opposites. Barthes says of wine that it "is above all a converting substance, capable of reversing situations and states, and of extracting from objects their opposites—for instance, making a weak man strong or a silent one talkative" (1972, 58). This has been a constant source of poetic trope: in classic Greece—

> wine can of the wise their wits beguile,
> Make the sage frolic and the serious smile—

or the middle ages—

> Thanks to me, dumb speak, deaf listen,
> Blind folk see, the senses glisten,
> And the lame man finds his feet.
> Eld through me to youth returneth,
> While thine influence o'erturneth
> All a young man's lustihead.[4]

And of dramatic tropes, as in the opening of *The Taming of the Shrew*.

Among the most prominent opposites that alcohol combines are fire and water—Gaston Bachelard called it "firewater," both dry and wet, and Galileo was fascinated by "the paradox of the fiery liquor born from cold water, the Heraclitean mystery of water that becomes fire and fire that dissolves into water" (Jennings 182; Camporesi 58). The interpenetration of these opposites textures a poem like the following, "A Fly about a Glass of Burned Claret" by Richard Lovelace:

> Forebear this liquid fire, Fly,
> It is more fatal than the dry,
> That singly, but embracing, wounds;
> And this at once both, burns and drowns.
> (82)

Civilization can be said to have developed out of a dialectic between excessive and social drinking. The excess of drink may be magical or divine, but it was dislodged from the social register at a very early date. Theognis wrote that "wine drunk in excess is an evil; if we drink it wisely it is not an evil but a blessing" (Lissarrague 1990, 9). Moderation and excess attains the status of an ultimate binary, like good and evil, god and beast, or heaven and hell. The Plato of *The Laws* was the great spokesman for this distinction, which persisted in social history and became the basis, in the nineteenth and twentieth centuries, for the construction of alcoholism.

Intoxication may be regarded as a utopian supplement, but Plato and others want to make a radical division in it, between an anarchic core (still pleasant, perhaps, but destructive) and an ideal displacement, a "just enough." The archaic Greek philosopher Zeno announced that a "wise man will drink but not be drunk" (Raymond 74). Ecclesiasticus, a book of Old Testament Apocrypha, similarly records that "wine was created from the beginning to make men joyful and not to make them drunk" (McNutt 50). George Herbert specified such a miraculous point of demarcation in his "Stanzas from *The Church-porch*":

Drink not the third glasse, which thou canst not tame,
When once it is within thee; but before
Mayst rule it, as thou list; and poure the shame,
Which it would poure on thee, upon the floore.
(472)

Plato's dialogue stipulates convivial drinking as a norm between excessive drinking and abstinence (1237–38, 1245). But is there really a civilized stage of drinking pleasure that exposes intoxication as a now unwelcome excess?[5] If so, where might intoxication begin? Does it have a social as well as a chemical point of origin? Are being "tiddly" or "having a buzz on" earlier stages in a process that ends in drunkenness? In a *Tatler* essay on contemporary drinking, Richard Steele implies that it is all intoxication, that "we are less masters of ourselves when we drink in the least proportion above the exigencies of thirst" (4.229). "For one must not," says Plato, "simply give pleasure full rein." The guests must "flirt with," but not succumb to, intoxication (Jeanneret 63). Yet even Plato cannot imagine an instance of this social drinking: "I suppose we may reckon a drinking party and its members as one kind of social activity? . . . Then has anyone ever seen such a party conducted as it ought to be? Neither of you can hesitate to give the answer 'never.' . . . And for my own part . . . I have never seen or heard of one rightly managed" (1239).[6] Drinking pleasure and intoxication are separable only as an impossible ideal, as in a Mohammedan afterlife where it means drinking without hangover.

Alcoholic drink, then, is both excessive and social, wild and tame, savage and civilized. In *The Bacchae,* intoxication (in the form of Dionysus) is a wildness that threatens the social order.[7] In Euripides' *Cyclops,* on the other hand, Dionysus's gift is regarded as a civilized pleasure. As with Polyphemus in Euripides' satyr play, so in the *Gilgamesh* epic, drink makes Enkidu, a savage who lives among the beasts in solitude but who will later become a friend of Gilgamesh, enter the human community (Maffesoli 132).

There were even two types of Dionysiac myth, Theban and Attic. The Dionysus of Thebes was the savage enemy of Pentheus and Lycurgus, but the Dionysus "who made his way through Attica appeared in a totally different guise. He was a discreet, patient god, a benevolent and generous power—the opposite of his Theban character" (Detienne 27). In the latter myths, Dionysus is portrayed as a culture hero who leaves the gift of wine and viticulture as his farewell present to the mortals he visits: "The 'inventor of wine' and bringer of civilization through viticulture," Albert Henrichs writes, "coexisted in deceptive harmony with the savage 'Raw-Eater' who led the mythical maenads to their prey" (1979, 1).

It is a close question whether drink civilizes or the watering of drink does. The first position corresponds to a line of anthropological inquiry claiming that "uncivilized" peoples did not have fermented drinks. Maguelonne Toussaint-Samat instances a Dr. A. Maurizio, who "unequivocally stated that 'savages still at the gathering stage did not have alcoholic liquors.' . . . But it is my view," she continues, "that they appeared in the latter period of this stage of civilization, and perhaps not until the time of cultivation with the plough" (36). An opposite position follows Owen Felltham, who wrote in his essay "Of Drunkenness," "We may observe that drink ever takes its footing, in the most barbarous nations" (171).

The opposition between excessive and social drinking is often expressed through the binary unmixed/mixed, answering Athenaeus's call for a drinking that proceeds with "due measure" (1.163). The practical equivalent of the indeterminate border between wild and civilized drinking is the proper proportion of wine to water, and this was anxiously calibrated in antiquity. Dionysus was not only the wine; he was also the mix, as he announces in a play by Ameipsias, *Men Playing at Kottabos:* "For you all I am Dionysus, five and two" (Wilkins 227).

Mixing wine with philosophical talk was another way to achieve this civilized goal, hence, the symposiac tradition. Plutarch felt that "when drinking we ought to engage in conversation that has . . . some instruction in it. . . . when conversation like this accompanies indulgence in wine, the wild and manic element is hidden away, benevolently restrained by the Muses" (1961, 111). In a metaphor in *The Birth of Tragedy,* Nietzsche says that the Greeks during their great period attained that "glorious mixture that one finds in a fine wine, which both fires the blood and turns the mind to contemplation" (100).

Marcel Detienne reads this duality of the wild and tame Dionysus diachronically as the gradual bourgeoisification of drink, the gradual politening of society:

> [Dionysus] offered the unprecedented spectacle of a deity of the vine and of unwatered wine gradually shedding his savagery, setting aside his wrath, and ending his murderous violence. He did so to the point where the inventor of the alcoholic drink was transformed into a patron saint of the tranquil life, of good health and marital felicity. Sublime actor, he sat, cantharus in hand, sipping tempered wine among the bourgeois and rentiers of the agora. (39–40)

This civilizing process is expressed through the myth of Amphictyon, king of Athens, who learned from Dionysus the art of mixing wine and water: "In order to retard inebriation, so the story went, Dionysus instructed Amphictyon to mix five parts water with every two parts of wine" (Hoffman 96). As a result, men learned to remain upright while drinking. The earlier Dionysus is the one who "makes men stagger, who keeps them from walking straight or standing up, who knocks their feet out from under them—he is Dionysos Sphaleotas or Sphaltes, 'the one who trips you'" (Lissarrague 1990, 72).

The civilizing effect of drink and intoxication would eventually become idealized and become part of the new transcendental dynamics of Christian humanism:

> Later in the Renaissance, Adrian Junius . . . stresses that his Bacchus signifies the spiritually quickening power of wine taken moderately. . . . He is no

mad god of drunken, earth-bound squalor; he symbolizes that spiritually liberating power of joyful wine, which classical and Christian man drank as a conscious act of wise and ennobling humanity, encouraging eloquence and the quest of truth. (Screech 1979, 454–55)

"Since the Greeks," Jean-Charles Sournia writes in his *History of Alcoholism,* drinking "has been equated with happiness, life, blood, well-being, warmth and virility" (1990, 9–10). In its positive modality, intoxication is an ultimate good that produces satisfaction with everyday life.

> Thou clears the head o' doited Lear;
> Thou chears the heart o' drooping Care;
> Thou strings the nerves o' Labor-sair . . .
> Thou ev'n brightens dark Despair.
> (Burns 174)

Thomas Randolph, the "jovial philosopher," declared that "Sacke is the life and soul and spirit of man, the fire which Prometheus stole, not from Jove's kitchen, but his wine-cellar, to increase the native heat and radicall moisture, without which we are but drousie dust and dead clay" (McNutt 90). Drink has a long history as a divine substance—the Vedic gods, who were originally mortal, acquired immortality by the drinking of *soma,* and mead was drawn from the udders of Odin's goat—and drink itself has been identified as a divinity: "The gift he brought was himself, for Dionysus was not just the god of wine; he was the wine itself."[8] In one of his poems, the Italian poet Giambattista Marini makes a pun on "divino" and "di vino" (Levarie 231).

Drink and intoxication have gathered to themselves a number of poetic and rhetorical figures. Foremost among them is a catalog of marvels that I mentioned earlier as a transformation into opposites, for example, "O, Dionysus. . . . Thou alone makest the humble to feel proud, and persuadest the scowler to laugh, the weak to be brave, the cowardly to be bold" (Athenaeus 1.155). Philostratus identified this figure as an illusory effect of intoxication itself: "This river [of wine] makes men rich, and powerful in the assembly, and helpful to their friends, and beautiful and . . . tall; for when a man has drunk his fill of it he can assemble all these qualities and in his thought make them his own" (97–99).

Another effect of intoxication, also mentioned earlier, is a feeling that one can do or be anything; as Robert Herrick says in his "Hymne to Bacchus," "Each Cobler is a King" (259). Such an absence of limitations may simply be a transcription of alcohol's primary effect, the numbing of inhibitions. Intoxication produces or releases feelings of personal intimacy—a secular variant of the "oceanic feeling"; it dissolves self-consciousness and our sense of difference. The community that drink creates, however, is traditionally male (even though, in nineteenth-century painting, the figure seated at a table in the café was most often a woman). Women are usually left out of such generic formulations, which emphasize the strong connection between alcohol and homosocial pleasure, embodied, for example, in the image of Ganymede, Zeus's boy and cupbearer. Plato's drinking party, *The Symposium,* is devoted to homosexual love.

A sudden access of intelligence and wit are virtues commonly associated with intoxication. This is what Plutarch alleged in his *Table Talk:* "Some people, who have a talent for invention but are too diffident and stiff when sober, will, when they immerse themselves in wine, find their spirits rise within them, like incense" (1961, 101). And Falstaff will later announce

> a good sherris-sack hath a twofold operation in it. It ascends me into the brain; dries me there all the foolish and dull and crudy vapors which environ it; makes it apprehensive, quick, forgetive, full of nimble fiery and delectable shapes; which deliver'd o'er to the voice, the tongue, which is the birth, becomes excellent wit. (Shakespeare 460)

True to its dual nature, the effects that flow from intoxication are also bad: Plato tells us that Bacchus "was bereft of his wits by his stepmother Hera, and that this is why he afflicts his victims with Bacchic possession and all its frenzied dancing, by way of revenge—that that and nothing else was the motive for his gift of wine" (1268). "What, make the story public?" Lucian's Lycinus says to Philo, "give a full description of what men do in their cups? A veil should be drawn over such things" (4.128).

The conversion-into-opposites trope moves in the other direction as well: "Wine does wonders—so it does! For it transforms a rational creature into an ass; a valiant man into a bully; and a man of property into a beggar" (Watson 27). Another common figure for intoxication is a sequence that moves from better to worse as consumption increases, often expressed as a sequence of cups. The figure is both sequential and polar, since the border crossed, like the equator in Herman Melville's *Moby-Dick,* turns everything into its negative. In a lost comedy by Euboulos, Dionysus himself explains:

> Three bowls only do I mix for the temperate—one to health, which they empty first, the second to love and pleasure, the third to sleep. When this is drunk up wise guests go home. The fourth bowl is ours no longer, but belongs to violence; the fifth to uproar, the sixth to drunken revel, the seventh to black eyes. The eighth is the policeman's, the ninth belongs to biliousness, and the tenth to madness and hurling the furniture. (Athenaeus 1.157)[9]

Drowning, poisoning, and possession by the devil are common metaphors for the negative aspects of intoxication. Xenarchos wrote:

> I'm starting to nod off;
> that cup I drank in honor of Zeus the Savior
> has completely wrecked me, the sailor, and sent me
> to the bottom, as you can see.
> (Lissarrague 1990, 108)

In Sebastian Brant's *Ship of Fools:*

> The wine, 'tis true, our thirst will slake
> But later stabs one like a snake,
> And poison through the veins will pour,
> As Basiliscus found of yore.
> (218)

There is a Jewish proverb that where Satan cannot go in person he sends wine to represent him (Tek Chand 243). "Every inordinate cup is unblessed and the ingredient is a devil," Michael Cassio says in *Othello* (Shakespeare 956).

From the sixteenth to the eighteenth centuries, toasting was a perfect image of intoxication gone bad, conviviality turned into a nightmare. Drinking begins with a verbal form, often a poem, called the toast, which, ironically, devotes drinking to the cause of health. This act of mingled medicalization and erotic desire was repeatedly denounced over the course of early modern history as the plague of social drinking—"to drink health is to drink sickness" was a British Georgian phrase (R. Porter 61). An eighteenth-century Scots jurist, Lord Cockburn, wrote that

> healths and toasts were special torments; oppressions which cannot now be conceived. Every glass during dinner required to be dedicated to the health of some one [and] . . . no sooner was the table cleared, and the after dinner glasses set down, than it became necessary for each person, following the landlord, to drink the health of every other person present. (Daiches 53–54)[10]

While sociability and courage are two of the vaunted good effects of intoxication, intoxication also turns the social occasion into a scene of anger and violence, as one of the earliest poets of intoxication, Anacreon of Teos, was well aware. "The revel brings blows," Euripides wrote, "insult and out-rage"; "whence," Athenaeus adds, "some declare that Dionysus and Hybris ('Violence') were born at the same time" (1.159). Intoxication also erodes the social compact by numbing our sense of shame and modesty, thus lead-ing to "indecent" behavior. The standard examples of this in the poetic and painterly traditions were Hebraic—Noah (who planted a grapevine after the ark landed, got drunk from the wine, and let his sons see him sleeping naked) and Lot (whose daughters seduced him under the influ-ence of wine).[11]

Intoxication turns the drinker into an animal: "That we should, with joy, pleasance, revel, and applause, transform ourselves into beasts," Cassio laments (Shakespeare 956). In fifteenth- and sixteenth-century art, four animals were used to depict drunkenness, either as four stages or as four varieties of the condition (Janson 246). Thomas Nashe divided drunkards into those who got ape-drunk, lion-drunk, swine-drunk, and sheep-drunk (207); in Erhard Schön's *Four Characteristics of Wine* (1530), an illustration for Hans Sachs's poem of that name, "the sanguine, or moderate drinker remains as gentle as a lamb, the choleric drinker becomes violent [as a lion], the phlegmatic vomits like a pig, and the melancholic degenerates into simian madness" (Kunzle 1990, 217). According to Gerard Manley Hopkins, "Drunkenness . . . makes man a beast; it drowns noble reason, their eyes swim, they hiccup in their talk, they gabble and blur their words, they stag-ger and fall and deal themselves dishonorable wounds, their faces grow blotched and bloated, scorpions are in their mind, they see devils and frightful sights" (Bold 9).

chapter 2

Drink Poetry; or, The Art of Feeling Very, Very Good

Stranger, passing near the tomb of
Anakreon,
Pour me a libation as you approach,
For in life I was a drunkard.
—*Greek Anthology*

"This Omar seems a decent chap," said Flapjack Dick one night,
When he had read my copy through, and then blown out the light.
"I ain't much stuck on poetry, because I runs to news.
But I appreciate a man that loves his glass of booze.
And Omar here likes good red wine, although he's pretty mum
On liquors which is better yet, like whiskey, gin, or rum."
—EUGENE FIELD, *Klondike Ballads*

In Greek antiquity, when poetry devoted to drink was common, Anacreon of Teos (c. 570 to c. 485 BC) was notorious for poetry praising drinking and intoxication. Anacreontic poems, both then and later, claimed that drinking strong liquor was productive of all value and converted the limitations of ordinary life to a condition of supreme satisfaction.

According to Simonides, Anacreon was the "first of Bacchic votaries," and his poetry or his name gave rise to an extensive Western poetic tradition that enlisted as colleagues in the creation of drinking songs many European poets—Pierre Ronsard, Ben Jonson, Gavriil Derzhavin, Johann Wolfgang von Goethe, Juan Meléndez Valdés, Giacomo Leopardi, and many others. Anacreon became the center of a body of lyric imitation without parallel in Western literature and an alcoholic celebrity matched, perhaps, only by Omar Khayyám (who represents an equally abundant Arabic and Persian tradition of drink poetry) or Robert Burns. In *The Poetics of Imitation: Anacreon and the Anacreontic Tradition,* Patricia A. Rosenmeyer writes, "It is impossible to say with any assurance why this imitative impulse occurred when it did, and why it continued to flourish for so many years in changing circumstances" (62).

The motive for such repetition, however, may have something to do with the fact that Anacreon's name served as a code word for drink through the modern era. Robert Herrick, a prominent English drink poet, has a vision of his ancestor:

> Me thought I saw (as I did dreame in bed)
> A crawling Vine about *Anacreon's* head:
> Flushed was his face; his haires with oyle did shine;
> And as he spake, his mouth ranne ore with wine.
> Tipled he was; and tipling lispt withall.
> (313)

In an early version of his poem "Romance," Edgar Allan Poe recalls himself as

> an idle boy lang syne,
> Who read Anacreon, and drank wine;

and George Bernard Shaw can still refer in 1948 to "Anacreontic writers" who "put vine leaves in their hair and drank or drugged themselves to death."[1]

Drink poetry is found in all literary cultures, found, for example, "in all periods of Arabic literature," in some of which, according to F. Harb, "the theme of wine dominated poetic production" (219). In the European Middle Ages, Sedulius Scotus and the Archpoet agree "on the superiority of verse well-soaked, '*carmina saturata*'" (Waddell 1929, 319). I could have organized the network of drink poetry in this chapter around the names of Li Po, Tu Fu, Omar, Olivier Basselin, and Robert Burns; or T'ao Ch'ien (the first Chinese poet to sing of wine and its pleasures), Abu Nuwas (who brought Persian wine poetry to fruition), the Archpoet (author of the "greatest drinking song in the world"), Ronsard (the greatest "*poète biberon' depuis Alcée et Anacréon*," as Paul Laumonier calls him), Esteban

Manuel de Villegas ("*el padre de la anacreóntica*"), and Alexander Brome ("the foremost exponent" of Interregnum drinking songs, easily punnable as "Bromius," one of Dionysus's epithets), as well as Anacreon.[2] Many poet names can stand, like his, for transnational bodies of poetry praising alcoholic drink. However, the adjective "Anacreontic" is well established in cultural discourse and has a wide circulation in Western poetic commentary, identifying a region of lyric poetry that spreads out analogically through tropes like the German or the Sicilian Anacreon, the Anacreon of Painters, and so on.[3]

Little categorical or critical thought has been given to this poetry: there has been almost no comparative study, in fact, little comparative acknowledgment apart from the analogical phrases just mentioned or a bare listing (here, for example, from an American poet, Bayard Taylor) that might point to an international connection:

Oh for Hafiz—glorious Persian!
Keats, with buoyant, gay diversion
Mocking Schiller's grave immersion;
Oh for wreathed Anacreon.
(1855, 134)[4]

This chapter is not that study, although it surely is comparative. It is an attempt to tease out a partial discourse of intoxication from the nature and spread of drink poetry and its various connections; and it assembles a chain of evidence, authority, and argument along which such a discourse runs. The other alcoholic discourse is that of addiction, and, although the chapter registers that shadow area from time to time, it ends when it comes up against the chronological divide between them.

A sense of the constructed differences between Western and Eastern literatures helps explain this failure in comparatism, as in the embattled orientalism of this passage by Walter Savage Landor:

A taste which has once been accustomed to the delicacies of Athens and of Rome, will naturally loathe the heady spirits and high-seasoned garbage of Barbarians. It must surely result from the weakest or most perverted understanding, that the *gazel* has ever been preferred to the pure and almost perfect . . . pieces of Anacreon and Tibullus. (544)

An orientalist bias may even be the reason why Omar was so fantastically lionized by the West: because he seems to convict Islam of hypocrisy in its ban against alcohol.[5]

The great irony of the Anacreontic tradition is that the poetry in question was never written by Anacreon. His name became mistakenly attached to a later body of poetry (the poetry of "Anacreon," or pseudo-Anacreon). It is now generally agreed that the *Anacreontea* consists of shallow treatments of drink and love by a mix of many writers from several periods, but "as it happened, the mediocre had a powerful influence and gave rise to whole movements" (Lesky 177).[6] The misattribution was known in antiquity and the Renaissance, but this knowledge was generally disavowed.[7]

While the delusion held, the poetry was extravagantly praised, so much so that René Rapin, who, Tom Mason writes, "was not given to easy praise," called the *Anacreontea* "*Flowers, Beauties,* and *Graces* perpetual. . . . there is nothing comparable in all Antiquity." However, "as soon as the Anacreontea were discovered to be spurious," Mason continues,

> they were despised—they were pronounced trivial, coarse, self-indulgent, incoherent. Where they had been felt for generations to be wise, they were now discovered to be foolish. . . . For the last hundred years, classical students seem to have been quite sure that the three hundred years of European admiration for "Anacreon" was merely an aberration.

"But the fragments of the real Anacreon," he continues, "seem never to have touched anyone's heart—as the false had done" (105–7).

A false tradition, taking nominal strength from a genius who had nothing, or nothing clearly, to do with it, nonetheless possessed more strength than any of the true lineages: the Alcaic, Sapphic, even the Pindaric. If, as Gordon Braden states, "Anacreon" has a "fame like no other poet," one must conclude that the name alone has a powerful signatory force, that a discourse of intoxication operates through it, providing the core of its fascination (1978, 206). Ovid is clear about this and other acts of signing: "What was the lesson of the lyric Muse of the old man of Teos? Surely it was sex—and a flood of wine. What did Lesbian Sappho instruct girls in but love?" (Russell 293). When Anacreon resurfaces in the Renaissance, his name will still stand for drinking and intoxication, even though the corresponding subject matter fades from the poetry.

Other bodies of drink poetry also float free, detached from a historical author, and this, as Helen Waddell suggests, may be the fate of drink poetry in particular and lyric poetry generally: "As for authorship, it is the paradox of letters that the lyric, the most personal, most individual of literary kinds, is often likely to go fatherless, the love-child of the Muses" (1927, 150). In the drink poetry of the European Middle Ages, another author, "Bishop Golias," took shape around a historical emptiness; like "Anacreon," he was a patron saint of drinking.

In a variation on this theme, studies of Omar and Hafiz generally fall into two groups: in one, scholars find all the drink poetry to be anonymous additions to a minuscule historical canon—according to Christopher Decker, it is even possible, though not likely, that Omar wrote no poetry at all, and J. C. E. Brown tells us that "the corpus of Khayyamic quatrains" has grown from 2 in 1221 to over 1,200 today.[8] In the other, scholars sublimate the body of drink poetry into its opposite, Sufi allegory, in which "wine is the symbol of spiritual ecstasy, 'saki' . . . of the divine love . . . the tavern of the heavenly monastery, and the rose and its fragrance of the hope of divine favor" (Pachori 16).

Also like "Anacreon," many drink poets have an energetic life of imitation, adaptation, and revival, especially Omar (Edward Fitzgerald's *Rubaiyat* had an enormous impact on cultural tastes and attitudes in England and America in the late nineteenth century); Hafiz (Goethe, in his *East-West Divan,* announced that he was the spiritual twin of the ancient Persian poet and desired to love and drink like him [1964, 237]); and Li Po (his verse, as rendered in Ezra Pound's *Cathay,* initiated one version of the modernist movement in poetry). And none has a more active legendary life than the father of Arabic wine poetry, Abu Nuwas, who "flits through the *Thousand and One Nights*" and eventually becomes a hero of folklore (Hakim Bey n.p.).

Drink poetry was generally performed to music at all-male gatherings, whether the Greek symposium or the medieval and early modern tavern.[9] The poetry extols the euphoria that comes from intoxication—nothing, Hafiz sings, can bestow as much pleasure as a goblet of wine, and T'ao Ch'ien prays that the wine will "drench" him "in bliss"—its power to dispel life's cares, to ease the burden of thought and anxiety, and to restore at least the illusion of youth (Hafiz in McNutt 70; Fang Dai 56).

Given the antiquity and widespread distribution of drink poetry, drinking and intoxication may well be one of the founding subjects of lyric poetry, as fundamental as this inscription in an Egyptian wine cellar from Ptolemaic times: "This is the place of wine and wine jugs when one gets drunk. Happiness is in it, joy of heart comes out of it"; or a song from the *Kojiki*, an eighth-century Japanese chronicle:

> Susukori brewed
> This august heavy liquor,
> And oh, how drunk I am!
> (Darby 567; Brower 44)

In his "Art of Poetry," Horace wrote as if this were common understanding:

> Gods, heroes, conquerors, Olympic crowns,
> Love's pleasing cares, and the free joys of wine,
> Are proper subjects for the lyric song.
> (135)

Jean Anthelme Brillat-Savarin proposed in 1826 to make a "methodical selection of gastronomical poems from the *Greeks* and *Romans* . . . to show the intimate connection which has at all times existed between the art of saying well and the art of eating well." These gastronomical poems turn out to be wine poems, since up to the middle of the eighteenth century [i.e., the discovery of the New World, which flooded Europe with a greater idea of good cheer] "such poems were chiefly made in praise of *Bacchus* and his gifts, for to drink wine, and to drink it without stint, was the highest degree of gustative exaltation to which man had thus far been able to attain" (314).

Wine drinking is one of the main subjects of the Persian lyric poem, the *ghazal*, in addition to having a genre of its own, the *khamriyya* (Arberry 1948, v). In *Twelfth Night*, Feste asks Sir Andrew Aguecheek, "Would you have a love-song, or a song of good life?" as if there were only the two choices (Shakespeare 305). One of the oldest devices in elegy and lyric poetry, the classical *paraclausithyron* (a lament sung by a lover at his mistress's door after he has been refused admission), is motivated by drunkenness, and F. H. Copley speculates that it may have derived from the *komos* of the symposium (1–5).[10]

Anacreontic poetry is dedicated to a world of drinking in which drink is only a pleasure, for "Anacreon"—"When I drink wine my veins ever with rapture thrill"—as for Burns in his "Epistle to John Goldie":

> There's naething like the honest nappy;
> Whare'll ye e'er see men sae happy,
> Or woman sonsie, saft and sappy,
>   'Tween morn and morn,
> As them wha like to taste the drappie
>   In glass or horn.[11]

Put another way, "Anacreon" is the poet of the honeymoon period of drinking, and the Greek epigrammatist, Dioscorides, imagines him in an appropriately paradisal setting:

> O Anacreon, delight of the Muses, lord of all revels of the night . . . may founts of wine bubble up for thee unbidden, and streams of ambrosial nectar from the gods; unbidden may the gardens bring thee violets . . . and myrtles grow for thee nourished by tender dew, so that even in the house of Demeter thou mayest dance delicately in thy cups, holding golden Eurypyle in thy arms. (*Greek Anthology* 7:31)

Drink may also be one of the original subjects of lyric poetry because the symposium was the occasion for most ancient poetry. According to L. Rossi, "The history of lyric is the history of the symposion," and Oswyn Murray states that "archaic poetry in almost all its aspects (with the exception perhaps of some political elegy and of religious choral lyric) was developed within the *symposion*—first by poets who were themselves full members of the sympotic group (Alcaeus, Sappho), and later by professional sympotic poets like Anacreon."[12] Michel Jeanneret writes that

"Anacreon and his followers only make sense against a background of conviviality where wine and words come together," and drink poetry continues
to be an expression of the convivial event, which is, by desire and definition, only euphoric:

> Souls of Poets dead and gone,
> What Elysium have ye known,
> Happy field or mossy cavern,
> Choicer than the Mermaid Tavern.
> (Jeanneret 149–50; Keats 225)[13]

Even when the poetry is released from its sympotic context, as with the
paraclausithyron, it still reflects it. Unlike reflective or meditative poetry,
drink poetry pretends to dwell in its occasioning moment. Unlike love
poetry, drink poetry reflects presence, not absence; it tells us what is being
done right now: "Come, come, my old crones and gay fellows"; "Trowl
the bowl, the jolly nut-brown bowl";

> Then while we are here, we'll drink ale and beer,
> And freely our money we'll spend;

or

> Fill, Fill, Fill the brimming glass;
> Each man toast his favorite lass.
> He that flinches is an ass.[14]

This insistence on the present, the unwillingness or inability to defer satisfaction, finds its anchor in the carpe diem thematics.

To maintain its hold on euphoria, drink poetry is governed by a logic
of intoxication, a code of limitations that suspends consequences. In *The
Classics and English Renaissance Poetry,* Braden explains it nicely:

> Relevant to the whole modus of these poems . . . is one of liquor's primary gifts
> to the race: the sudden adequacy of the banal . . . as rendered in a hundred
> commonplace and otherwise vapid declarations and images. Being young again
> and dancing with the kids is what, as it were, the Anacreontic tradition has

been trying to persuade the speaker that he really wants; the poem describes a state (drunkenness) in which wanting those things is somehow enough. (210)

"Anacreon" never takes his subject matter—whether drunkenness, sexual consummation, or death—to a close, for that would risk a mood change. Decontextualization keeps at bay the knowledge of how fragile this fantasy is.

As its primary theme, Anacreontic poetry endlessly announces the major psychological effect of intoxication, that it frees us from care. In the words of Horace:

> For, to the sober, Heaven makes every task more hard to bear;
> And by no other magic than by wine flies carking care.
> Who after wine grumbles at toils of war or stinted days?
> Who does not rather thee, Sire Bacchus, sing,—thee, Venus, praise? (18)

Edmund Waller:

> The burnished face oft decked with hoary hairs
> Shows drinking brings no death, but to our cares;

or Charles Stuart Calverley:

> Such power hath Beer. The heart which Grief hath canker'd
> Hath one unfailing remedy—the Tankard.[15]

If by chance Gargantua "was vexed, angry, displeased, or peeved, if he stamped, if he wept or if he screamed, they always brought him drink to restore his temper, and immediately he became quiet and happy" (Rabelais 54). This is the effect of drink that makes the song possible, and the effect that is repeatedly celebrated in the song, so "Anacreon" sings:

> Let's drink now the wine
> from beautiful Lyaios;
> for whenever we drink,
> our troubles slumber
> (Rosenmeyer 1992, 258)[16]

What he doesn't allow into the poem is the knowledge that when the effects of drink wane, the care or anxiety returns more strongly, as temperance poetry was eager to remind its reader:

> Grief banished by wine, will come again,
> And come with a deeper shade,
> Leaving, perchance, on the soul a stain
> Which sorrow had never made.
> (Sir William A'Beckett in Tek Chand 361)[17]

The enemy of drink and drink poetry is sobriety in two senses, the second being gravity of thought or seriousness. This is foremost among the cares that drink dispels in A. E. Housman's lines,

> Ale, man, ale's the stuff to drink
> For fellows whom it hurts to think.
> (89)

Anacreontic lyric identifies thought, analysis, psychology, anything that might expose the empty enchantment of the euphoric moment, as its enemy:

> You know, my Friends, with what a brave Carouse
> I made a Second Marriage in my house;
> Divorced old barren Reason from my Bed,
> And took the Daughter of the Vine to Spouse.
> (Decker 75)

And much poetry is written against this foe, from the clerks' songs in the medieval *Carmina Burana* to the college drinking song in Sigmund Romberg's operetta *Student Prince* (1924).

The opposition between Anacreon and philosophy was staged in the seventeenth century by Bernard de Fontenelle in a dialogue between the poet and Aristotle. The philosopher complains that Anacreon's title to wisdom is undeserved; Anacreon seems to agree with him: "I had done nothing but drink, sing, and wax amorous; and the wonder is that people called me 'the Wise' . . . while they have called you merely 'philosopher.'" The poet, however, proposes a revision of Western humanism in which the struggles of life are higher in value than philosophical thought (a materialist therapy that resembles modern alcoholic treatment more than alcoholic experience):

> I maintain that it is more difficult to drink and to sing as I have, than to philosophize as you have philosophized. To sing and drink, as I did, required that one should have disentangled one's soul from violent passions; that we should not aspire to things not dependent upon us, that we be ready always to take time as we find it. . . . [one who philosophizes] need not have cured oneself of either ambition or avarice. (15–16)

A related fantasy is the reinterpretation of all philosophy as drunken talk, as in the alcoholic burlesque of "The Tippling Philosophers" or the *Monty Python* sketch "The Australian Philosophy Department" (see Maynard 62).[18]

Nevertheless, Anacreontic euphoria seems to border on a gravity of its own, since it seeks its pleasure within the shadow of the grave. The most pervasive Anacreontic arguments are inflected by carpe diem: "Bring water, bring wine, boy. . . . the dead man has no desires," and

> All my care is for today;
> What's tomorrow who can say?
> Come then, let us drink and dice,
> And to Bacchus sacrifice,
> Ere death come and take us off,
> Crying, Hold! th'hast drunk enough.
> (Rosenmeyer 1992, 260; Thomas Stanley in Levarie 225)

Before the day of Herrick's death comes,

> Still I be Bousing;
> For I know, in the Tombs
> There's no Carousing.
> (197)[19]

Drinking against death can easily modulate into poetic arguments that oppose drinking to the "death" of ordinary life or to the swift passage of time. These empty categories, against which the rapture of intoxication means everything, would eventually be packed into a concept of modernity. Charles Cotton's "Clepsydra, a poem on the water clock," orchestrates drinking and time while it also alludes to the traditional dialogue between water and wine, where water (like time) threatens alcoholic euphoria:

> Why, let it run! who bids it stay?
> Let us the while be merry;
> Time there in water creeps away,
> With us it posts in Sherry.
> Time not employ'd's empty sound,
> Nor did kind Heaven lend it,
> But that the Glass should quick go round,
> And men in pleasure spend it.
> (217)

Drink also has a place in the *beatus ille* trope, which urges withdrawal from public life, after Horace's second epode:

> Happy the man, who far from town's affairs,
> The life of old-world mortals shares;
> With his own oxen tills his forebears' fields,
> Nor things of usury and its yields.
> (113)

The burden of Anacreontic poetry had always been private pleasure rather than public achievement or duty. In making an initial choice to withdraw from public life, it acts out its literary history, its opposition to the great odes of Pindar. The motif of withdrawal reflects a thematic shift in the poetry from epicureanism to a defensive stoicism; it acknowledges the reality of pain and defeat in a way that carpe diem never did. Euphoria is now either promissory or hard-won, as in a quietly desperate triplet by Cotton:

> Let mee have sack, tobacco store,
> A drunken friend, a little whore,
> *Protectour*, I will ask no more.
> (222)

The motif of withdrawal strongly marked English Cavalier poetry for reasons that were much dwelt on in the texts: the Puritans could have the world; they would be happy somewhere else. The Cavalier of the drink narrative has already withdrawn, not to a farm or valley but to a tavern, which is, paradoxically, both a prison and a sphere of untrammelled freedom and pleasure:

> Though we're in hold, let cups go free,
> Birds in a cage may freely sing;

and

> They onlie are besieg'd, whilst we
> By drinking purchase libertie.
> Wine doth enlarge, and ease our minds,
> Who freely drinks no thraldome finds.
> (Brome 117; Robert Heath in Sullivan 1981, 85)

In a countermove, the tavern is an everything: the court that was lost as well as a new and radiant cosmological dispensation.[20]

One withdraws to wine, but the wine is itself a withdrawal. Since this stoic impulse would have us give up anything contingent, only the pleasure of drinking (in this nonaddictive universe) is constant and under our control; Lord Byron wrote, "In the goblet alone no deception is found" (265). Even the love of the original Anacreontic formula has come to seem a distraction from the perfect happiness of drinking, as Sir Willfull Witwoud sings in William Congreve's *Way of the World,*

> He that whines for a lass,
> Is an ignorant ass,
> For a bumper has not its fellow;

or Charles Sedley rhymes in "To Phyllis Who Slighted Him":

> Since you no longer will be kind,
> But my embraces shun,

Bacchus shall ease my am'rous mind,
To his embrace I run.[21]

The figures and tropes that support carpe diem can also feed despair. In the Anacreontic fiction, death is not fearful, merely a ruse to heighten pleasure; but it is an anxious reality for Omar and other drink poets whose drinking is done against a more pressing horizon. Commentators agree that Omar's hedonism is a weary attempt to make a hopeless life bearable; his quatrains dissipate the comfort normally found in carpe diem:

Then to the Lip of this poor earthen Urn
I lean'd, the Secret of my Life to learn:
And Lip to Lip it murmured—"While you live,
Drink!—for, once dead, you never shall return."
(Decker 101)

This is a note seldom heard in early modern Western song, although there are exceptions, like Cotton's triplet and this passage by Sedley:

Dear Friend, I fear my Heart will break;
In t'other World I scarce believe,
In this I little pleasure take:
That my whole Grief thou may'st conceive;
Cou'd I not Drink more than I Whore,
By Heaven I wou'd not live an Hour.
(Sedley in Robinson 72)[22]

Edward Fitzgerald comes late in the nineteenth century, after Friedrich Nietzsche has read even the original Greek euphoria as anxious terror in *The Birth of Tragedy*.

In his book on Dionysian poetics, Charles Segal opposes the innocence of Anacreon to the ambiguity of the Platonic *pharmakon* where drugs can either cure or kill. The Dionysus of Euripides is also savagely dual. Of course the dark side of drinking (a drinking that lives with hangover, remorse, and shame) was known to classical antiquity, for example, in Tibullus's fifth elegy:

Often with drink I seek to rout these sorrows,
But sorrow turns wine itself to tears;

or Lucian's "Saturnalian Letters" where water drinkers "get up next morning without either the headache the rich man's wine leaves behind, or the disgusting queasiness that results from his surfeit of food" (Tibullus in Lind 222; Lucian 4.122). Even the bright side of drinking had its dark side: "Athenaeus quotes sources, including Aristotle, who say that the ivy wreath, often worn by symposiasts, did not have its origin in Dionysian cult practice but was used to bandage throbbing temples in order to thwart the effects of drinking too much" (Lynch 9). So why was the Anacreontic delusion persisted in?

Anacreon was not always acknowledged as the poet of intoxication and euphoria; in learned classicist readings, his poetry is already shadowed and fallen. That honor should go to his predecessor, Alcaeus of Lesbos (b. 625–20 BC), who stands out as the "toper" among the Greek lyric poets: in the matter of mixing wine with water, for example, "Anacreon recommends 2:1 for restrained drinking," while "the more boisterous Alcaeus prescribes 1:2." Alcaeus was the *real* poet of drunkenness for whom "any pretext was good enough to justify a drinking party," and his poems keep up a steady refrain of "Drink!": "Rejoice and drink this . . . Come, drink with the rest!" "Drink, Melanippus!" "Drink, why wait for the lamp?" "Let's drink, the star now shows in the sky."[23] Nevertheless, Anacreon's name is used to designate this motif, not Alcaeus's.

Albin Lesky writes that there is a "striking contrast between Alcaeus singing to his carousing club-mates of his well-stocked armory, and Anacreon at the wine-bowl expressing distaste for the mention of conflict or hateful warfare" (176). "Anacreon"'s poetry may well mark an awareness of the pain of drinking in the regularity with which it forbids anger and fighting to cohabit the drinking scene, the steadfastness with which it repudiates the connection between drinking and violence.[24] What "Anacreon" banishes from the scene is precisely the excess of drinking, the mark that would rob intoxication of its euphoria. In a world where drink produces only euphoria, excess itself looks like moderation.

The injunctions against aggression and violence remind us of the actual consequences of drinking. The violence that the singer fears would result in the death of the feast, and this explosive closure is illustrated by the various centaur myths, both the adventure of Hercules with Pholus and the battle of the centaurs and the Lapithae. Any Titanomachy, Gigantomachy, or Centauromachy, Miroslav Marcovich remarks, must be banned from the symposium, for "they all sing deeds of violence which have no place at such a holy celebration" (11). Banning violence from the drinking scene can also be read as a self-reflexive boundary between the drink poetries of Anacreon and Alcaeus, since the latter "was overfond of war but no less fond of drinking . . . as all the critics from Athenaeus downwards have observed" (Giangrande 106).

Rosenmeyer laments the reduction of Anacreon to "Anacreon," who is *only* a poet of love and drink: "The legends which grew about Anacreon after his death contributed greatly to a reduced image of a drunken old man singing love-songs, an image which seemed to mesh perfectly with the newly recovered texts": Alexandrian realism "turned Anacreon into the complete drunkard" (1992, 3, 19). The poetry attributed to this "complete drunkard" would eventually come to be regarded as slight and meretricious, so that the reductiveness Rosenmeyer deplores would be aesthetic as well as canonic. "Pretty as they often are," J. M. Edmonds says of the *Anacreontea,* "their silver-gilt could not but suffer close comparison with the true gold [of the genuine Anacreon . . . or of Sappho]" (Silver 323). Braden characterizes our present sense of this poetry: "The speaker of these poems is intelligible mostly as a convergence of repeated clichés: he is old and usually broke, fond of dancing and roses and young boys and girls, and especially liquor, which is valued mainly for the quick relief it provides from the vaguely defined menace of *merimna,* anxiety." All the more reason to ask why "Anacreon"'s poems had the drawing power that they had; Braden goes on to say that "it requires some historical reconstruction to understand why the Renaissance took them very seriously indeed" (1978, 207, 196).[25]

   This poetry exerted a powerful draw up to the present century, and if its source is not the poet or the poetry, it must be a more diffuse discourse that "Anacreon" signs. "These poems, clearly, offered something that could not be found elsewhere," Tom Mason writes, "something that found an answering resonance in minds very different from one another" (106). "Anacreon" stages alcoholic desire and literalizes every drinker's dream to have the good times go on forever.

So extreme is the identification between "Anacreon" and strong drink that he thirsts for it even from the grave:

> Stranger who passest by the simple tomb of Anacreon . . . pour some drops, that my bones may rejoice refreshed with wine, that I who delighted in the loud-voiced revels of Dionysus, I who dwelt amid such music as loveth wine, even in death may not suffer without Bacchus my sojourn in this land to which all the sons of men must come. (Antipater of Sidon in *Greek Anthology* 7.26)

Such a postmortem existence attaches to other wine poets, notably the Persian Hafiz and the Chinese Cheng Chuan. The following verses, for example, are inscribed on Hafiz's grave:

> If you sit above my grave with music and wine
> At the fragrance of you I shall rise from that narrow place and dance.
> (54)

Cheng once said, "Bury me at the side of an oven and, after a few hundred years, I may turn into a *sake* jar" (Bownas 235).

The reduction of Anacreon to a "perfect drunkard" also became the data of biography, so André Simon declares that "of all Greek lyric poets, none had a greater love of wine and none a more tragic end for a wine-bibber than Anacreon" (1948, 21). He was "charged," Judson Davidson asserts, "with licentiousness and inebriety. It has also been said that his erratic habits finally unfitted him for little else than the pursuit of pleasure" (38–39). According to Leslie O'Bell, his legendary biography was as much a topic of the Anacreontic tradition as the verse itself; every edition published the life as a preface (80).[26] Anacreon's death performs a witty turn on this mode of construction: it was said to have been caused by his choking on a grape pip—"Anacreon . . . surpassed the common span of human life but perished when a single pip obstinately stuck in his withered throat as he sustained his poor remaining strength with raisin-juice"—"a fate," Leigh Hunt remarks, "generally thought to be a little too allegorical to be likely" (Valerius Maximus in Campbell 1988, 2.29–30; Hunt 1865, 110).

Despite the reduction model offered by Rosenmeyer, it is hard to see the sequence leading to it: an original and diverse Anacreon replaced by a caricatural drunken old lover. Even Rosenmeyer admits, "There seems to be no strictly chronological degeneration: the anacreontic, drunken, love-sick poet appears as early as 515 B.C., while the sober, archaic hero re-appears seventy-five years later" (1992, 36). The chronology may be difficult here because the original citations are already ambiguous, caught in the confusions of an Anacreon who might be only "Anacreon": When Michael Grant writes that Anacreon's reputation among the ancients was that of a poet exclusively devoted to love, wine, and song, one suspects a crossing of traditions; is his reference a representation of the original poet or of the editorial processes that are at this very time constructing "Anacreon" (19)? Are the slim remains of Anacreon themselves shaped by the later reputation?

Anacreon's other role as lover is not unconnected to his drinking. He is not merely a lover but an old lover, and wine conventionally makes a man feel young.[27] Conversely, F. R. C. Bagley writes that it is "hard to accept the picture of Khayyám shown in many modern Tehrani editions of his *roba'iyat,* with their illustrations of a tired old man being consoled by a flimsily clad maiden holding a flask in her hand" (85).

When "Anacreon" was recovered in the Renaissance, his name continued to designate drinking, as, for example, in John Southern's *Pandora* (1584):

> But like the olde poet Annacron,
> It pleases mee well to be Bibern,
> And thus in a Sellor to quaffe—

or Ronsard's poetic address to Rémy Belleau—

> Belleau, you don't drink enough
> To do Anacreon justice;

and a type of poetry called anacreontic was distributed through all the national lyric traditions of Europe (Southern, "Odellet," n.p.). Paolo Possiedi claims that the *Anacreontea* "enjoyed for a long period a tremendous success, both as classical poetry and as unsurpassed models for modern poetry" (107). "Anacreon" had a crucial part to play in the development of vernacular poetries until the nineteenth century when the attraction waned or, actually, shifted downward into a popular song tradition (the poetry of the Caveau in France, for example, or Anacreontic Society songs in England and America, including, as colleagues pointed out when I told them about this chapter, the song whose melody was adapted for "The Star-Spangled Banner").

No other Greek poet was as instrumental in the development of the modern lyric as "Anacreon": Anacreontic poetry served to create an affective "lyric" space that could offset the authority of public poetry, the inheritance of Pindar. Although of little poetic value in themselves, translations and imitations of the *Anacreontea* made space for the development of lyric poetry. Pierre Hart writes that "the lightness and grace of such poetry was a welcome alternative to the solemn ode, while its emphasis on experience more intimate than the celebration of national events encouraged the cultivation of lyric elements" (378). In German literature, according to Newell Warde, Anacreontic and lyric were synonymous terms (15).[28]

In 1549 Henri Estienne, a French scholar and publisher of Greek texts, discovered the sixty odes of "Anacreon" appended to an eleventh-century manuscript of the *Greek Anthology* and published fifty-five of them with his own Latin translations five years later. Estienne was jubilant over the recovery of this lost poet: "It was supposed that Anacreon had been irrevocably doomed; and now, breaking the adamantine fetters that had held him so long, he had emerged from captivity"; as was Julius Caesar Scaliger: "Who will rouse gentle Anacreon, that elegant old man, to dance to his uncomplicated measure? Come, friends of Bacchus, loosen the Muse's yoke, so that with generous love we may rediscover those ancient mysteries of song" (Bullen ix; Braden 1978, 203). In one of Ronsard's poems, "Corydon" (a classical name for a cupbearer) is asked to bring together a "squadron of men of letters" for a literary banquet to toast Estienne and the discovery of Anacreon (Jeanneret 126).

Soon after Estienne's publication, Ronsard wrote several imitations of these newfound odes, and "Anacreon" soon became a major influence on Ronsard's poetic development as well as part of the Pléiade's program for vernacular literature. A sequence of nationalist recoveries followed: an English translation in 1651; a Dutch translation in 1656; Spanish, in 1657; Italian, in 1670.[29] The first German translation appeared in 1698, and Warde states that "Anacreonticism became a movement to which practically every German poet in the second half of the eighteenth century devoted some of his creative energies" (1). "Anacreon" did not enter Russian poetry until 1791 (O'Bell 80).

As I mentioned earlier, the wine tended to disappear from the poetry after the Renaissance, particularly in the French, Spanish, and Russian adaptations. Writing in early-nineteenth-century France, Pierre Béranger called on anacreontics to enter history: "Love and wine could no longer furnish more than the mere framework of the ideas possessing a people that had risen from the Revolution" (Pollock 11). A prominent Russian poet, Mikhail Lomonosov, attacked both the hedonism and the personal nature of Anacreontic poetry and "corrected" these faults in his own work (Hart 100). As a consequence of this public morality, Russian Anacreontic poetry has few identifying characteristics beyond passion (but is there really no connection between the suppression of Anacreontic content and an alcoholic culture?).[30]

For all his enthusiasm about "Anacreon," even Estienne had worried about the possible immorality of the poetry: if anacreontics no longer dealt with drink, they could still signify erotica, even pornography. On his death-bed Sir Philip Sidney "blushed at even the most casual mention of his Anacreontics, and once again begged his brother, by their tie of common birth, by his right hand, by his faith in Christ, that not any of this sort of poem should come forth into the light" (Duncan-Jones 226). In his life of Abraham Cowley, Samuel Johnson describes anacreontics as "songs dedicated to festivity and gaiety, in which even the morality is voluptuous, and which teach nothing but enjoyment of the present day" (Levarie 238–39). Christoph Martin Wieland denounced as immoral the poetry of Johann Peter Uz, a leading German Anacreontic poet, and S. T. Aksakov found the anacreontics of another Russian poet, Gavriil Derzhavin, unpleasant and embarrassing, particularly as the latter insisted on having them read to young women (McCarthy 24; O'Bell 65). In J. C. Mardrus's translation of the *Arabian Nights,* Shahryar threatens to bring Scheherazade's "story-telling career to a sudden end," not when she runs out of stories but if she tells him any more stories about Abu Nuwas, "this debauchee who respected neither Caliphs nor laws" (Ingrams 28).

An instability had entered the valence of the name: "Anacreontic" could still signify wine and love, but it could also refer to a meter; the qualities of simplicity, softness, and lightness in tone and form—"All agreed," Mason writes, "that Anacreon possessed sweetness, ease, freedom of metre, and a particular form of wisdom"; lyrical or personal poetry; as well as poems about small things (doves, swallows, bees, grasshoppers); poems instructing painters how to paint their beloveds; or aristocratic or court poetry.[31]

The eighteenth-century French philosopher Charles Batteaux distinguished three sorts of enthusiasms in his treatise on the lyric: the sublime, or Pindaric; the moderate, or Horatian; and the soft, or Anacreontic. "The clarion tone of Estienne's introduction," O'Bell writes, "derives from the momentary illusion of having discovered an alternative and better lyric tradition" (82); Estienne suggests in his preface that readers who find Pindar hard will enjoy Anacreon (Levarie 222). The great obstacle to the development of modern lyric was the tradition of the Pindaric ode. Pindar, as Braden explains, was "a notoriously difficult poet whose odes had hitherto constituted the only substantial body of classic Greek lyric available" (1978, 203). "Anacreon," on the other hand, was granted the essential lyric quality of spontaneous utterance:

> The notion of a great naturalness and lack of artifice in Anacreontic poetry, for example, was accepted by all readers and imitators of the Teian poet. . . . Anacreon became the singer of primordial desire and pleasure, the poet whose voice did not need planning or artifice, but, on the contrary, was marked by an overbearing spontaneity and by a healthy and beneficial naturalness. (Possiedi 108, 111)[32]

The opposition between Pindar and "Anacreon" was played out in the ode that Estienne and most modern translators insisted on putting at the head of the collection:

> Give me the lyre of Homer
> without its bloody chord
> (Rosenmeyer 1992, 127)

This editorial error was actually a boundary statement, explaining how the genre originated: I tried to sing an epic or Pindaric ode, but my lyre would only sing of love.[33] The ban against fighting and violence discussed earlier also came to mean, in this specific Renaissance context, "Anacreon" not Pindar, intoxication and dalliance not public events.

The poetic careers of Ronsard and Goethe were major battlefields on which the opposition of Pindar and "Anacreon" were fought. Both of these writers underwent dramatic conversions from the influence of the former to the latter. Ronsard "renounced the triadic sinuosities of the Pindaric ode with profound relief," and "the *ode grâve* of the Theban poet was repudiated in favor of the *ode légère* of Anacreon" (Silver 352).[34]

But the reign of "Anacreon" would come to a sudden end: since the days of Byron and Thomas Moore, A. H. Bullen states, "poets, in a genuine sense, not mere versifiers, have left Anacreon severely alone" (xiv). And George Saintsbury writes that

> an essayist who should not fear to touch the titles of Charles Lamb might perhaps take a worse subject than the decay of drinking-songs. For the last half-century it would be difficult to find any instance in the more prominent literatures of Europe of a Bacchanalian poet, and the instances of those who have recently tried to make themselves exceptions to the rule are rather more convincing than the silence of the majority. The *maladie du siècle* does not seem to have had any unfavorable effect on the consumption of fermented liquors, but it certainly has interfered with their poetical celebration." (377–78)

Some poets, like Leconte de Lisle, C. S. Calverley, A. E. Housman, Norman Douglas, and Richard Aldington, continued to write anacreontics, but they were fewer and farther between than in past centuries.

The Anacreontic impulse, however, thrived well into the twentieth century in a body of literature that would eventually become popular poetry: newspaper and magazine verse, the productions of Anacreontic societies, choral societies, and glee clubs. And in this verse literature, the term *anacreontic* still meant drink.[35]

Romantics turned against the Anacreontic equation because it was lacking in "real" passion: only poetry in which authors are "expressing their real feelings and beliefs deserves the dignity of being called 'lyric'" (Warde 1).[36] This waning of Anacreontic influence in Europe, however, coincided with a second hit of Greek intoxication, the concentrated infusion of "Dionysianism" imported into the West by German scholars and philosophers. The poetry of drink splits in the work of Romantics like Samuel Taylor Coleridge and John Keats: the major poetry becomes infected by a pathology of indolence, that is, turns into a poetry of addiction that would become the dominant modality for drink or drug poetry in the twentieth century, culminating in a performance like John Berryman's *Dream Songs*. The older branch, the poetry of intoxication, turned very light indeed:

> Cry, Avaunt, New Potato!
> And don't get drunk, like old Cato!
> Ah beware of Dys Pipsy,
> And there*fore* don't get tipsy!
> For tho' Gin and Whisky
> May make you feel frisky,
> They're but Crimps for Dys Pipsy.
> (Coleridge in Taylor 1994, 231)

chapter 3

Double Dionysus: Ambiguities in the Discourse of Intoxication

> He is Bromius who leads us! *Evohé!*
> —With milk the earth flows! It flows with wine!
> It runs with the nectar of bees.
> —EURIPIDES, *The Bacchae*

In Euripides' tragedy, the universe pulses with intoxicating liquid. Dionysus is the lord of this nature, like Christ, turning water into wine:

> One woman
> struck her thyrsus against a rock and a fountain
> of cool water came bubbling up. Another drove
> her fennel in the ground, and where it struck the earth,
> at the touch of god, a spring of wine poured out.
> (223)

It may, however, be difficult to make *The Bacchae* tell us much about intoxication, since no drinks or drugs are ingested during the play. The accusations of intoxication are most likely puritanical fantasies of Pentheus, the king of Thebes. In this play, Dionysus, attended by a band of maenads, has returned home after his conquest of India. He appears in the guise of a Lydian priest and lures the women of Thebes to the mountains outside the city, where they spend their time in ritual festivity. Pentheus is outraged and accuses Dionysus and his followers of drunkenness and sexual orgy. In retaliation, the god transforms the king into an infantile voyeur and sends him, dressed in female clothing, into the midst of the frenzied maenadic band, where he is torn apart by the revelers, one of whom is his mother.

Just as the wild behavior in the play may have nothing to do with drink, so in the commentary Dionysian intoxication readily slips its tether and becomes an index of transcendental states or the protean stuff of the self. Uncertainty about the nature of Dionysian feeling and behavior in Euripides is matched by a similar confusion about the meaning of this god in antiquity. Dionysus is either the god of wine or the god of so many things that readings of his presence in art become impossibly overdetermined, and he begins to sound like the disease of alcoholism itself, whose symptoms multiply until no diagnosis has credibility. A sequence of three quotations from Albert Henrichs illustrates this multiplication: "Throughout antiquity, Dionysus was first and foremost the god of wine. . . . In the eyes of most Greeks and Romans, Dionysus was the inventor of wine, and nothing more" (1980–82, 140, 160).[1] "Dionysus was essentially the god of wine and vitality; of ritual madness; of the mask and the theater; and of a happy afterlife. These were his four major provinces, in which he was firmly established by the fifth century B.C. and which he never gave up" (1984a, 205).

> Dionysus is different. His divine identity oscillates bewilderingly between extreme and even opposite characteristics. . . . Dionysus is essentially a paradox, the sum total of numerous contradictions. Other gods are clearly delineated. . . . By contrast, Dionysus is composed of ambiguities which are irreconcilable if seen separately. (1979, 1–3)

The multiplicity model is held in place by ratcheting up to a higher level of abstraction: "Dionysus appears to signify not a discrete being with a definable identity," Michelle Gellrich writes, "but a condition prior to or other than 'identity.' He does not so much destroy or confuse distinctions as configure the nondifferentiation out of which such distinctions eventually arise—notably, the foundational ones of female/male and nature/culture" (53). And, Jean-Pierre Vernant adds, "he blurs the frontiers between the divine and the human" (390).

If Dionysus is multiple, it may be because he is the god of transgression itself. According to Charles Segal, "As Apollo imposes limits and reinforces boundaries, Dionysus, his opposite and complement, dissolves them. . . . In this 'space between,' order and disorder lose their familiar clarity of definition and energies are released to combine in new ways. . . . It is the spirit of the carnival" (12–13). But if Dionysus dissolves limits, we must remember that this is also a special feature of alcoholic drink.

Dionysus's later career in pagan and Christian Rome is to be only a drunk, "depicted as a kind of congenial cherub who was always tipsy" (Evans 60). Lucian specializes in this Dionysus—in "The Gods in Council": "You may all see him [Dionysus] for yourselves: an effeminate, half-witted creature, reeking of strong liquor from the early hours of the day," and in "Dialogues of the Gods": "I should be ashamed, Jupiter, if *I* had such a son [as Bacchus]; so effeminate, and so given to drinking, tying up his hair in a ribbon, indeed! and spending most of his time among mad women" (4.166, 1.76). For "the Middle Ages Bacchus was a drunkard and tutelar of drunkards" (Stock xiv).

The Bacchae is traditionally read within the context of Greek religion as a statement about otherworldly ways of being like ecstasy, possession, and madness. The appearance of Dionysus brings with it a kind of wild energy that is constantly referred to the spiritual side of the soul-body split: this is apparently what happens when a god manifests himself or invades one's being. What is gained or lost if we add material intoxication to this list, either as another term in the series or as an unvoiced master term?

What are ecstasy, possession, and madness that intoxication is not? The three abstract terms are generally defined in terms of one another—for example, "She was mad, stark mad, possessed by Bacchus" (Euripides 1960a, 242)—and all three are defined through metaphors of intoxication. In much that is written on *The Bacchae,* the word *intoxication* appears as a way to bring home what the other, presumably more appropriate and important words, like *ecstasy, possession,* or *madness,* mean, because "drunkenness is the only realm of human experience which can be used to describe the ecstasy of union with God" (Cave 20). Intoxication is used to anchor the other terms, as in Kenneth J. Reckford's statement that "Dionysian ecstasy must have seemed to Heraclitus a crazy 'drowning' of the soul, akin to drunkenness" (460).

Jane Harrison describes a figure on a London stamnos as "the Thracian Dionysus drunk with wine, a brutal though still splendid savage" (450), while C. Bérard and C. Bron call the same figure "the prince of maenads and satyrs in the paroxysm of the ecstatic crisis" (Carpenter 193). The confusing relationship between intoxication and ecstasy is examined at length in chapter 7. The overlap between drunkenness and madness is easily documented: Homer, for example, makes their equivalency evident in the lines,

Disastrous folly led me thus astray,
Or wine's excess, or madness sent from Jove";

Anacreon sings:

Let someone bring for me
the juice of Dionysus' harvest,
in order that he may see the strength of an old man,
one who . . . knows how to drink,
and gracefully to be mad;

and Chaucer's Pardoner explains that drunkenness is merely a brief form
of madness:

Senec seith a good word doutelees;
He seith he kan no difference fynde
Betwix a man that is out of his mynde
And a man which that is dronkelewe,
But that woodnesse, yfallen in a shrewe,
Persevereth lenger than doth dronkenesse.[2]

In Dionysian myth, the god's invention of wine occurs during a period of
madness inflicted on him by Hera (Sutton 210).

More to the point, how are we to understand ecstasy, possession, or
madness as they are produced by a god who *is* wine? "The gift he brought
was himself, for Dionysus was not just the god of wine; he was the wine
itself" (O'Brien 1992, 3). Dionysus is the god *in* the bottle or *in* the wine:
in *The Bacchae*, Tiresias states that "when we pour libations to the gods,
we pour the god of wine himself"; Charles Baudelaire called Dionysus "the
mysterious god hidden in the fibers of the vine"; and Walter Otto wrote
that the "wine carries within it the wonders and secrets, the boundless wild
nature of the god."[3] The text of the play need not concern itself with literal intoxication as long as one understands that Dionysus *is* drink, and
this understanding brings the play to the edge of a narrow allegorical reading whereby everything that occurs is also happening in the register of
material intoxication. If I write a story about someone I identify as the god
of drink or as drink personified, I force the reader to infer propositions
about intoxication, its angry sweep and its dual personality.

The Bacchae sets the stage for certain ambiguities in the discourse of intoxication, whereby a god who is wine produces the effects of intoxication, but it is called something else. This tendency toward misdirection will be extremely influential in discussions of a certain order of artistic creativity that takes the form "not drink but god," that is, not the fruits of intoxication but a *furor poeticus* or some other divine afflatus. The language of literary criticism descends in part from narratives such as this.

Dionysus has little to do with actual wine, but he produces drink's primary effects in those around him. *The Bacchae* is set in an arena where festive and antisocial behavior—carnivalesque behavior—occurs. The first citizen of Thebes, Cadmus, is overtaken by an impulse to "dance night and day, untiringly beating the earth with his thyrsis" (200). If the presence of wine is minimal, behaviors that belong to intoxication nonetheless organize this universe and its actions. Still, the obvious connection to intoxication is rarely made: the extremes of maenadic behavior, according to Henrichs, invite "comparison with medieval examples of religious mass hysteria, with clinical cases of possession, and with various tribal rituals"— but not with drunkenness (1978, 122).

The formulations constructed to express transcendental meaning fit drink and drugs just as well—for example, R. P. Winnington-Ingram: Dionysiac happiness is an escape "into a mindless joy in the present"; Jean-Pierre Vernant: "Their gambols and leaping give animated expression to another aspect of Dionysianism, the joyful, liberating delirium that seizes whoever does not reject the god"; or Charles Segal: "Like his bacchants, Dionysus himself embodies the volatility of emotion, that within us which lies beyond our full control and, if released from the usual discipline and restraint, may suddenly rush to its diametrical opposite." "As the Scythians in Herodotus put it," E. R. Dodds wrote, "'Dionysus leads people on to behave madly'—which could mean anything from 'letting yourself go' to becoming 'possessed.'"[4]

The absence of drink parallels another absence in the play: the curious omission of satyrs, and this imbalance speaks directly to a buried relationship between ecstasy and intoxication. In the Renaissance, Dionysus is attended by both maenads and satyrs who constitute a gender pair and a species pair (woman and man/human and animal).[5] In antiquity, according to Henrichs,

Wine and maenadism, the two major provinces of Dionysus, were kept strictly separate: wine-drinking maenads are as unheard of in real life and actual cult as male maenads. Not even in the *Bacchae* of Euripides, with its extremely ambiguous portrayal of maenadism, do the maenads drink wine or mingle with men: both charges, though repeatedly made by Pentheus, are refuted by the first messenger, an eyewitness. (1984b, 70)

Christopher Faraone agrees that Dionysus's worship is "strangely conditioned by the gender of the worshiper—men exalted him by drinking wine in symposia, while women danced on the mountain" (1993, 1). "Dionysus can," Lissarrague states, like his maenads, "enter into a trance (just as, like satyrs, he can get drunk)" (1993, 215).[6]

Maenads and satyrs thus struck different (but coordinated) thematic keys. Maenads offered "women the 'blessings of madness' within the institutional limits of ritual maenadism," and satyrs offered "to men the gift of wine and its ritualized consumption" (Henrichs 1980–82, 160). These gender communities wrote two different but parallel languages, a first one of ecstasy and madness, a second of literal intoxication.

Euripides' *Bacchae* has Dionysus attended only by maenads. Euripides' *Cyclops* is devoted to the adventures of that missing band of satyrs. One is a tragedy, the other a comedy or satyr play, and satyr plays, according to Roger Green, originally concerned themselves "with some adventure of Dionysos in person, dealing often, for example, with the many legends of his introduction of wine into the various countries of the world" (Sophocles viii–ix).[7] The first is filled with drunken behavior without any intoxicating substance; the second is given over to drink and drunkenness. Where there are men, there can be literal intoxication, as in *The Symposium,* which is dominated by the image of Socrates as a satyr.

Some writers deny such a neat separation of female and male, claiming that the sobriety of maenads is a matter of representation more than of fact.[8] Still others opt for full-scale maenadic intoxication: Helene Deutsch, for example, sees the maenads in a state of "wine-induced exaltation" (28).

The separation of women and wine may be connected to a deep revulsion felt against drinking women in antiquity. Juvenal blamed the decay of religion on increased female drinking. Petrarch commiserated with the "poor matrons of early Rome, for whom drinking was a capital crime, since when a man killed his wife for drinking he was not only unpunished, but not even reproved" (446). He was possibly thinking, André Simon suggested, of Egnatius Mecenius (as we can read in Pliny's *Natural History*), who, in 650 BC, beat his wife to death and "being brought before Romulus on a charge of murder was acquitted when he claimed justifiable provocation because his wife had been drinking his wine" (1948, 31). "*Censoriall Cato* was so curious in the observation of this ordinance," Thomas Nashe writes, again after Pliny, "that hee customably caused certaine men to kysse the women, to know whether theyr breath smelled of wine" (39).

One Euripidean effect in particular points to literal intoxication: Pentheus's double vision. Clement of Alexandria assumed that Pentheus, "like other double see-ers," is merely drunk with wine (O'Brien-Moore 141).[9] A. W. Verrall and Gilbert Norwood have argued that the entire tragedy must be understood to be driven by drink and drugs. Verrall claimed that Pentheus's collapse is caused by a potion, "for the king on emerging gives the familiar sign of drunkenness, the double sun and double city; and his tormentor's first words allude to wine-libations" (52). Vernant also states that Tiresias "goes so far as to accuse him [Pentheus] of being delirious, a prey to *mania,* regarding him as so cruelly mad, having so completely lost his wits, that his derangement can only be explained by a drug" (403–4). Verrall had even speculated that Dionysus's identity in the play as a Lydian would lead the audience to suppose that he carried drugs with him.

> In such a time as the fifth century B.C. . . . the connexion of enthusiasm with intoxicants must have been notorious, and it must . . . have been applied, long before the date of the *Bacchants* . . . to explain some of the performances attributed by legend to Dionysus and his votaries. The Athenian audience, the educated part of it, would probably expect the exhibition of a drug to figure as an element in a Bacchic story. (115)

I don't want to endorse such a narrow reading of the play, but I also do not want intoxication to be generalized out of existence, lost in the more "profound" regions of ecstasy, possession, and madness.[10] As I mentioned earlier, an alcoholic reading of the play is offered to us and rejected as without foundation. Pentheus tries to turn Dionysianism into nothing more than sensual derangement, but Erwin Goodenough thought that the king's guess was eminently reasonable: "I am forced by the ribaldry of Greek comedy and the contemporary vases, however, to believe that Pentheus's description of the licentiousness which he thought was going on in the bacchanalia would have been recognized by every Athenian who saw the play as a true account of what often happened" (18).

Dionysus and Pentheus are generally read as opposites, but the opposite of ecstasy, possession, and madness should be sobriety or proper rationality. This is not the case here, since Pentheus initially seems to embody an overly rigid, excessive rationality. Pentheus's later pathology culminates in the very hallucination and madness he had set himself against: the intoxication and lust that he projected onto the dramatic scene on the mountain now operates at the level of his own mind and body.[11]

Within the binaries along which the play seems to operate, Pentheus should be opposed to intoxication; yet he becomes the identifiable drunk, the bearer of symptoms, while Dionysus stands apart, calm and smiling.[12] The most notorious sign of his intoxication is, of course, his double vision, but in general, as R. D. Stock and Ainsworth O'Brien-Moore suggest, Pentheus is "led in tow by Dionysus as a drunken, effeminate fool," and "his silly questions about the proper holding of the thyrsus, his fancy that he can carry Cithaeron, reflect only the muddled mind of drunkenness" (Stock 66; O'Brien-Moore 142). Pentheus is transformed from a king to a clown, a fulfillment of the marvels of drink.

The opposition between the two can also be read alcoholically, with Pentheus as a figure of hysteria, Dionysus one of control. Pentheus may be the intoxicated one, but Dionysus can be compared to the alcoholic filled with narcissistic rage. He is a god, and grandiosity and perfectionism become the tenor of his being:

> Dionysus destroys those who fail to recognize his divinity, which defines his own narcissistic grandiosity. . . . So, what is wise? What is rational? What works? Apparently nothing, unless the strategy of Dionysus remains the best: to stay calm, cool, collected, but all in the service of one's narcissistic grandiosity. This is what psychoanalysts call narcissistic rage, a cold, calculating rage that can wait calmly for revenge and then take it with no mercy and no pity. But this seems to work only for a god, who has the power to enforce his rage. (Alford 46, 48)

When Agave, the mother of Pentheus, is chastised by Dionysus for mocking him, she answers, "Should God be like proud man in his rage?" (Emboden 189).

Dionysus is not simply cruel but sadistically ensnaring. He imposes a double bind on Pentheus, who must accept him without Dionysus giving any proof of his godhead, except the proof from which reason cannot recover. At the beginning of the play, Cadmus and Tiresias call Pentheus mad simply for opposing the announcement of a new religion. Should every new religion be accepted as true? Shouldn't a ruler protect his people from false religions? To enhance the double bind, Dionysus has chosen the most repellent disguise to approach Pentheus with, the one best calculated to send him over the edge of sanity.

Rather than the drunk and the alcoholic, Carl Ruck reads the opposition between Pentheus and Dionysus as drugs and drink. In addition to bringing a new religion with him to Thebes, Dionysus has planted the first grape-bearing vine in this land where he was born, "for Thebes is a country that has yet to learn the art of viticulture. . . . Pentheus too knows of wine only by rumor, and he suspects" its effects are only a fiction (180). Ruck understands Dionysus to be bringing wine to a drug culture, and the culture explodes in that spectacular violence traditionally attributed to alcohol. In his book *Essential Substances: A Cultural History of Intoxicants in Society,* Richard Rudgely describes how easily prehistoric drug cultures succumbed to the alcoholic habits that arrived with European colonists (36).

The story is complicated by having Dionysus come from the East. Is he an insider, a Western imperialist himself, coming back from the East after having conquered it, or an outsider? Dionysus is, after all, Zeus's son, destined to reign over the West.[13] Edward Said, however, sees him as the outsider: he reads *The Bacchae* as one of the first Western orientalist fictions, which tells of the invasion of the West by the East (57). And the East here is turning the West on, as it would do so often in the future within the Western imperial imaginary.

Dionysus is not simply cruel. Like wine, which is both a scourge and a source of health, the god has a dual effect: "Dionysus, son of Zeus, consummate god, most terrible, and yet most gentle, to mankind." The chorus sings of this benign and fostering god:

The deity, the son of Zeus,
in feast, in festival, delights.
He loves the goddess Peace,
Generous of good,
preserver of the young.
To rich and poor he gives

the simple gift of wine,
the gladness of the grape.
(209)[14]

There is a deep division in this god: he is the one "who snatches his victims
by surprise, who trips his prey and drags it down into madness, murder, and
defilement; yet he is also the god of vines that ripen in a day, of fountains
of wine, of the drink that intoxicates, that creates effervescence" (Detienne
2). In a different register, the Dionysus of Aristophanes' *Frogs* alternates
between bravado and cowardice, "between the heroic costume of the great
Heracles and the mundane garments of a slave" (Hubbard 1991, 200).

Although the passages belonging to the tame Dionysus seem to have
wandered into the play from elsewhere—they may in fact be interpola-
tions—this duality does perplex the tragedy. It corresponds to a larger
problem whereby a play devoted to a wild Dionysus who subverts social
order is staged within a civic institution dedicated to the tame god—"the
Dionysus of the tragic representation" versus "the Dionysus of the civic religion": the wild, amoral, and cruel trickster of the representation is opposed
to and undermined by the Dionysus of the Dionysia, the patron of sociability and community (Vernant 382). "The drama says the opposite of the
institution," Mera Flaumenhaft writes: "Instead of lightning appearances
and the removal of the population to the mountain, here a man-made
statue of the god is deliberately carried within city walls, through gates
and streets, and placed in a building made for institutional worship" (69).

The Bacchae tells the sort of atrocity story that the state loves to tell about
any set of practices that makes it feel uneasy, like stories of the instant sexual abandonment of nice girls in films with titles like *Reefer Madness* or
stories about people high on LSD walking out of high-rise windows or
blinding themselves by staring directly into the sun. These are the stories
that people like Pentheus tell about Dionysus and his followers, and a tale
of barbaric violence is even better than one of intoxication and sexual
abandon. Following this line of thought, one might conclude that Pentheus is not defeated in the play, but that he triumphs, simply because *The
Bacchae* is the story that Puritans tell about intoxicatory experience. In the
very manner of his punishment and his death, Pentheus's anxieties and
concerns are vindicated.

chapter 4

Socrates Undrunk: Literature Writing Philosophy in Plato's *Symposium*

We must, first of all, dismiss from our minds Fite's misleading implication that the moral atmosphere of the *Symposium* is simply that of an "all-night drinking party," attended by idly rich addicts of the aristocratic Greek vice of *paiderastia,* and that the program of successive speeches in praise of Love is merely a "parlor game." This is a serious confusion of the cultural perspective.

—RONALD B. LEVINSON, *In Defense of Plato*

And if men skilled in dialectic should converse on the subject of syllogisms when they have gathered for a drinking party, one might protest that they were acting in a way alien to the occasion, when even a polite gentleman might get drunk.

—ATHENAEUS

In Plato's *Symposium,* only the twenty-one pages of Socrates' speech are read as "philosophy." According to Randall Craig, this speech "transcends the occasion entirely, standing in relation to the earlier speeches as spiritual love to physical, and as philosophy to rhetoric" (167). In the reading that Philosophy claims for itself, only a central thread of reasoning (or assertion) is acknowledged, and there is little uncertainty in the reading community about where this center is to be found.[1] Anything that might call such a declarative reading into question is ignored or denied. In the philosophical reading, all the other uses of discourse are as flute girls to Socrates' wise entertainment.

Another tradition of commentary on *The Symposium,* however, suggests that it should be the last of the Platonic dialogues to be read in this way.

This dialogue has long been praised as a unique contribution by a philosopher to the domain of Literature.[2] It is commonly admitted that *The Symposium* has a rich dramatic setting and contains almost no dialectic (that is, no philosophy, properly speaking). Even philosophical readers like George Kimball Plochmann take their fellows to task for finding in this work "not much more than a unitary doctrine, a dogma of love," playing down "all the dramatic and poetical touches as being delightful but excrescent" (328). In general, Drew Hyland denounces "a multitude of 'continental' philosophers who completely misrepresent 'Platonism' by ignoring the dramatic aspects of the dialogues. Especially given their commitment to 'literary sensitivity,' this misrepresentation is particularly deplorable" (115).

But this appeal to poetry and drama never includes anything subversive; the touches referred to can only enhance the philosophical core: the difference between philosophy and literature, according to Plochmann, is the difference between "doctrine" and "doctrine and an embodiment of it" (328). However, within the dialogue, Socrates voices a fear that all the truth will be used up before he has a chance to speak (the opposite of the traditional reading in which almost no truth is used up *until* he speaks), and this catastrophe would be a function of literature: "It will, of course, be unfair to those of us who occupy the last places, but if fine performances by earlier speakers exhaust the subject, we shan't mind" (41).[3]

Nonetheless, traditional commentary desires to assign literature to philosophy; as Walter Hamilton puts it, "the philosopher in Plato has not yet banished the artist and the poet" (Plato 1951, 9). Another common argument also speaks to such a desire: Socrates is the artist who truly knows how to write both comedy and tragedy because he is a philosopher, and so it is he, not the tragedian Agathon (in whose honor the symposium is being held), who should win the prize for the highest art: "On another level, the Platonic dialogue replaces a celebration of Dionysus with a celebration of philosophy, and the *eiron* takes the place of the tragic hero on centre stage" (Wilson 1987, 227). *The Symposium* enacts what Friedrich Nietzsche later feared, the philosopher triumphing over and replacing both tragedian and comedian.

For all of its acknowledged magnificence as literature, *The Symposium* has not been held to account for one of the basic laws of literature: that ground conditions figure, that is, that people in extreme affective states, in love, in despair, drunk, or getting drunk, think and talk differently than they otherwise would. The dialogue that champions the transformation of love from a carnal to an ideal state takes place amid merrymaking and excessive drinking. Why should we assume that, like its hero Socrates, it is able to drink inordinately but never get drunk? There is no greater demonstration of a mind-body split, for which Plato has been credited, than to keep putting strong drink into the body and have the mind remain unaffected. I believe this to be true of neither the man nor the work.

The symposium is "an all-night drinking-party," and if the dialogue is really as dramatically apt as many of its critics allege, then intoxication should be writing some of it (Fite 158). Manuela Teçusan says that intoxication should make a difference in our reading: "Sympotic dialogues . . . are distinct from other kinds of philosophical dialogue because of the mark left on them by the background against which they are supposed to take place" (264). Alcibiades thinks so, too, because when Eryximachus proposes that he deliver a speech like the others, he replies, "An excellent idea . . . but it can't be fair to make a man who is drunk compete in speaking with men who are sober" (99).

Nevertheless, the dialogue acts as if philosophy can stave off drunken excess and keep the participants sober (the naive reading of Socrates' relationship to drink). And the dialogue contains as its ultimate truth an unbelievable overevaluation of philosophy and of Socrates. Philosophy, it seems to say, protects you not only from the effects of intoxication but also from human vulnerability. A contemporary commentator writes that by the time Alcibiades is finished speaking, "we are bound to think that in charging Socrates with jealousy he is indulging in wishful thinking: Socrates can no more be subject to base emotions such as jealousy than he can be overcome by drink" (Waterfield xxxviii). His core is "self-disciplined, divine, precious, and marvelous" (Morgan 95). According to Erasmus, Socrates is a "god rather than a man, a great, lofty and truly philosophic soul, despising all those things for which other mortals jostle and steer, sweat and dispute and struggle" (Phillips 269).[4]

The dialogue reproduces the condition of its own reading: Socrates and philosophy are a vein of gold in a world of dross. They are the only matters worth attending to, as Alcibiades acknowledges to his pain, "I have been wounded and stung in my heart or soul . . . by philosophical talk which clings more fiercely than a snake" (105). Figures such as this sound ludicrously exaggerated, like the braggadocio that often attends intoxication, a comparison that Alcibiades himself makes:

I myself, gentlemen, were it not that you would think me absolutely drunk, would have stated on oath the effect which his words have had on me, an effect which persists to the present time. Whenever I listen to him my heart beats faster than if I were in a religious frenzy, and tears run down my face. (101)

But Alcibiades *is* drunk. Since the author of all this extravagance about philosophy is a philosopher, one can read it as self-promotion just as easily as truth.[5]

At the urgings of feminism, Plato's *Symposium* has been prodded and read, if not against its grain, at least against the abstract regard of philosophical tradition. By attending to signs that philosophy conventionally ignores, feminist readers have noticed, for example, that the dialogue rests on two contradictory premises: the condition of philosophic discourse is the expulsion of women (the flute girls), but philosophy comes from a woman (Diotima). In this dialogue, the truth comes to a truly ignorant Socrates (usually he only pretends that he is) from a woman who treats him the way he treats his disciples, and in her presence Socrates uncharacteristically abandons irony. According to Barbara Freeman, Plato's dialogue "may be read as an allegory of the position of women in Western philosophy: she is present either as a crucial, initiatory absence—for example, as the flute-girl who is asked to leave the room before the symposium proper can begin, or as the image of plenitude personified by Diotima, guardian of and spokesperson for Platonic truth" (172).[6]

It should be difficult to read *The Symposium* as the simple communication of truth because the dialogue is so treacherous, mined with narrative twists and excessive narrative armature (Hamilton finds the "curiously elaborate machinery" of the dialogue a problem that he cannot explain [Plato 1951, 10]). For one thing, the text is scored by an extensive motif of joking and mockery.[7] The account, moreover, is relayed from a long distant past that renders communication problematic: "Aristodemus did not recollect precisely everything that each speaker said, and I do not recollect everything that Aristodemus told me. . . . This or something like it, according to Aristodemus, was the speech of Phaedrus. It was followed by several others which he did not quite remember" (41, 45). That Socrates may not have said exactly this or that remains a rich and evocative literary possibility throughout, but such a supposition should play havoc with philosophy.

I began by saying that there is a disjunction in Plato's dialogue between the carnivalesque frame and the philosophical message that Socrates presents and commentary accepts. *The Symposium* is presumably about love, but it floats on a sea of drink, and these two constitutive elements are not allowed to be seen as connected. Drink is a barely discernible figure in the work even though it clamors for our attention. Intoxication study has a claim on this text.

We are told a great deal about past and present drinking: the drinking of the night before and the hangover of the morning of the event. Aristophanes says that he was "one of those who were pretty well soaked yesterday"; Pausanias tells the company "that yesterday's bout has left me in a very poor way"; and Agathon is feeling "very weak indeed" (38–39). Alcibiades' entrance returns the symposium to heavy drinking: "Good evening, gentlemen. Will you welcome into your company a man who is already drunk, utterly drunk, or shall we just put a garland on Agathon, which is what we came for, and go away?" (96).[8] Toward the end of the evening there is a second wave of drunken energy as a "crowd of revellers came to the door, and finding it left open by somebody who had just gone out, made their way into the dining-room and installed themselves there. There was a general uproar, all order was abolished, and deep drinking became the rule" (113).

Drink is embedded in the very center of the text. The inset narrative about the birth of love is a drunken narrative: love is the child of blind intoxication:

> On the day that Aphrodite was born the gods were feasting, among them Contrivance the son of Invention; and after dinner, seeing that a party was in progress, Poverty came to beg and stood at the door. Now Contrivance was drunk with nectar—wine, I may say, had not yet been discovered—and went out into the garden of Zeus, and was overcome with sleep. So Poverty, thinking to alleviate her wretched condition by bearing a child to Contrivance, lay with him and conceived Love. (81–82)

The dialogue demands, as a condition of its status as philosophy, that no connection be made between the eros of the superstructure and the alcohol of the base. Outside the dialogue, however, excessive drinking has an intimate connection with eros, as ancient writers like Achilles Tatius ("Cupid and Dionysus are two of the most violent of the gods, they can grasp the soul and drive it so far towards madness that it loses all restraint. . . . for wine is the very sustenance of love" [61–63]); Philostratus ("Dionysus comes to the side of Aphrodite, 'drunk with love' as the Teian poet says of those who are overmastered with love" [63]); Apuleius (the god of wine "always aids and abets the Goddess of Love" [33]); Aristotle ("Wine also makes men amorous; this is shown by the fact that a man in his cups may even be induced to kiss persons whom, because of their appearance or age, nobody at all would kiss when sober. It is for this reason that wine excites sexual desire, and Dionysus and Aphrodite are rightly said to belong together" [21]); and Plato knew full well. The connection between drunkenness and love is not a sublimated but a carnal connection. One might be tempted to say that it describes sexual addiction except that it is an asymmetric equivalent of sexual addiction, a sexual symptom of alcohol addiction, a similar but very different thing.

Love and drink are connected in the dialogue as well. There is a problem as to what god the dialogue addresses, Eros or Dionysus: "Why is the last word in this dialogue about love given not to Eros but to Dionysus, the god of tragedy and comedy and wine? If this scene, like the final scene of the 'Phaedo,' is a poetic summary of what has been said and enacted in the dialogue, then Dionysus must have some connection with Eros" (Bacon 415).[9] Commentary even assigns actors to these two roles: Socrates as Eros, Alcibiades as Dionysus.[10]

The praise of Socrates that starts as extravagant idealization ends, oddly enough, as a comparison to Silenus and satyrs: "He is like no other human being, living or dead. . . . you will never be able to find anyone remotely resembling him either in antiquity or in the present generation, unless you go beyond humanity altogether and have recourse to the images of Silenus and satyr" (Plato 1951, 110). The choice of Silenus is very curious, for in Plato's antiquity Silenus is only a figure of appetite. With the exception of M. E. Screech, who claimed, "There is an element of wilful, playful paradox on Plato's part, when he applies the term *silenus* to Socrates, his teacher, the wisest and the best of men," commentators have seen nothing strange in the comparison (1979, 128). This was not the first time in antiquity that Socrates had been compared to Silenus, but, earlier, it had clearly been a joke based on the visual resemblance between Socrates and stock images of Silenus: "His eyes were prominent, his nose upturned, and lips thick—features customarily attributed by the Athenians to satyrs and silenoi" (Dover xxxii).[11]

Plato's text, however, denies such joking intent and asserts the propriety of a simile that rests on the proposition that both Silenus and Socrates are wise. Who or what is Silenus; what are his connotations in antiquity? He is the aged leader of the band of young satyrs who attend Dionysus, and in his primary classical appearance, in Euripides' *Cyclops,* there is nothing wise about him, only silly and greedy drunkenness. By 1872 Nietzsche can look back to an antiquity that harbors an infinitely wise Silenus, but where could Plato have found such a creature? Almost all of the available evidence suggests that he was not to be found.

In section 3 of *The Birth of Tragedy,* Nietzsche tells the "old story" that

> King Midas had long hunted wise *Silenus.* . . . When Silenus had finally fallen into his clutches, the king asked him what was the best and most desirable thing of all for mankind. The daemon stood silent, stiff and motionless, until at last, forced by the king, he gave a shrill laugh and spoke these words: "Miserable, ephemeral race . . . why do you force me to say what it would be much more fruitful for you not to hear? The best of all things is something entirely outside your grasp: not to be born, not to *be,* to be *nothing.* But the second-best thing for you—is to die soon. (22)

For Nietzsche this would be *the* salient anecdote from mythology to express his sense of Greek civilization: this story condensed "the terrible wisdom of Silenus," against which Greek mythology and art were a defensive response.

Various scholars and critics declare there was a tradition of a wise Silenus in antiquity. According to George Butte, Nietzsche's account follows that of Plutarch in the *Moralia,* but that was written five hundred years after Plato's dialogue, and, with the possible exception of Pindar (c. 522–443 BC), the other references to a wise Silenus come long after Plato (427–347 BC)—in Theopompus (380 BC), Cicero (160–43 BC), and Aelian (AD 170–235) (Butte 156–57).[12] The earliest location for such a paradoxical character is a dialogue of Aristotle's (384–22 BC), "Eudemus or, On the Soul" (Hubbard 1975, 55).

There is another wise Silenus in antiquity to put alongside Nietzsche's, but he is wise in a very different way than Socrates, as a poet rather than a philosopher. This Silenus is the subject of Virgil's "Sixth Eclogue": the

Silenus "of the dominant classical tradition: merry, wine-loving, full of charming songs about the creation of the world and the metamorphoses of gods" (Butte 163). Virgil's figure is radically split: in the narrative frame he is a buffoon, while the persona, the singer Silenus, is a Lucretian poet. Two boys come upon him lying in a drunken sleep, and they bind him with garlands until he sings for them. Silenus sings the creation of the world and various other mythic events.

The accounts of Silenus before Plato make no mention of wisdom—obviously not, in the case of the many vase paintings that feature him, but some scholars even claim that wisdom can be read into the graphic text.[13] There seems to be a tautology at work to anchor the wisdom of Silenus in Greek antiquity because Plato had associated him with Socrates in *The Symposium,* but the wise Silenus is actually a figure without an origin. Commentators, particularly writers of handbooks, feel free to weave all these Silenuses into a connected narrative, so the pessimistic Silenus also sings the joys of cosmogony, and, like a third wise Silenus, the Silenus of Theopompus, tells "wonderful tales of an immense continent lying beyond the Ocean stream— altogether separate from the conjoined mass of Europe, Asia or Africa— where splendid cities abound, peopled by gigantic, happy, and long-lived inhabitants, and enjoying a remarkable legal system" (Graves 1.281).

The riddle of why Socrates is like a silenus is a good one. However, the answer given by Plato—because both have divine interiors beneath uncouth facades—rests on shaky ground.[14] A second answer, that both Socrates and Silenus are ugly, is not given. A third answer cries out to be heard: "Because they're both drinking all the time." It is Alcibiades' figure, and in explaining it he says nothing about drunkenness; yet the outstanding association to Silenus in antiquity was as a drunken fool, a "bibulous monster": "Silenus, the chief friend of Bacchus, was represented as a jolly old man with a bald head and puck nose, fat and round like his own wineskin, which he always carried," and he "had a temple at Elis, where Methe (Drunkenness) stood by his side handing him a cup of wine (Coleman 203; Smith 1967, 3.823).[15]

Ovid (43 BC–c. AD 17) wrote antiquity's longest extended treatment of the capture of Silenus in his *Metamorphosis.* There is, however, not the faintest shadow of wisdom, just boozing: Ovid's Silenus is too heavy to accompany Bacchus, "For the old man weighed half a ton with wine." He is tripped up by Spartan peasants, who carry him to Midas.

When Midas saw the old man was Silenus—
They had been filthy drunken good old friends—
He ordered up a dozen rounds of drinks,
Then more and more, and drank ten days and nights.
When the eleventh dawn streaked hills with red
Midas, still cheerful-drunk, took gay Silenus
The road to Lydia, nor did he stop till he delivered
The old man to the ruler he loved best,
His foster child in drink, the young God Bacchus.
(300)

In his *Symposium* Xenophon makes clear who his Silenus Socrates is being compared to: the Silenus "in the satyr plays" (149). The only extant satyr play is Euripides' *Cyclops,* and that Silenus, according to David Grene, "is at every point the ancestor of Falstaff—lewd, fat, bald, drunken, boastful, knavish, and foolish" (Euripides 1960b, 4). How perverse of Plato to choose this character to signify ideal virtue!

Nietzsche perpetuates a Silenus who is not so much wise as pessimistic. This Silenus is more than drunk all the time: he is the earliest alcoholic; and his vaunted wisdom is the wisdom of that disease, aptly named the "white logic" by Jack London (Crowley 33–34). What Nietzsche claimed to be the truth would later be identified as alcoholic despair. What is philosophy in 1898 in Germany is alcoholic thinking in America in 1912. It makes sense that the heaviest drinker in the culture should be given the white logic as a vision.

We are regularly told that Socrates is a great drinker, but unlike Silenus he is never drunk. He outdrinks everyone else in *The Symposium* but never suffers the effects of intoxication himself: "He will drink any quantity that he is bid, and never be drunk all the same" (Plato 1951, 98). This is illustrated at the very end of the dialogue, when,

[toward daybreak, Aristodemus] woke up, and found that the rest of the party had either fallen asleep or gone away, and that the only people still awake were Agathon and Aristophanes and Socrates. They were drinking from a large cup which they passed round from left to right, and Socrates was holding forth to the others. . . . Aristophanes fell asleep first, and when it was fully light Agathon followed him.

Then Socrates . . . got up and went away. . . . He went to the Lyceum
and washed, and spent the day as he would any other, and finally towards
evening went home to bed." (113–14)

How are we to read Socrates' remarkable hollow leg? Can it be true, as I
asked earlier, that philosophy protects one against intoxication?

"Socrates, after all the others had succumbed, went off, took a bath, and
spent the day as usual, not taking any rest until the night following. That
is to say," Warner Fite declares, "he was able to carry through the pretense
(like many a seasoned hard-drinker) that a night's debauch had made no
difference" (276).[16] Even in antiquity, Seneca had distinguished between
"those who drink without getting drunk and . . . others who succumb with
the greatest of ease" (Sournia 1990, 11). This tendency in Socrates resembles nothing more than alcoholic tolerance, a magical characteristic that lies
at the center of the system of alcoholism and makes it go. It remains in
place until the late stages of the disease. It is as if the person destined to
be an alcoholic is equipped with a potency that allows him to drink to
excess without ill effect. (Surely, it cannot be an unconnected historical
fact that Socrates died of drink, "drinking the hemlock with as cheerful a
face as he wore when drinking wine, and joking with his friend Phaedo
even as he lay dying" [Erasmus in Phillips 269].)

It is ironic that Plato, who argued against symposia as the very antithesis of philosophy (and would only be reconciled to them in his last work,
The Laws), would choose to stage philosophy at a symposium. Teçusan calls
it a "spectacular" change when, in the first two books of *The Laws,* Plato
allowed that symposia might have a social function, which is to teach
sobriety by associating drinking pleasure and drinking behavior with shame
(244).

A notorious symposium occurred in Athens in 415 BC, thirty years before
the writing of *The Symposium* but only one year after the date on which
Plato's dialogue was set, an event marked by excessive drinking and followed by criminal activity in which Alcibiades and Phaedrus were both
said to be deeply implicated. "The events of the summer of 415 BC in
Athens," Oswyn Murray declares, "affected the lives of many individuals for
the next twenty years; and, in the larger political view, they can be held to
have been ultimately responsible for the fall of the Athenian empire, in
that they opened up a fatal breach of mistrust in Athenian political life,

between the *demos* and its traditional aristocratic leaders" (1990, 149). The events of that summer were ultimately responsible for Socrates' death.

That summer, shortly before the Sicilian expedition, the Athenians were shocked by an act of blasphemous vandalism: the statues of Hermes customarily placed in front of houses had been defaced and damaged one night. Apparently, a silent band of irreligious men had perpetrated the crime. Amid the confusion and anger of the following days, it was established that Alcibiades and Phaedrus had a part in the affair (Navia 127).

Two explanations are given for this occurrence: first, that it was "no more than an unusually grandiose and spectacular piece of vandalism of a kind which appeals to some people at a certain stage of drunkenness," and, second, that it was a preparation for oligarchic revolution (Dover in Murray 1990, 153).[17] The destruction of the herms was not unlike a typical consequence of the *komos,* "the ritual drunken riot at the end of the *symposion,"* which often consisted of "the greatest pleasures and acts of *hybris* and all types of madness" (Murray 1990, 150; Megillus in Fisher 28). These mad acts were "performed in public with the intention of demonstrating the power and lawlessness of the drinking group" (Murray 1990, 150). In Aristophanes' *Wasps,* Philokleon, "the converted man of the people . . . attempts to follow the aristocratic life-style of his sophisticated son." He ends "by successfully imitating the wildest sympotic behavior, and returns home in a traditional *komos,"* drunk, with a stolen flute girl, pursued by outraged citizens claiming damages for assault (Murray 1990, 150).

Socrates' relationship with Alcibiades haunted Socrates all his life: "The fact that Alkibiades' teacher was Sokrates had raised dark suspicions that Sokrates, or perhaps his kind of thinking, had led Alkibiades to desecrate the herms and to defect—a suspicion which . . . was believed to have played a significant role in Sokrates' trial and death" (Anderson 105).[18]

If, from the vantage of the present, the philosophy of Nietzsche's Silenus can be thought of as alcoholic despair, in another tradition of cultural discourse, philosophy becomes a power temporarily granted by intoxication. In the first part of this chapter philosophy inhibited intoxication (or so conventional readings of Socrates suggest); now, intoxication produces philosophy. In chapter 1, I mentioned the long-standing belief that drinking makes dull wits philosophical. Even more has been claimed for intoxication in the nineteenth and twentieth centuries: that it induces a liminal experience, allowing one to experience transcendentally or divinely—

Bacchus's gift of the grape "opens men's eyes to the sight of the invisible world" (Fehl 37). Alcohol performs truly what the Neoplatonists only meant metaphorically when they used the language of intoxication for ecstatic experience.

But the cosmic insight produced by intoxication (and in the modern period this is usually predicated of drugs other than alcohol) is delusory. Alathea Hayter describes the subjective intensity felt by some drug users: the "immensely stimulated" "power of associating ideas . . . in long unfolding links and networks of thought," and the projects for "huge philosophical works which will be a synthesis of all knowledge and will explain the pattern of existence" (1968, 43). But these come to nothing. High on nitrous oxide, William James discovered the secret of the universe, but when he looked at it the next day, it read

Higamus, hogamus,
Woman's monogamous,
Hogamus, higamus,
Man is polygamous.
(Goodwin 1993, 9)

chapter 5

"Out, loathed med'cine! O hated potion, hence!": The Magic of Literary Drinks

In every mannes mouth it is
How Tristram was of love drunke
With Bele Isolde, whan they drunke
The drink which Brangweine hem betok

—JOHN GOWER

In a recent review of Pete Hamill's *Drinking Life,* Dan Wakefield (one drunk speaking for two) quotes Hamill on the lure of cartoons in his adolescence:

> For most American kids of our pre-TV generation, the comics provided not only entertainment but education, like "the lesson of the magic potion." Hamill recalls that "the comics taught me, and millions of other kids, that even the weakest human being could take a drink and be magically transformed into someone smarter, bigger, braver." (166)[1]

Seventeen centuries earlier, a Sophist named Flavius Philostratus wrote the same thing about a river of wine in an imaginary painting of Bacchus on the isle of the Andrians: "This river makes men rich, and powerful in the assembly, and helpful to their friends, and beautiful and . . . tall; for when a man has drunk his fill of it he can assemble all these qualities and in his thought make them his own" (97–99).

As part of this larger effort to uncover buried traces of intoxication, I want to ask of potions that work magic on the drinker what they have to do with attitudes toward alcohol and narcotics. The substances in question may confer youth and immortality (as in fountain of youth legends and nineteenth-century "elixir of life" fictions by Mary Shelley, Honoré de Balzac, Nathaniel Hawthorne, and others)—the equation is written into the word *whiskey*, "the water of life"— or they may induce love (as in the Tristan narratives or Shakespeare's *Midsummer Night's Dream*). In Shakespeare's play, many of the elements that Mikhail Bakhtin finds central to carnival (the world upside down and the dethroning of the official king for the space of the holiday) are driven by drink, the "liquor" of the "juice," a magical fluid that releases sexual inhibitions and unleashes violent feelings. I survey these and other examples of the literature and art of magic drinks and take a closer look at two multidetermined fictions that revolve around drinking—Bram Stoker's *Dracula* and Robert Louis Stevenson's *Strange Case of Dr. Jekyll and Mr. Hyde*—as fables of addiction.

If I am literalizing and thus reducing these old potions, the drift of history is much more declarative in that respect, for, in Gaetano Donizetti's version of the Tristan story or Philip Barry's version of *A Midsummer Night's Dream* (*L'elisir d'amore* and *The Philadelphia Story*, respectively), Isolde's love potion and Puck's eyedrops are nothing else but liquor. What is metaphorically crossed with liquor in the earlier periods becomes more and more literalized as strong drink in the nineteenth century, as narrative and language come to demonstrate that "potion" and "elixir" have nothing to be but alcoholic drink. Certainly, drink best meets the conditions of Occam's razor, as that is fancifully acted out in the temperance parable of the man who was tempted by the devil to do one of three things: kill his neighbor, commit adultery, or become intoxicated. Thinking that he was choosing the least evil, he elected to get drunk and so was led to both adultery and murder (Eddy 431).

Many tropes that come into play through these potions and elixirs belong to the discourse of intoxication (and addiction), like personality transformation or animal metamorphosis; as Hamill declares, magical potions narrativize surprising acquisitions of strength and endurance that resemble the condition of tolerance. Intoxication has long been credited with rejuvenating capability, by "Anacreon" and Erasmus, for example: "As we pass the bowl around . . . we old men seem young again"; "The secret of their ascribing a youthful appearance to Bacchus is that drinking wine rids our minds of cares and anxieties and induces a certain cheerfulness. Hence it seems to restore old men themselves to youth" (Anacreon in Davidson 1915,

63; Erasmus 1965, 596). In Samuel Butler's *Characters,* the "Sot" has "found out a Way to renew, not only his Youth, but his Childhood, by being stewed, like old *AEson,* in Liquor" (Digby and Digby 222).

The first mention of a fountain of youth appeared in *The Letter of Prester John,* a popular literary forgery of the late twelfth century: "At the foot of Mount Olympus bubbles up a spring which changes its flavor hour by hour, night and day, and the spring is scarcely three days' journey from Paradise, out of which Adam was driven. If any one has tasted thrice of that fountain, from that day he will feel no fatigue, but will as long as he lives be as a man of thirty years" (Baring-Gould 30). Narratives about the fountain of youth and two other fairy fountains were featured in the *Romance of Alexander.* Alexander and his army discover them on their march to India, which is undertaken in imitation of Dionysus's earlier conquest of the East (Nonnus xiv). He captures four gigantic old men who tell him the story of the three marvelous fountains. Antigonus, "who had white hair and had lived so long that he was bent," bathes the prescribed four times in the "dear fountain of sweet water that rejuvenated," and when "he came out of the water he was straight and strong and there was no more handsome knight in the host. He was thirty and full of strength" (Devereux 89–91).[2]

An American legend concerned the Spanish explorer and colonizer Ponce de León: "As related by Peter Martyr, there existed on an island north of Cuba named Boiuca or Bimini, 'a spring of running water of such marvellous virtue, that the water thereof being drunk, perhaps with some diet, makes old men young again'" (Morison 504). In Hawthorne's "Dr. Heidegger's Experiment," the doctor asks his four ancient acquaintances, whom he has gathered in his study for an experiment in rejuvenation, if they have ever heard of the fountain of youth, "which Ponce de Leon, the Spanish adventurer, went in search of, two or three centuries ago."

> [He never found it] for he never sought it in the right place. The famous Fountain of Youth, if I am rightly informed, is situated in the southern part of the Floridian peninsula, not far from Lake Macaco. Its source is overshadowed by several gigantic magnolias, which, though numberless centuries old, have been kept as fresh as violets, by the virtues of this wonderful water. An acquaintance of mine, knowing my curiosity in such matters, has sent me what you see in the vase. (9.231)

At the end of Hawthorne's tale, after the experiment has failed, the quartet set off to discover the fountain and drink more of the waters.

In fountain of youth legends the miraculous water remains at the center of the story, while in Tristan narratives the love potion diminishes in visibility. Central to early versions of the story, it becomes subsequently marginalized. The magic potion is a dominant motif in the twelfth-century poems of Beroul, Thomas d'Angleterre, and Eilhart von Oberg; as these three poets tell the story, passion has absolute power over Tristan and Isolde from the moment the potion is drunk: it "comes into the narrative suddenly and unexpectedly, and its effect is to bind together two people who have no reason to like each other and whose relations are indeed more hostile than friendly" (Beroul 1970, 10). The potion subsides in the commentary as it does in the history of the text; in the regard of humanist criticism, it virtually disappears.

Although Shakespeare's magical eyedrops produce radically violent results, they also seem to be of no importance to readers of *A Midsummer Night's Dream*. The holiday transformation in the play is motivated by an extremely potent, mood- and reality-altering liquid, but the material substance is forgotten by the participants and invisible to those who look back at it. The status of potions or elixirs in literature is signatory, meaningful only to the extent that they can be made allegorical or symbolic.

The love potion occupies a liminally unstable position and can be easily discarded as having no proper weight of its own; it is only a symbol of something elemental inside or outside the two lovers: "The medieval motif of the philtre is so effective because it is basically only a symbol for the powerful and overpowering passion which takes hold of them, a symbol for the magic quality of love"; "There is no outside magic in the potion. What they drink is their own desire"; "It represents, so to speak, the hand of Fate, for it is something quite external to the lovers. The passion which joins them irresistibly to each other comes not from within themselves" (Curtis 8; Bandera 45; Fedrick 25). Whether a symbol for an internal or external force, critics have always seen the potion as something other than the drink itself.

But these magical narratives are also awash with ordinary drink. It is rare to find a potion in literature, art, or music that is not identified in some way or other with alcohol. In the Tristan stories, the potion regularly crosses positions with wine. The lovers, for example, drink the potion because they believe it to be wine: "The third day was very hot . . . [and Tristan] called for a drink. By mistake, Brangain brought the love potion and handed it to Tristan, who drank and passed it to Yseut. Both thought it was good wine: neither knew that it held for them a lifetime of suffering and hardship and that it was to cause their destruction" (Beroul 1970, 44). This mistake is understandable, since the potion is repeatedly said to resemble wine (von Strassburg 192, 194). In addition, it actually is wine:

> On the fourth day Tristan was playing chess with Isolt, and it was so hot that Tristan became very thirsty, and he asked for wine. Gouvernal and Brangien went to get it for him, and they found the love potion among the other silver vessels. . . . Brangien took the cup of gold and Gouvernal poured into it the drink, which was clear as wine. And wine it was indeed, but other things were mixed with it. (Beroul 1973, 27)

In Shakespeare's comedy, the juice of the flower "love-in-idleness" is an aphrodisiac, but wine is the oldest and most basic of the aphrodisiacs as well as the most common solvent for other aphrodisiacs (Faraone 1992, 97).

In Eurasian legend, as I mentioned, the fountain of youth became intimately connected with the figure of antiquity most closely associated with excessive drinking and alcoholism, Alexander the Great. Fountains of youth appear frequently in "Schlaraffenland" (glutton's paradise) legends along with rivers and fountains of wine (Ackermann 80–84). The three fountains in the Alexander legends are of milk, honey, and wine, everywhere conjoined in early narratives, all three versions of the same magical liquid. At the festival of the Roman goddess Bona Dea, women drank wine and performed Bacchic dances, "but the name of the wine was avoided, and it was called milk instead" (Bell 1982, 275). This three-way conjunction occurs frequently in Late Antiquity and the Middle Ages: Greek sibylline oracles proclaim that God will send righteous souls to a land where there is abundant fruit and "fountains three, of honey, wine and milk"; in the ninth-century *Voyage of Maeldúin,* the hero comes to an island with a golden rampart, on which is a fountain: "It gives water on Wednesdays and Fridays, milk on Sundays and feasts of martyrs; on the feasts of the Apostles, of Mary and John the Baptist, and on the hightides of the year, it gives ale and wine"; and in *The Travels of Marco Polo,* the valley enclosed by the Old Man of the Mountain flows "freely with wine and milk and honey and water" (Patch 85, 32, 160).

In the sixteenth century, Hans Sebald Beham, the Nuremberg engraver, made several woodcuts titled "The Fountain of Youth." His title referred narrowly to a bathhouse, but Beham doubled the reference by including as half of the work a scene of convivial drinking on the roof of an adjacent building: the right half of the roof is taken up by a single drinking party seated at a table, and the middle railing is lined with ewers, flagons, pitchers, and glasses—it is signed by drink (Bartsch 206–7). By juxtaposing a scene of bathing with a scene of drinking, Beham did spatially what the literary texts do metaphorically.

In the nineteenth century, the magic potion or elixir is well on its way to being literalized as liquor. Many nineteenth-century writers were drawn to stories of an elixir of youth—William Godwin (*St. Leon*), Mary Shelley ("The Mortal Immortal"), Honoré de Balzac ("The Elixir of Life" and *The Wild Ass's Skin*), and Alexandre Dumas ("The Man Who Lived 4000 Years"), while Hawthorne returned to this motif throughout his literary career, dealing with it most centrally in "Dr. Heidegger's Experiment," the *Dolliver Romance,* and *Septimius Felton*. In each text, the magical liquid is juxtaposed with wine or other alcoholic liquor, confused with wine, or covertly identified with wine.

The language of earthly intoxication moves irresistibly into these otherwise magical drinking tales: Balzac's Don Juan, for instance is "so interested in holding the mysterious phial to the lamp, as a drinker holds up the wine-bottle at the end of a meal, that he had not seen his father's eyes fade" (3.10). In Hawthorne's "Dr. Heidegger's Experiment," there is an "almost immediate improvement in the aspect of the party, not unlike what might have been produced by a glass of generous wine. . . . the three gentlemen behaved in such a manner, as proved that the water of the Fountain of Youth possessed some intoxicating qualities" (9.232–34).

Both the Balzac and Dumas tales are divided (like the Beham engraving) between an elixir or fountain of youth and a drinking party, and, as in the engraving, the division produces an equation between them. In Balzac's story, the encounter between Don Juan and his father takes place in a private room of a palace otherwise given over to wild orgy, while the Dumas contains two separate stories, one about a magical Tokay and another about immortality, and they seem to have only the most casual connection with one another.

In keeping with his commitment to problematize marvelous events,

Hawthorne even denies that the potion in "Dr. Heidegger's Experiment" has magical properties, suggesting instead that the tale records a mass hallucination:

> Never was there a livelier picture of youthful rivalship, with bewitching beauty for the prize. Yet, by a strange deception, owing to the duskiness of the chamber, and the antique dresses which they still wore, the tall mirror is said to have reflected the figures of the three old, gray, withered grand-sires, ridiculously contending for the skinny ugliness of a shrivelled grand-dam. (9.236–37)

Heidegger's potion is not really an elixir of life, but something that temporarily produces the energy and illusion of youth. How can we read this fiction? Why should the effects of the elixir be only degenerative? The narrative is clearly being ironic in all its talk of a second chance, but why shouldn't people be able to do better the second time around? All that this magic potion does is return the characters to early bad behavior (sexual acting out and brawling). Hawthorne renders the marvelous as fantastic, but if the potion is not marvelous, then it is alcohol.

In *Septimius Felton,* the elixir of life is split into an Eastern and Western branch, a formula discovered by Roger Bacon that has been imperfectly transmitted through the English aristocracy, and a Native American potion possessed by the Indians: "At one of those wizard meetings in the forest, where the Black Man used to meet his red children and his white ones, and be jolly with them, a great Indian wizard taught the secret to Septimius's great-great-grandfather, who was a wizard, and died for it" (13.86).

Both of these trade routes are associated with an alcoholic or heavy drinker, the first with Dr. Portsoaken, described as constantly "imbibing of strong liquor," and the second with Septimius's Aunt Keziah ("And then, having drunk, she gloated over it, and tasted, and smelt of the cup of this hellish wine, as a wine-bibber does of his most fragrant and delicate wine") (13.74, 83). Portsoaken drinks liquor, while Keziah drinks "something else" like an alcoholic: these are the two drinking positions in all these texts. The drift of metaphoric crossover is extreme in this romance, as in the Rabelaisian rendering of one of Hawthorne's inveterate tropes, the illegible text (this one contains the formula for the magical potion) as itself an alcoholic drink: "It was an unintelligible mass, conveying some-how an idea that it was the fruit of vast labor and erudition, emanating from a mind very full of books, and grinding and pressing down the great accumulation of grapes that it had gathered from so many vineyards, and squeezing out rich, viscid juices, potent wine, with which the reader might get drunk" (13.49).

There is also, in this romance, a great emphasis on the notion of the one last or one missing ingredient that would make the potion truly magical. This motif echoes and combines several cultural formulas—the perfect drink; the "one drink" of the alcoholic, the first drink as the one drink that sets the alcoholic off; and the "one drop" of blood that characterizes American racial romance.[3] The missing ingredient is both semantic ("Then he began to see that there must have been some principle of life left out of the book, so that these gathered thoughts lacked something that had given them their only value") and textual ("Septimius was surprised, or strangely impressed, to see that through this paper . . . had gone his fatal bullet—straight through the midst—and some of the young man's blood, saturating his dress, had wet the paper all over") (13.14, 30).

One form of the legend says that the central ingredient is "the heart's blood of a pure young boy or girl" (13.94). Most of the legends, however, identify it as a rare flower:

> This drink was compounded of many ingredients, all of which were remem-bered and handed down in tradition, save one, which either because it was nowhere to be found, or for some other reason, was forgotten; so that the drink ceased to give immortal life as before. They say, it was a beautiful pur-ple flower. (13.85)

In the Western branch, however, the one last ingredient is liquor: The potion "came down to me from the chiefs, and sachems . . . and from the old wizard, who was my great grandfather and yours, and who, they say, added the firewater to the other ingredients, and so gave it the only one thing that it wanted to make it perfect" (13.83–84).[4]

The metaphoric relationship between the magic potion and strong drink can also be expressed as a denial. The potion in Shelley and Hawthorne cannot be compared to wine because, we are told as it is being compared to wine, it is so much stronger or weaker than wine: "I remembered the glorious drunkenness that had followed my stolen draught. . . . Cornelius had brewed a soul-refreshing drink—more inebriating than wine—sweeter and more fragrant than any fruit"; "The Water of Youth possessed merely a virtue more transient than that of wine" (Shelley 1990, 321; Hawthorne 9.238).

Even without naming alcohol, these narratives borrow structural elements from paradigms of intoxication and addiction. The potion registers a "hit"—"the next moment, the exhilarating gush of young life shot through their veins. . . . They were a group of merry youngsters, almost maddened with the exuberant frolicksomeness of their years"—and produces euphoria: "Words would be faint and shallow types of my enjoyment, or of the gladness that possessed my bosom when I woke. . . . Earth appeared heaven, and my inheritance upon it was to be one trance of delight" (Hawthorne 9.235; Shelley 1990, 319). The liquor in "Dr. Heidegger's Experiment" whets a craving: the drinkers cry eagerly for more, and drinking leads immediately to venery and violence (9.233). The liquor of *A Midsummer Night's Dream* does not merely produce love but impulsive actions, mood swings, inappropriate erotic behavior, and then blackout, amnesia, and shame: Titania "does not remember ever having desired him. She remembers nothing. She does not want to remember anything. . . . All are ashamed in the morning. . . . Even Bottom" (Kott 1965, 188).[5]

In commentary on Tristan, much is made of the fact that the potion drives the lovers to act in defiance of their value systems—"'Good Heavens, ma'am!' retorted the others. 'Your thoughts are not honest and straightforward, you are very double-tongued'" (von Strassburg 211). According to Alan Fedrick,

> It is the tragedy of the lovers that their comportment is so often and so fundamentally in direct conflict with the attitudes required by social, family, and feudal obligations. Love inspires Tristan and Iseut to sin against every moral law that surrounds them. They commit adultery persistently and flagrantly. (23)

The Tristan texts stress that before drinking the potion, the couple do not dream of committing what will be called a "vilenie," but after they have drunk, they do commit it with enthusiasm; and the potion is the only determinant for this radical shift in behavior. If we are to understand that there is a demonic form of love that can override will, conscience, and good sense and lead people helplessly to destroy themselves, then it is fatally confusing to have the sign of that love be drink, since drink produces those effects on its own.

Alcoholic drink is the inevitable metaphor for the potion because it is the only metaphor for a potion that is otherwise "magical" (i.e., unthinkable as itself), and if that is the case, the distance between metaphoric tenor and vehicle collapses. The potion has nothing else to be but alcohol. In Walter Besant's *Inner House*, when a professor announces a new discovery to arrest aging and tries to explain it to a lay public, alcohol is the only explanatory vehicle at hand: You all know, he says, "how at a dinner a single glass of Champagne revives the spirits, loosens the tongue, and brings activity to the brain. The guests were weary; they were in decay; the Champagne arrests that decay. My discovery is of another kind of Champagne which acts with a more lasting effect" (15–16).

In an article in *Ulster Folklife* titled "Grinding Old People Young," J. B. Smith refers to a "Belfast print of the early nineteenth century showing elderly people entering a mill and emerging from it as maidens with their beaux." However, a more realistic gloss for this phrase is provided by the fact that it was a common pub name: two Irish pubs were called "'The Mill for Grinding Old People Young' in Belfast and 'The Old Grinding Young' at Harold's Cross, Dublin" (1991, 62). The magic drink in E. T. A. Hoffmann's *Devil's Elixir* and Washington Irving's "Rip Van Winkle" *is* liquor, even if it is also magic liquor. Hoffmann's consists of certain flasks of wine that "were offered by the devil to St. Anthony as part of his temptation. Whoever drinks from them, and Medardus does, falls prey to mad and evil impulses" (Romero 579). In "Rip Van Winkle," the liquor puts the drinker into a deep sleep from which he wakes confused and disoriented, and one of the long-standing effects of the drink is the breakup of his family.

Silvio Malaparto's "Il filtro" was the basis for two identical libretti— Daniel Auber's *Le philtre* and Gaetano Donizetti's *L'elisir d'amore*. In both, the peasant hero, Nemorino, wants an elixir that will cause a woman he loves to fall in love with him. Earlier his beloved, Adina, had been reading a Tristan story in which Tristan yearns for a cruel Isolde, so he seeks out a magician to concoct a potion for him. "What a marvelous potion," Nemorino sings, "I wish I knew the recipe of that magic brew." A famous scientist, Dr. Dulcamara, enters, and Nemorino asks him if he has the "love potion of Isolde?" "Of course, I distill it myself," the doctor replies. "But it's in great demand." What little money Nemorino has turns out to be the exact price, and the doctor slaps a label reading "elisir d'amore" on a bottle of red wine: in an aside he even informs us that "it's Bordeaux wine, not elixir." He tells Nemorino to hold it to his lips and "drink in small sips and astonishing results will ensue."[6]

The elixir in Alphonse Daudet's story of that name is a "green, golden, warm, sparkling, exquisite liqueur," which will become a treasure for the Order of the White Fathers and save them from their wretched poverty. Compounded by an old woman from five or six kinds of simples, the elixir is produced by Frère Gaucher, who has a good face with "grayish goat-like beard" and "somewhat wild eyes." It soon becomes very popular: there was not a farmhouse that had not "a little brown earthenware flagon, sealed with the arms of Provence, with a monk in ecstasy on a silver label." This elixir is both alcoholic drink and magical elixir simply because the good fathers have made of it something mysterious and terrible. And it has a terrible effect on Frère Gaucher:

> Just fancy that one evening, during service, he arrived at the church in a state of extraordinary excitement—red, out of breath, with his cowl awry, and so agitated that in taking holy-water he wet his sleeve to the elbow. They thought at first it was embarrassment at arriving late; but when they saw him make low obeisances to the organ and the pulpit instead of to the high altar, cross the church like a whirlwind, and wander about the choir for five minutes in search of his stall, and then, when seated, bow right and left with a maudlin smile, a murmur of astonishment ran through the three naves.

A victim of his own discovery, Gaucher tests the elixir on himself and finds that he likes it very much. His superior orders him to limit himself to twenty drops, but, "Alas! it was in vain that the poor father counted his drops; the devil had hold of him and never let go": "The drops would fall from the graduator into the silver goblet. The father would swallow these twenty at a gulp, almost without pleasure. It was only for the twenty-first that he longed. Oh, that one-and-twentieth drop!" (Digby and Digby 197–205).

Bram Stoker's *Dracula* and Robert Louis Stevenson's *Strange Case of Dr. Jekyll and Mr. Hyde* are two fictions that revolve around magical and transformative drinks. In Stevenson's tale, the first thing that the lawyer Utterson sees when the fog lifts at Hyde's door is a "gin palace, a low French eating-house . . . many ragged children huddled in the doorways, and many women of many different nationalities passing out, key in hand, to have a morning glass" (48). *Dracula* also opens with a great thirst, although it is not alcoholic: on his first night in Transylvania Jonathan Harker has "paprika hendl" for dinner: "A chicken done up some way with red pepper, which was very good but thirsty. (*Mem.,* get recipe for Mina)." Consequently, he has all sorts of queer dreams, which "may have been the paprika, for I had to drink up all the water in my carafe, and was still thirsty" (1–2).

Dracula can be read as a fountain of youth fable, since its central figure lives by drinking a liquid that renders him immortal. Alcoholics have frequently been figured as the living dead:

Recklessly drunk, it leaves the body cursed
more than a fever . . .
wickeder far than fire or fetid snake . . .
Think of the trembling limbs, the void for mind,
the hamstrung shambling walk, the eyes half-blind,
the deafened ears, the tongue that none can mark.
Speak drunkard, are you dead or living now?
(Lindsay 39–40)

Drinking is a center of some anxiety in the novel: Renfield, for example, says, "'What's the use of spiders? There isn't anything in them to eat or—' He stopped suddenly, as though reminded of a forbidden topic. 'So, so!' I thought to myself, 'this is the second time he has suddenly stopped at the word "drink"; what does it mean?'" (271). Earlier, Harker had observed: "It is strange that as yet I have not seen the Count eat or drink. He must be a very peculiar man!" (26)

The vampire's constituting act can be variously understood as biting, sucking, or drinking. Whatever it is, it is, Joan Copjec states, "an *oral relation . . .* a *jouissance*" attained through sucking (33). Christopher Craft suggests that it is "about our bodily fluids . . . semen, milk, blood" (109; see also Rickels 320). This biting/sucking/drinking is kept strongly in view by criticism and treated as extraordinarily meaningful, constantly being displaced and interpreted as sexual penetration, masturbation, homosexuality, syphilis, castration (i.e., the fear of being devoured by women or dark [Jewish] aliens).[7] It is culturally displaced onto metaphors like the vampirism of capitalism (see, for example, Ernest Jones in Bentley 27; Howes 104; Showalter 98–99).

Wine enters the picture along lines of symbolic displacement insofar as the vampire's ingestion of blood is often read through imagery of the Eucharist. The two great feasts of Christianity are Cana (wine and water) and the Last Supper (wine and blood). Wine is often a surrogate for blood and vice versa. "Then he spoke to me mockingly. . . . 'And you, their best beloved one, are now to me flesh of my flesh; blood of my blood; kin of my kin; my bountiful wine-press for a while'" (Stoker 287–88).[8]

In his *Pleasures and Pains: Opium and the Orient in Nineteenth-Century English Culture,* Barry Milligan proposes another model for Dracula, that of the Chinese opium master, who is also credited with a hypnotic power over English women, elaborating a national fantasy "that living-dead foreigners will colonize England by subsuming all of its women and making them invincible living-dead monsters like themselves" (92).[9]

Stevenson's *Jekyll and Hyde* hinges on a chemical draught that confers youth and savage energy on the drinker. Nevertheless, there has been little critical interest in the potion itself (in fact, it has provoked some critical discomfort). Critics have been largely interested in the meaning of the effects it produces, both a transformation and a release that Jekyll both desires and fears.[10] A number of discursive contexts have been proposed for the fable, and, in a general way, *Jekyll and Hyde* has proved easy enough to understand, but it has been difficult to read the fine print. It clearly involves a redefinition of man as innately depraved or degenerate, and the most obvious readings work through an "other Victorian" model, a Jack the Ripper paradigm in which the respectable Victorian gentleman sneaks out at night in disguise to indulge his filthy pleasures.

What is so frustrating to this and other readings of the relationship between the two characters is that we are never told what Hyde does in pursuit of his pleasures: his desire is never even identified, much less texted. As the novella says, "Into the details of the infamy . . . I have no design of entering"; "What he told me in the next hour I cannot bring my mind to set on paper" (87, 80). The center is not only empty, it is eroded: "The worst of my faults," Jekyll tells us, "was a certain impatient gaiety of disposition, such as has made the happiness of many." The formulations we are given counter whatever acts of a violently sexual nature we could imagine at the buried center of the book: "Many a man would even have blazoned such irregularities as I was guilty of; but from the high views that I had set before me, I regarded and hid them with an almost morbid sense of shame" (81). In a letter to Gerard Manley Hopkins, Stevenson foreclosed the relationship of Hyde to any simple sense of pleasure: "'People are so filled full of folly and inverted lust, that they can think of nothing but sexuality for him. . . . 'the beast Hyde' who is let out 'is no more sensual than another, but . . . is the essence of cruelty and malice, and selfishness and cowardice: and these are the diabolic in man'" (Heath 94).[11] What, then, did Jekyll find initially attractive about that other state?

We also get slips and errors, the aftermath of Hyde's pleasure, where his viciousness either chooses to or is forced to display itself as murder. The murders, we presume, are not themselves the sins around which this tale is constructed but supplementary acts. On the other hand, they are all that we are given to actualize the wealth of suggestion in the work.

Shadowy, deep urgings that cannot be resisted suggest compulsions like sexual addiction, sexual "deviation," or alcohol/drug addiction: as Joyce Carol Oates says, "Dr. Jekyll's uncivilized self, to which he gives the symbolic name Hyde, is . . . a shameless indulgence of appetites that cannot be assimilated into the propriety of everyday Victorian life. There is a sense in which Hyde, for all his monstrosity, is but an addiction like alcohol, nicotine, drugs" (604).[12] Sexual addiction may be the first form of particularity that we attach to the tale, but homosexuality and substance addiction cannot be far behind.

Insofar as sexual addiction rides on a release of inhibition, it is also a drinking effect. Instead of a metaphoric perspective where drinking the potion symbolizes the release of pleasure, we shift to a metonymic one where drinking puts one in a position to pursue sexual pleasure. The films made from Stevenson's fiction all doggedly follow this path. In the John Barrymore, Fredric March, Spencer Tracy, and Jerry Lewis versions, the newly transformed Hyde goes immediately to a tavern or club where he orders a drink, gratuitously beats up a man, and charms a woman who becomes his lover.

"As [George] Levine points out," Denise Herd writes, "the story of Dr. Jekyll and Mr. Hyde 'magnificently captured the broader nineteenth century fear of, and fascination with, a liquid which could transform repressed civilized men and women into uninhibited beasts'" (365). The potion is drunk as an alcoholic drink: "Hyde had a song upon his lips as he compounded the draught, and as he drank it pledged the dead man" (91). After drinking, Jekyll loses his inhibitions and acts out his deepest desires. Whatever the strange brew, it produces euphoria: "There was something strange in my sensations, something indescribably new and, from its very novelty, incredibly sweet. I felt younger, lighter, happier in body; within I was conscious of a heady recklessness, a current of disordered sensual images running like a mill race in my fancy" (83).[13]

In his dissertation on the representation of the drunkard in English fiction, D. M. Thomas identified a binary trope of intoxication that is pertinent to *Jekyll and Hyde.* It asks if intoxication transforms the drinker into something new or simply brings out his essential character, as in "in vino veritas." At the core of intoxication's negativity lies the mystery of the self: drink introduces a division in the self, either by transforming us into something new or revealing hidden depths. Thomas articulates this binary through opposing attitudes of Joseph Addison and Henry Fielding. According to the first, "drunkenness may betray the hidden faults of a man, and show them in the most odious colors, but [it] often occasions faults to which he is not naturally subject. Wine throws a man out of himself, and infuses qualities into the mind which she is a stranger to in her sober moments" (37). In a chapter in *Tom Jones,* titled "THAT DRUNKENNESS SHEWS THE MIND OF A MAN, AS A MIRROR REFLECTS HIS PERSON," on the other hand, Fielding writes,

> Nothing is more erroneous than the common Observation, That Men who are ill-natured and quarrelsome when they are drunk, are very worthy Persons when they are sober: For Drink, in reality, doth not reverse Nature, or create Passions in Men which did not exist in them before. It takes away the Guard of Reason, and consequently forces us to produce those Symptoms which many, when sober, have Art enough to conceal. (Thomas 36)

The "effect of the wine, does but remove Dissimulation"; "It shakes out the folds as it were, where duplicity and rancour lurk in the mind, and reveals every trait of character and every secret feeling in transparent language" (Hobbes 143; Plutarch in Jeanneret 98).

This issue cannot be resolved either in social histories or in the textual relations between Jekyll and Hyde. The question of whether the drink transforms or releases the essential Jekyll is answered as yes to both. We are told that the potion attacked "the very fortress of identity," that "Hyde was indifferent to Jekyll . . . [remembering him only] as the mountain bandit remembers the cavern in which he conceals himself from pursuit" (83, 89). But we are also told that Hyde was a "familiar that I called out of my own soul" (86). In the following statement, Stevenson says both things at once: I "managed to compound a drug by which these powers [that made up my spirit] should be dethroned from their supremacy, and a second form and countenance substituted, none the less natural to me because they were the expression, and bore the stamp, of lower elements in my soul" (83). The author or narrator who can utter these statements is already divided into his Jekyll and his Hyde.

In the fiction as opposed to the language, however, transformation is paramount and quite in keeping with traditional figures for intoxication and addiction. The potion turns Jekyll into a monster and a criminal ("devil" and "bandit") and, in the films, into the virtual beast indicated by the tale: "I still hated and feared the thought of the brute that slept within me" (94).

Drink has universally been a potion that turns a man into a beast: Michael Cassio exclaims, "O God! that men should put an enemy in their mouths to steal away their brains; that we should, with joy, pleasance, revel, and applause, transform ourselves into beasts," and Thomas Nashe divided drunkards into those who got "Ape drunke," "Lion drunke," "Swine drunke," and "Sheep drunke," as in the drinking song from John Lyly's *Mother Bombie:*

> O the deare bloud of Grapes
> Turnes us into Anticke shapes
> Now to shew tricks like Apes.
> Now Lion-like to rore
> Now Goatishly to whore.
> Now Hoggishly ith' mire.
> Now flinging Hats ith' fire.[14]

More than any of the fictions treated in this chapter, *Jekyll and Hyde* betrays the shape of addiction.[15] As Stevenson said in "A Chapter on

Dreams," "All that was given me was the matter of three scenes, and the central idea of a voluntary change becoming involuntary" (Geduld 96). To the idea of an involuntary change are added the forms of craving—"I began to be tortured with throes and longings" (90)—loss of tolerance and acceleration of effect. Jekyll has to double, even treble the dosage to produce the same effect (see 108).[16] There is an asymmetry in the doubling of characters as well as in the doubling of the dosage: the latter doubling speeds up, becomes autonomous, and Jekyll loses control of it "like any addict," according to Oates, although Jekyll still deludes himself that he can control the transformation: "I will tell you one thing: the moment I choose, I can be rid of Mr. Hyde. I give you my hand upon that" (Oates 606; Stevenson 44). Addiction even fits the terms of Stevenson's letter to Hopkins, since it overwrites pleasure with a sadistic script and turns it toward "cruelty and malice." And it is a doctor who is addicted. Doctors were (and remain) an extremely high-risk category for this condition, since they and pharmacists were (and are) the only legal dispensers of such drugs.

Eve Sedgwick takes the presence of addiction in Stevenson's tale for granted, although she finds in it a metaphor for sexuality:

> In *The Picture of Dorian Gray* as in, for instance, *Dr. Jekyll and Mr. Hyde,* drug addiction is both a camouflage and an expression for the dynamics of same-sex desire and its prohibition: both books begin by looking like stories of erotic tensions between men, and end up as cautionary tales of solitary substance abusers. The two new taxonomies of the addict and the homosexual condense many of the same issues for late nineteenth-century culture. (1990, 172)

This context is even scripted by the tale: "I do not suppose that when a drunkard reasons with himself upon his vice, he is once out of five hundred times affected by the dangers that he runs through his brutish, physical insensibility" (Stevenson 90). And Stevenson's text often reads like the cautionary prose of temperance fiction: "'And now, you who have . . . derided your superiors—behold!' He put the glass to his lips, and drank at one gulp. A cry followed; he reeled, staggered, clutched at the table" (80).

The core of Stevenson's tale expresses a basic addiction trope: that continued drinking splits the subject, makes the subject feel divided against himself or occupied by a presence alien to himself. As Jekyll says, "I saw that, of the two natures that contended in the field of my consciousness, even if I could rightly be said to be either, it was only because I was radically both" (82). How well Coleridge's opium addiction, as described by Anya Taylor, fits *Jekyll and Hyde*:

> His disgust with himself arises from the dividedness of being that sottishness reveals, causes, or requires, the sinking of the human elements of his nature into the bestial and brutish, the abandonment of will and control. This sort of collapse sickens him; his disgust makes him relinquish yet more self-control, believing himself not worth the bother. (1991, 362)

One can imagine, as precursors of Jekyll and Hyde, the two original opium eaters, Coleridge and De Quincey. According to Christopher Herbert, "the crux of De Quincey's most original thinking, is the many-sided idea of self-division. . . . division between a desired identity and the guilty one forever visible to one's conscience" (257). In the "English Mail Coach," De Quincey "finds evidence of frightening complexities in human nature":

> The dreamer finds housed within himself—occupying, as it were, some separate chamber in his brain—holding, perhaps, from that station a secret and detestable commerce with his own heart, some horrid alien nature. What if it were his own nature repeated—still, if the quality were distinctly perceptible, even that—even this mere numerical double of his own consciousness— might be a curse too mighty to be sustained. But how if the alien nature contradicts his own, fights with it, perplexes and confounds it? (Herbert 258)

chapter 6

Spiritual Intoxication and the Metaphorics of Heaven

Excess is, in short, for the body what the mystic's ecstasy is for the soul. Intoxication steeps you in fantastic imaginings every whit as strange as those of ecstatics.

—HONORÉ DE BALZAC, *The Wild Ass's Skin*

The sway of alcohol over mankind is unquestionably due to its power to stimulate the mystical faculties of human nature, usually crushed to earth by the cold facts and dry criticisms of the sober hour. Sobriety diminishes, discriminates, and says no; drunkenness expands, unites, and says yes. It is in fact the great exciter of the *Yes* function in man.

—WILLIAM JAMES, *The Varieties of Religious Experience*

The strongest cultural imperative encountered in the study so far has been the insistence that many statements about drink and intoxication are to be read metaphorically, which has left deep traces in the discursive practices of religion. Such a reading habit was so pervasive that in sectarian Judaism "wine" meant "allegory": "Turning water into wine" was the way one read the Torah so as to reveal its true meaning. This figure is elaborated into a similitude by Ivan Illich in his *In the Vineyard of the Text: A Commentary to Hugh's Didascalicon*:

> When Hugh [of Saint Victor] reads, he harvests; he picks the berries from the lines. He knows that Pliny had already noted that the word *pagina*, page, can refer to rows of vines joined together. The lines on the page were the thread of a trellis that supports the vines. As he picks the fruit from the leaves of parchment, the *voces paginarum* drop from his mouth. (Feeley-Harnick 60; Illich 57)

So, according to Charles Baudelaire, does hashish mean allegory: "Allegory—a deeply spiritual art-form, which, although incompetent painters have accustomed us to despise it, is really one of the primitive and most natural forms of poetry—regains, in an intellect enlightened by hashish, its legitimate dominion" (110).

Perhaps the most important function of drink and intoxication in the history of culture has been to provide the metaphors through which transcendent states of consciousness are expressed: ecstasy that cannot be grasped in its own right takes shape as "spiritual intoxication." Much of what will now follow is anticipated by a passage in Aldous Huxley's 1956 essay, "The History of Tension":

> William James's characterization of alcohol as an exciter of the mystical faculties is strikingly confirmed by what the mystics themselves have said of their ecstatic experiences. In the mystical literature of Islam, metaphors derived from wine and winebibbing are constantly employed. Precisely similar metaphors are to be found in the writings of some of the greatest Christian saints. Thus St. John of the Cross calls his soul *la interior bodega di mi Amado*— "the inward wine cellar of my Beloved." And St. Teresa of Avila tells us that she "regards the center of our soul as a cellar, into which God admits us when and as it pleases Him, so as to intoxicate us with the delicious wine of His grace." The experience of self-transcendence and the release of tension produced by alcohol and the other consciousness-changing chemicals is so wonderful, so blessed and blissful, that men have found it quite natural to identify these drugs . . . with one or other of their gods. (Huxley 1977, 122)

This chapter asks first why despised material processes should be appropriated as an indispensable index of religious truth. I also ask from where (or where else than intoxication) the otherness of religion could have come, and I answer the second question in an obvious, possibly a naive, way: I accept the truth of metaphor, expressed in the common phrase "spiritual intoxication" as it modulates back into "spiritual" intoxication, and imagine that heaven was originally constructed out of our drunkenness. Rather than intoxication being used to characterize heaven or ecstasy, ecstasy and heaven were originally carved out of the experience of intoxication.

As soon as you scratch the various postings of a phrase like "spiritual intoxication," you discover that literal intoxication was also spiritual and that spiritual intoxication was always also literal: the separation that is announced to be so radical that the two terms, *ecstasy* and *intoxication,* can only be understood as correlatives by an impossible stretch of the imagination turns out to be no separation at all.

Spiritual intoxication is a common metaphor for spiritual experience of an intense order, like ecstasy: "When the worshipper reaches the highest ecstasy," Florence Weinberg writes, "all intellectual clarity vanishes in a state which Plotinus compares to intoxication by nectar" (156)—a condition which Philo Judaeus called a "sober intoxication, more sober than sobriety itself" (Wolfson 2.49) and Richard Crashaw, a "sweet inebriated extasy" (399). Since 1976, Ecstasy is also the name of a drug.

Spiritual intoxication is often claimed to be the perfect metaphor or the only metaphor for ecstasy.[1] The term is, of course, an oxymoron, not an intoxication but a sobriety. In Alexander Pope's version in "An Essay on Criticism"—

A little learning is a dangerous thing;
Drink deep, or taste not the Pierian spring:
There shallow draughts intoxicate the brain,
And drinking largely sobers us again
(70)—

the real effects are reversed. Since I began this project, I have encountered many variations on Pope's couplet, all boldly declaring that certain kinds of drinking, far from getting one drunk as is commonly supposed, actually make one more sober.

This metaphor was in constant use in the literature of Christianity from the time of Philo in the first century—"the first to introduce into mystical literature the famous oxymoron of 'sober drunkenness' to describe the way in which the mind is taken out of itself in the upward way"—through Latin writers like Augustine or Gregory the Great in the fifth and sixth centuries (McGinn 39–40). Alexandrian philosophers, church fathers, and Renaissance humanists all accepted the existence of a spiritual rapture that produced effects exactly like those of intoxication, a something that enlivened one spiritually as much as drink does materially.[2]

Metaphoric intoxication was used to hit off almost every ideal state, place, or agent in the religious vocabulary: ecstasy, mystical union, divine love or grace, God, Christ, the New Testament as the vital words of Christ, or the Holy Ghost.[3] Among the things that wine symbolized for Mechthild von Magdeburg in the thirteenth century was divine love, the "unio mystica," the liquid that flows from Christ's wounds, Christ himself, and the Holy Spirit:

> "The heavenly Father is the blessed server there and Jesus the chalice and the Holy Spirit the pure wine, and the entire Trinity is the filled chalice and love the mighty cellar—God knows I would gladly partake so that love would bid me dwell there." The Holy Spirit is the wine that flows to the soul out of the wine cellar that is divine love in general. (Franklin 146)[4]

The equation that I am tracing through Christianity also runs deep in Sufism. Powerful reading practices have dictated here and elsewhere that references to intoxication be read as spiritual:

> In the terminology of Islamic and particularly Persian mysticism . . . "drunkenness" is used figuratively for that type of ecstasy in which all sense of self seems to vanish away. . . . The mystics, after their ascent to the heavens of Reality, agree that they saw nothing in existence except God the One. . . . They became drunk with a drunkenness in which their reason collapsed. (Zaehner 42, 157)

The discourse of intoxication has long been subject to a ruthlessly allegorical regime that lets no drop of the real stuff remain on the page. In Islamic poetry, the wine is allegorical according to a fixed code: "The 'Friend' is God, the 'wine' His spirit irradiating mankind, the 'vine' is the material creation, the 'full moon' the spirit of the Prophet Muhammad . . . the 'stars' flashes of illumination experienced by the ecstatic mystic when infused ('mixed') with the divine, and so forth" (Harb 233). Such religious allegory tends to be imposed on almost all the Persian poets, even those it clearly doesn't fit, like Omar and Hafiz.

The insistence in Persian poetry that wine must be allegorical is associated with a second ruthless regime—the Islamic ban against alcohol. Earthly wine is forbidden in Islam, while spiritual wine is mandatory (or is it mandatory to the extent that its opposite number is forbidden?): "To drink that Wine is no sin, as some allege; rather is it the unforgivable sin not to taste of it" (Arberry 1971, 67).[5] This ban is usually read as complete and all encompassing (but such a reading is itself the product of an orientalist fiction used to establish the otherness of Islam). In fact, it was a gradual ban and never wholly successful for all Islamic peoples in all places. Preeminent among resisting populations were the Persians, who had a long-standing religious and secular alliance with wine through Zoroastrianism (Streit 59). Much Arabic and Persian poetry is devoted to actual wine and often written against religious zealots in general and the ban against alcohol in particular: Abu Nuwas begs his companion to sing to him and give him a goblet of wine to distract him from the muezzin's call (Harb 230).

Nevertheless, the allegorical insistence was strong. It was the great sin, for example, for Edward Fitzgerald, who claimed that "[Omar's] Worldly Pleasures are what they profess to be without any Pretense at Divine Allegory; his Wine is the veritable Juice of the Grape; his Tavern, where it was to be had." "Only the most scandalized among his audience took him at his word," Daniel Schenker writes, "everyone else went ahead and read it as an orthodox theological document" (62). Even in the secular West, allegory rules over texts devoted to ostensible drink and intoxication, like the fiction of François Rabelais or the painting of Jan Steen. For example, Weinberg (who is named for a drink paradise) declares that the "effect of the Rabelaisian drinking bout is not, as it appears on the surface, vulgar drunkenness, but a type of inspiration, or ecstasy" (53).

Ecstasy dramatizes the split between soul and body (already an a priori necessity for any transcendental ontology), and drunkenness is the sign of that rupture. The phrase *spiritual intoxication* suggests that intoxication occupies a position on each half of the broken line and that whatever happens in the lower has an equivalent in the higher. St. John of the Cross writes, "In the same manner that drink spreads and overflows through all the members and veins of the body, in the same way does the communication of God substantially spread and overflow the whole soul" (de Nicolás 210).

This practice is not confined to religious utterance. Intoxication is available in common language as a metaphor for a wide range of excitement. One can be drunk on almost anything: "With wine, poetry or virtue," as in Baudelaire's poem "Be You Drunken Ceaselessly" (145). Athenaeus claimed that "since thirst is the most insistent of human desires, poets use it figuratively of various strong desires," and Lionel Trilling writes that "ingestion supplies the imagery of our largest and most intense experiences: we speak of the wine of life and the cup of life; we speak also of its dregs and lees," as in Matthew Prior's quatrain,

> Who would, says Dryden, Drink this draught of Life
> Blended with bitter Woes and tedious Strife
> But that an Angel in Some Lucky hour
> Does healing Drops into the Goblet pour?[6]

It may not be correct to say that the trappings of intoxication were borrowed to clothe an ineffable spiritual reality, since literal intoxication was also understood to be spiritual. There had long been a persistent belief that drinking and its effects were immaterial: throughout Europe brandy was known as aqua vitae, the water of life; in Russia vodka was similarly praised as the elixir of life, or the living water. Wine was the spiritual other to material food. Writing on Euripides' *Bacchae,* Arthur Epstein casually mentions that "one deity, Demeter, provides food to sustain man physically; the other, Dionysus, brings to man the fluid of wine to nourish him spiritually" (166), and, according to Maguelonne Toussaint-Samat, Dumas "said perhaps all that needs to be said about wine and food in a couple of brief sentences: 'Wine is the intellectual part of a meal. Meats are merely the material part'" (277). We even seem to have forgotten what the literal of alcohol is, as in this note by M. A. Screech: "I suggest that Rabelais's 'wine' is mainly to be taken literally, as a means of spiritual enhancement. . . . [although it] has other meanings as well" (1980b, 259).

According to Mesopotamian legend, the grapevine is a microcosm of both the physical and spiritual universe: it is a cosmic tree that enfolds the sky; the stars are grapes and wine is embodied light. For Galileo and the academicians of the Cimento investigating the mystery of fermentation, the grape was a metaphysical-spiritual entity, and the desire of this scientific academy was "to unlock the mystery of the grape that captures the sun's rays and absorbs cosmic light, holds it and transforms it into chemical energy." They called wine "liquified sunshine," "tamed and bottled fire," and "a compound of humor and light" (Camporesi 57, 52, 54).

This mode of sublimated reference is common in the literature that treats wine, most notably Nathaniel Hawthorne's *Marble Faun.* Hawthorne constructs his Italian principal, Donatello, as an avatar of Dionysus himself and his vineyard as a divine precinct, the source of the original wine, "the wine that Bacchus himself was fabled to have taught his sylvan ancestors how to express." The wine of Monte Beni is sunshine itself, and more:

> As it stood in Kenyon's glass, a little circle of light glowed on the table roundabout it, as if it were so much golden sunshine. . . . to drink it was really more a moral than a physical enjoyment. There was a deliciousness in it that eluded analysis, and—like whatever else is superlatively good—was perhaps better appreciated in the memory than by present consciousness. (4.235, 223)

Referring to the use of wine in the ancient mystery cults, Walter Otto asks, "Is it conceivable that the ancients could have assigned to wine the miraculous power to lead man to the divine, without, at the same time, worshipping the spirit of the divine within it?" (145). The Aryan *soma*, too, was deified and projected into the heavens as brother-deity to Indra. The Rig-Veda tells us that the drinking of the potion makes the drinker immortal: "We have drunk Soma, we have become immortal, we have entered into light, we have known the Gods" (Farnell 122).[7]

Drink poetry, here the Archpoet's "Confessions of Golias," locates the place of drink, the tavern, in proximity to religious ecstasy—"The lamp of the soul is lighted with cups; the heart steeped in nectar flies up to heaven"— because inns and taverns, as Pierre Motin wrote, are "Paradises upon earth" (Wright 1968, 168; Brillat-Savarin 316). Drink and drugs are vehicular: in Henry Vaughan's "Rhapsody," for example, they lead to transcendence:

> Drink deep; this Cup be pregnant; & the wine
> Spirit of wit, to make us all divine,
> That big with Sack, and mirth we may retyre. . . .
> And by the influxe of this painted Skie,
> And labour'd formes, to higher matters flye.
> (18)

"Drunkenness," according to Gérard de Nerval, "while it disturbs the eyes of the body, enlightens those of the soul; the spirit, freed from the body . . . escapes like a prisoner whose warder has gone to sleep. . . . He flies easily through atmospheres of unspeakable happiness" (108). In Phillip Epstein's reading of "Jack and the Beanstalk" as a fable of psychedelic experience, the giant plant is the pathway "to new heights of awareness and reality," which enable Jack "to live a richer and fuller life" (178).

Painterly bacchanals like Titian's *Bacchanal of the Andrians* transport us to heavenly terrain on the wings of intoxication, where we casually encounter divine or ideal personages and events in their proper domain. But only bacchanals, as Philipp Fehl suggests, signify the necessity of Bacchus for such illumination, because intoxication bestows transcendent vision:

> The sponsors of such encounters are Amor and Venus, and Bacchus, whose gift of the grape also opens men's eyes to the sight of the invisible world. To represent in painting the joining of the two worlds in forms which are, as it were, true to nature, is necessarily one of the most difficult and challenging tasks of art. (37)

Drugs were and are widely believed to free the soul from the prison of ordinary consciousness so that it could participate in other orders of reality, and the history of our century is marked by moments when this ecstasizing power is reinvoked as a cure for the ills of modernity. "Life plunges man into darkness," Antonin Artaud wrote, "and henceforth such [originary] states can be recovered only by the grace of an abnormal lucidity, caused, for example, by narcotics" (Lyons 126). One major movement of psychedelic striving was said to begin with the publication of Aldous Huxley's *Doors of Perception* in 1954 (which celebrates, according to Walter Houston Clark, "the virtues of mescalin, as a safe and sane, non–habit forming means of producing mystical insight" [284]) and run through the drug counterculture of the 1960s. The drug culture was one of several contemporary movements of the spirit along with black liberation, anti–Vietnam War protest, hippie culture, women's liberation, and others.

Huxley appears in a sequence of psychedelic self-experimentation that began (after the extraction of mescaline from peyote) with the publication of drug accounts by S. Weir Mitchell, Havelock Ellis, and William James at the end of the nineteenth century. In the mid-twentieth, continued experimentation and the public response to it heated up in a number of locations in America, Canada, and Mexico until the situation exploded at Harvard University in 1963—when Timothy Leary and Richard Alpert were dismissed from their teaching positions—and in the Bay Area some time later. It spread on the waves of this publicity to the society at large to become a "drug culture": "What Leary did," according to Alan Harrington, "was to steal this sacred food from the gods (laboratory scientists) and, clad in his white robes, cast it among the children of the 1960's" (48). The psychedelic movement is usually understood to move between elitist and populist intentions, Huxley and the intellectuals versus Leary, Allen Ginsberg, Ken Kesey, and the hippies.[8]

Leary claimed that he and his associates had wanted to proclaim the *scientific* value of psychedelic drugs but were forced to retrench to a religious defense. Jay Stevens, however, argues that what was so immediately unsettling about psilocybin and LSD was that their effects and implications breached the division between science and religion (xv). In its scientific phase, psychedelic experimentation sought out a variety of applications for the new drugs: ESP (J. B. Rhine), alcoholic treatment (Humphrey Osmond), criminal reform (Leary), sickness and death therapy (Erik Kast, Stanislav Grof, and Sidney Cohen)—and, of course, plain old psychotherapy.[9] Its religious dimensions flowed into an abiding American interest in Eastern religions and stimulated new interest in Native American religions. The center of this flow was the presumed equivalence between the effects of LSD, mescaline, and psilocybin and the historical record on religious mysticism, that is, intoxication and ecstasy.

When asked whether the drug experience was similar to the mystical experience, Walter Stace, a philosophy professor at Princeton, answered, "It's not a question of being similar to mystical experience; it *is* mystical experience," and in 1953, Huxley wrote to Harold Raymond that the mescaline experience "is without any question the most extraordinary and significant experience available to human beings this side of the Beatific Vision" (Metzner 69; Huxley 1977, 42). In *The Varieties of Religious Experience,* William James had simply included "consciousness produced by intoxicants" as part of the philosophical study of religious mystical states (377). In the 1960s Walter Pahnke conducted a major study ("the miracle of Marsh Chapel") to determine "whether the transcendent experience reported during psychedelic acid sessions was similar to the mystical experience reported by saints and religious mystics," and his findings supported his hypothesis (Leary 89).[10]

Despite the periodic championing of drug-induced ecstasy, the standard cultural model for spiritual experience has long declared that drink and drugs entered the human regime only after a fall from some original spiritual plateau. In the matter of psychedelic mysticism, the expansive celebration on the Left was answered by a number of writers, most notably R. C. Zaehner, Spalding Professor of Eastern Religions and Ethics at the University of Oxford, who accepted the civilizing mission of refuting Huxley and controlling the damage done by *The Doors of Perception* and *Heaven and Hell* (1956).

For those who thought like Zaehner, psychoactive substances represented degeneration from a state of authentic ecstasy: first there was true ecstasy; then there was drunken or drugged ecstasy. For Carl Jung, aqua vitae is not the water of life and spirits are not "the spirit"; that act of naming is based on a false analogy (1988, 1039). Coleridge planned to write a long poem on this fall: "Man in the Savage State as a water-drinker . . . possessed of the Heavenly Bacchus." His fall left him mentally "vacant," and so "the bastard Bacchus comes to his relief" (Taylor 1999, 123). Baudelaire is generally credited with articulating the attack on what he called "artificial paradises": The "visible lord of visible nature (man, I mean) has therefore sought to construct Paradise from drugs or fermented drinks—like a maniac using stage-sets, painted on canvas and mounted on frames, as a substitute for real furniture and gardens" (77). However, a recent critic of drug-induced ecstasy, Mircea Eliade, has had this degenerative model of shamanic development dismissed by a number of younger scholars who find it to be a compound of middle-class propriety and wishful thinking.[11]

Just because the story of drugs as spiritual degeneration is insistently repeated doesn't make it true. True and false states of exaltation may not be as different as cultural arbiters claim, since the institutions and images that compose our religious history have been airbrushed by denial, or, shifting to Terence McKenna's similitude: "There are skeletons in the closet of human origins and of the origin of religion. I would wager that those skeletons are all plant psychedelics" (54). States we are taught to regard as spiritual, like religious ecstasy, may have been largely or partially material as well.

An exemplary meditation on this topic is found in Hans Peter Duerr's *Dreamtime;* he asks why the Inquisition and later writers on the persecution of witches never thought to ask what the salves and ointments that they rubbed on their bodies were made of. He answers that if the question were asked, flights through the air and orgies with the devil would have to be classified as hallucinatory experience. And if these were known to be subjective, the devil would lose his purchase on the world, and Christianity would falter (6).

On the other hand, when Christianity cast its glance backward at pagan religions or sideways at ritual cults, a materialist bias was gladly entertained. Psychotropic substances were allowed to enter easily into discussions of other religions, as though such intoxication were a decisive step toward proving their falsity. St. Augustine believed that "ecstatic experiences sought through drunkenness carried with them the implicit stigma of paganism and even heresy" (Bowers 419). So it has been speculated that the Eleusinian mysteries employed a sacred mint or ergot; the Delphian Pythia was drugged with hemp or laurel; and the Dionysiac maenads were high on wine, hallucinogenic drugs, or hashish.[12] Surveys of this kind also include Indian religions, *soma,* and hemp; the Aztecs and their divine mushroom; the Incas and coca; and the Sufi opium ritual, which "permits them to carry out their self-mutilations."[13]

Within Christianity, the "abnormal" condition of witchcraft attested, as many commentators looking back from the 1960s allow, to the active presence of a drug culture:

> Recent work in nutrition, biochemistry and pharmacology suggested that the craze resulted from the deliberate or unknowing ingestion of drugs. Bernard Barnett noted that "since the concept of hallucinatory drugs was not defined, the Devil, not surprisingly, got the blame," and Michael Harner suggested that "once the use and effects of these natural hallucinogens are understood, the major features of past beliefs and practices suddenly seem quite logical and consistent." (Sidky 249; Quaife 5)

Modern researchers speculate that witches were drugged at the time of their initiation, at the time of their practice—the flamboyant aspects of the reconstructed witch experience, flying through the air and copulating with the devil—and, most intriguing, at the time of their interrogation when Christianity fought drugs with drugs: torture specialists, Homayun Sidky writes, made witches "imbibe a 'witch-broth,' a foul drink allegedly made from the ashes of burnt witches," which "contained psychomimetic drugs (substances producing psychosis-like conditions), and their use can conceivably account for the bizarre and detailed confessions on record"

(139).[14] There has been speculation that these episodes in the religious history of the West may have been early skirmishes in the drug wars, that the clergy resented the village healers who "had wide knowledge—insights into telepathy, hypnotism, and the use of drugs, especially hallucinogens capable of controlling and influencing the moods of clients" (Quaife 92).

The archives of Christianity are well stocked with materialist rereadings of the religion, but these have been officially received as parodic or reductive, thus not to be taken seriously, as in Robert Burns's "Epitaph on John Dove, Innkeeper":

> Strong ale was ablution,
> Small beer persecution,
> A dram was *memento mori;*
> But a full flowing bowl,
> Was the saving his soul,
> And port his celestial glory.
> (263)

There are many drink rewritings of Christianity in the form of mock sermons: Peter the Great established a church of Bacchus with mock liturgies and rituals burlesquing those of the Orthodox Church, which included the scattering of vodka for Holy Water (Juniper 62). Still, why can't we read sermons like the following, "On Loving Wine," as both literal and parodic, particularly if we suspect that intoxication is not the antithesis of ecstasy but its analogue or perhaps even its model?

> The first and greatest commandment is: Thou shalt love the Lord thy Wine with all thy mouth and with all thy stomach and with all thy entrails. . . . "Thou shalt love" is said not in command but in prophecy, knowing that you will love Wine. For who is there today in Holy Church who does not love Bacchus? . . . Not without cause, indeed, is Jesus said to have turned water into wine at Cana. . . . I baptize you not with water but with wine. (Dronke 38)

Most religions, major or minor, institution or cult, can be said to have a drug of choice. Morris Carstairs wrote that "communities choose certain drugs to the exclusion of others, praise these, often invent legends of their supernatural origins; and denounce alien drugs 'with a ferocity which

betrays a fear of their powers,'" and he instances "a village in Northern
India, where the warrior Rajputs drank wine and despised the local *bhang*
or hashish, and the Brahmins took *bhang* and proscribed wine" (Laski 259).
D. T. Suzuki writes, "If tea symbolizes Buddhism, can we not say that
wine stands for Christianity? . . . Wine first excites and then inebriates. In
many ways it contrasts with tea, and this contrast is also that between
Buddhism and Christianity" (273).

The most obvious instance is Christianity and wine (although Zoroastrianism, Taoism, and Judaism also have strong connections to wine and
intoxication).[15] "To drink is a Christian diversion," sings William Congreve's Sir Wilfull Witwoud, "Unknown to the Turk or the Persian" (351).
Christianity is, after all, a religion whose kerygmatic god referred to himself as "a gluttonous man and a wine-bibber" and "the true vine," whose
first miracle was the turning of water into wine, and who, after his death,
is drunk by his worshippers as wine.[16] "It is reasonable," Origen asserted,
"that he who brings the wine which cheers the heart of man is the 'true
vine'" (1989, 75).

As a drink religion, Christianity absorbed earlier Dionysus worship, and
the drinking and intoxication become metaphoric, or more metaphoric
than they had previously been.[17] P. Corrado Leanardi has shown that early
Christian icons and theological literature made extensive use of the vine
and grape motifs found in Asia Minor, Greece, and Italy (Demetz 524), and
Albert Henrichs agrees, writing that

> Long after the final victory of Christianity, familiar Dionysiac motifs such
> as vines, drinking cups, peacocks, and even Erotes continued to appear fre-
> quently on Christian mosaics and sarcophagi, which projected a vision of a
> luscious paradise that owed more to the world of Dionysus than to the Bible.
> (1984a, 213)[18]

In his *Survival of the Pagan Gods,* Jean Seznac recalls that "the Christian
art of the catacombs borrowed from mythology the symbolic motif of *amor-
ini* as vintagers which later caused the Basilica of Constantine to be mistaken for a temple of Bacchus" (105).

"This concept of the Son of God who is physically present on the altar
in the form of wine," Arthur Evans writes, was "to have a significant impact
on Christian mythology" (59). Christ was compared to Dionysus, just as
Dionysus, who was very different from the other Olympian gods, was read

as a prototype of Christ. According to Caroline Houser, "both were the son of a father god . . . and a mortal mother, both dwelt among mortals, and both gave their followers the promise of resurrection after death" (15). The Italian playwright Dario Fo sees the mirthful Jesus as a continuation of Dionysus-Bacchus, the god of wine who comes to earth to bring back the spring. This aspect of Christ, Fo claims, is dear to the spirit of the folk and stands in opposition to and in defiance of the severity of official dogma (Scuderi 286).

As a glorious corollary to this metaphoric regime, the Christian Church drank long and deeply:

> [The Church drank] to the greater glory of *God;* bumpers were drained *au bon père* and drunkenness was so much less a sin when the malt was ecclesiastical. Person pitted himself against person, and he with the largest swallow proved the godliest; parish challenged parish [in the Whitsun-ales, clerk-ales, give-ales, etc.] and the fabric of the Church, fairer than heathen strumpet, rose from the froth of a blessed sea of ale. (Juniper 133)

"Ale even entered into the body of the Church," William Juniper notes, "for it was believed that mortar mixed with ale had greater durability than that mixed with water" (133).

Clerical drunkenness was a popular theme in medieval and later satire on ecclesiastics. The ninth abbot of Angers

> would have his wine all times and seasons.
> Never did a day or night go by
> But it found him wine-soaked and wavering
> (Seward 9),

while Alexander Pope referred

> to happy convents, bosom'd deep in vines,
> Where slumber abbots, purple as their wines.
> (246)

In his chapter on banquet literature, Mikhail Bakhtin cites the eleventh-century "Treatise of Garcia of Toledo"—a parody of the litany that detailed "continuous feasting of the Roman curia with the Pope and cardinals. The Pope drinks from a large golden cup; he has an unquenchable thirst. He drinks to all and to everything. . . . Nor do the cardinals lag behind" (290). Desmond Seward also mentions "Peacock's 'bottle-cracking' Brother Michael and the boozy abbots and priors of *The Ingoldsby Legends*," Rabelais's Friar John, and Alphonse Daudet's Canon Gaucher (13).

Christianity was the great wine-producing as well as the great wine-consuming religion. One of monasticism's services to Western civilization was its contribution to wine growing and to the distillation of strong drink:

> Monks largely saved viticulture when the Barbarian invasions destroyed the Roman Empire, and throughout the Dark Ages they alone had the security and resources to improve the quality of their vines slowly and patiently. For nearly 1300 years almost all the biggest and the best vineyards were owned and operated by religious houses. (Seward 15)[19]

Christianity, then, is a drink religion with a great drink or drunk, the Eucharist, at its center, since the purpose of the Eucharist is to produce spiritual intoxication (notice that in this case one attains spiritual intoxication not by unspeakable or transcendent means but by *drinking wine*). The two great feasts of Christianity are Cana (wine and water) and the Last Supper/Eucharist (wine and blood).

Carl Jung identifies the wine miracle at Cana with a miracle in the temple of Dionysus, and Dionysus is associated with several wine miracles of this kind (transforming water into wine or making springs of wine gush forth from the earth) (Kott 1973, 204; Hedreen 78–79).[20] Cana is Christ's first miracle, and, in allegorical interpretations of the event, the wine is usually read as the new dispensation of his gospels, while the old wine, the superseded Mosaic law, has become literal intoxication: according to Ludolphos, it "brought forgetfulness of God and kindled a desire for the flesh" (Sterling 29, 62). George Herbert rhymes

> But much more him I must adore,
> Who of the Law's sour juice sweet wine did make.
> Even God himself being pressed for my sake.
> (79)

As it had been in the worship of Dionysus, the wine and bread of the Eucharist are the deity himself, and Michel Maffesoli hints at a secret history of Bacchanalian orgy behind the symbolism of the eucharistic wine:

> Even though every effort has been made to bar them from memory, there exist through all the history of the church multiple groups of deviants who have taken to its ends the logic of communion. From the Adamites to the Nicolites, the list of Christian sects who, with eroticism or sometimes cruelty, took seriously the communion of the sacred wine is long. (124)

If turning water into wine is a figure for the process of biblical exegesis (as I mentioned in the opening of this chapter), the bread and wine of the Eucharist stand for two different modes of reading. Bread is denotative, wine connotative language: Origen wrote that the "difficult and wandering journey by which the soul returns to God begins from the clear 'bread' of direct scriptural language, but can only advance through ingestion of the 'wine' of scripture, its obscure and poetic speech, which intoxicates and draws upward" (McGinn 116).

The great poet of the eucharistic moment was the American Puritan Edward Taylor. He takes the implications of the Lord's Supper most literally, for example, in his *Holy Meditation* 1.10, which begins with an image of the intense thirst of the poet's soul:

> My Soule had caught an Ague, and like Hell
> Her thirst did burn.

In answer, a "Well of Aqua-Vitae" springs from Christ's wounded side: "And down came running thence t'allay my thirst."

The poem describes a heaven of wine cellars and servants, and the speaker commands,

> Lord make thy Butlar draw, and fill with speed
> My beaker full: for this is drink indeed.
> Whole Buts of this blesst Nectar shining stand
> Lockt up with Saph'rine Taps, whose splendid Flame
> Too bright do shine for brightest Angells hands
> To touch, my Lord. Do thou untap the same.

Oh! make thy Crystall Buts of Red Wine bleed
Into my Crystal Glass this Drink-Indeed.
. . . Nay, though I make no pay for this Red Wine,
And scarce do say I thank-ye-for't; strange thing!
Yet were the silver skies my Beer bowle fine
I finde my Lord, would fill it to the brim.
(21–22)

In an article on drink in Taylor's poetry, Jon Miller argues that the poetic celebration is in inverse proportion to the material wealth of the society—when scarcity ruled the Massachusetts Bay Colony, Taylor's eucharistic sentiments were clothed in metaphors of abundance and excess (36). This is a point that bears directly on the metaphor of spiritual intoxication and its missing referent: Taylor can praise drink only when it isn't present.

It is common to argue that there are many ways to induce ecstasy: through spiritual disciplines as well as a wide variety of material practices, like "hypnotic suggestion, rapid over-breathing, the inhalation of smoke and vapors, music, and dancing" (Lewis 1971, 39). Only intoxicating substances, however, have given texture to this glory, and ecstasy, as this chapter has tried to show, is intoxication whether the devotee has gotten drunk or not—ecstasy is never a spiritual hyperventilation. This chapter has been waiting to ask the question, Why drink? Particularly because, of all the ways to induce ecstasy, drink and drugs alone are stridently condemned by the same societies that celebrate their metaphoric implications.

The metaphoric language praises what the religious culture otherwise condemns. The problem that dominates the discourse of addiction—that intoxication is good in moderation, but bad in excess—disappears, for example, in Wenzel Hollar's seventeenth-century engraving *Three Useful Schools of Wine, for the Preservation of Body and Soul,* where the wine of the Holy Ghost *must* be drunk to excess (as opposed to the wine of health, which should be drunk to moderation, and the wine of the devil, which should not be drunk at all); Abu Yazid al-Bistami, a ninth-century Sufi mystic, wrote to Yahya ben Mu'adh and asked him, "What do you say of one who, if all the oceans in the world were composed of the wine of Love, would drink them all and still cry for more to slake his thirst"; and Gregory of Nyssa, writing on "Song of Songs" (2.4–5), imagines that the bride "asks to be brought into the very wine cellar, and have her mouth held right beneath the vats bubbling over with sweet wine" (Kunzle 1973, 217; Smith 1928, 208 94; and Danielou 176).[21]

Aelfric, an eleventh-century British abbott, seems to have felt this discrepancy. According to Hugh Magennis,

> [He was] extremely reticent about using this kind of imagery. Perhaps his moral concern about the dangers of drunkenness made him unwilling to introduce to his relatively unsophisticated audience a metaphor which might be unfortunately misunderstood. His often-expressed warnings about the vice of drunkenness indicate that he may have been too concerned about inebriation in its immediate, literal sense to wish to explore the finer points of its spiritual exegesis. (1986a, 4)

Aelfric and other Old English writers, Magennis goes on to say, were reluctant to use metaphors of spiritual intoxication even when they occurred in the Latin texts that those writers were following.

In the Christian tradition it has been conventionally understood that the intoxication referred to is metaphoric; in Sufism, despite an insistent allegorical imperative, that fact has to be continually reasserted and argued. Neither the allegorical nor the literal reading of intoxication ever wins out. "How are we to know," Michael Sells writes, "that references to the eternal or to the day of resurrection are not the irreverent hyperboles of the wine poets? Although the distinction is sometimes made later in a Sufi poem, or in a poet's commentary, the poet will often heighten and play upon the ambiguity rather than clarify it" (89). Critical commentary is helplessly caught between these two poles of meaning, and the range of testimony from experts is so contradictory that the discussion often reads like a parody of scholarship:

> Between the judgement of Jami, that Hafiz was undoubtedly an eminent Sufi, and that of Von Hammer, who, playing upon his names, declared that the Sun of the Faith gave but an uncertain light, and the Interpretor of Secrets interpreted only the language of pleasure—between these two there is a wide field for differences of opinion. For my part, I cannot agree entirely either with Jami or with Von Hammer. (Bell 1928, 66)[22]

In a culture like Persia's, which once had a great tolerance for wine (and a personal mythology attending it) but was now subject to a discipline forbidding this pleasure, might you not find a schizophrenic poetic culture suffused with details of drink, intoxication, and drunken love, but so poised and hedged about that neither the original culture nor later commentary could tell whether it was an actual reference or a metaphor for ecstatic truth? The poets themselves even fostered such allegorical hinting, so it was said, as a form of "protective dissimulation" in order to shield themselves from the authorities (Bürgel 8; Bagley 84).[23]

Even the Christian discourse keeps impaling itself on certain general and specific problems with metaphoric language, mainly the incommensurability built into the transcendental mode. Diurnal metaphor can be understood to work by similarity or equivalence, but how can spiritual metaphor do so? If it can, heaven and earth are not as different as they are alleged to be. Certain Christian writers didn't think that gulf was impossibly wide, but others believed that spiritual metaphors could only work by opposites. According to Robert Daly, Taylor's

> insistence on the inadequacy of metaphor goes well beyond Bradstreet's belief that earthly beauties were literally vain but figurally portentous, that while they could not compete with heaven, they could figure it. Taylor repeatedly insists that all metaphoric predications are equivocal, that, applied to God and heaven, all earthly metaphors become inverted, showing forth the glory of God, not by similarity, but by opposition. (188)

This is the general problem of metaphor. The specific problem is one I have raised often, the contemptible status of intoxication. Could there also be spiritual vomit, or spiritual shit?

While there may be correspondences and equivalences between material and spiritual intoxication, their opposition of value is so great that comparison quickly nullifies itself. So, for example, Origen claims we must "recognize the fact that besides this wine which is pressed from the dogmas of truth and mingled in Wisdom's bowl, there is another wine of an opposite nature with which sinners and those who accept the harmful dogmas of false learning wickedly get drunk" (1957, 187), and St. John Chrysostom writes:

> And lest you, hearing the word *inebriates*, be surprised and think it to be the same as that which produces infirmity of body. . . . it is wonderful and strengthening. It is a new kind of drunkenness, that gives strength, and

makes men strong and powerful; for it flows from the spiritual rock. . . . Let us then be drunk with this wine; but let us abstain from that other. (Toal 2.196)[24]

According to many official voices, intoxication is much less than even a metaphor for ecstasy or creativity: it is an utterly unworthy material signifier for spiritual truths that transcend it so completely as to strain any metaphoric connection and render it oxymoronic, hence a "sober" intoxication, another way of being under a mark of erasure.[25] And yet the linguistic connection remains active. However much beyond drunkenness ecstasy may be, drunkenness is the only intelligible term avowed in its construction, just as it is regularly disavowed in its understanding.

The metaphoric drift of the writers I have been considering makes intoxication an earthly type of ecstasy; but they never seem to entertain the notion that it might be ecstasy that is derivative, that ecstasy may be a spiritualized and despirited intoxication. The connection between intoxication and transcendental thrills would make more sense if heaven were a projection of our altered states, and this origin was then forbidden and forgotten. We can trace such a process at work in Christa Karoli's analysis of *ekstasis* in antiquity. She observes that ecstasy was "originally a purely bodily heightening of the self" through physical intoxication in ancient religious cults. The Greeks modulated the concept into a "creative state of excitement as the bodily and spiritual forms of intoxication merge" (Warner 147).
    Huston Smith and Mary Barnard would agree:

> More interesting than the fact that consciousness-changing devices have been linked with religion is the possibility that they actually initiated many of the religious perspectives which, taking root in history, continued after their psychedelic origins were forgotten. Bergson saw the first movement of Hindus and Greeks toward "dynamic religion" as associated with "divine rapture" found in intoxicating beverages; (Solomon 1964, 153)

and:

> Which was more likely to happen first: the spontaneously generated idea of an afterlife in which the disembodied soul, liberated from the restrictions of

time and space, experiences eternal bliss, or the accidental discovery of hallucinogenic plants that give a sense of euphoria, dislocate the center of consciousness, and distort time and space, making them balloon outward in greatly expanded vistas? (Barnard 583–84)

On the level of verbal imagery the equation between intoxication and religious ecstasy works in this way. There, it is heaven, ecstasy, and paradise that are metaphors for the effects of intoxication. Heaven, ecstasy, and paradise come into existence as the ne plus ultra of intoxication: "This box contains the paradise your prophet promised to his believers," says a character in a tale by Nerval, "[and in one hour I will put you] in the arms of the houris without making you pass across the bridge of Alsirat" (107).

Heaven was made out of our intoxication, and in an intriguing Persian painting by Sultan Muhammad we see various simultaneous stages of heavenly and mundane intoxication:

"Hafiz himself, popeyed with drink or religious inspiration, sits in a window with the huge wine jar," under a roof on which angels are dancing and drinking, while in the lower level wild-looking dervishes produce strange music. It is indeed a picture "which demolishes the conventional split between the effects of wine and divine ecstasy. In this extraordinary transcendental painting, low comedy and high religion meet . . ." And thus the problem that has puzzled generations of scholars and admirers of Hafiz, whether to interpret his poetry as sensual or mystical, seems to be solved by the brush of one of the greatest Persian painters. (S. C. Welch in Schimmel 1986, 938)

chapter 7

Drinking in Style:
A Horatian Aesthetic

I'd like to ask why the ancients called Bacchus, whom they liked to think the inventor of wine, the god of poets. What has that tipsy god to do with poets, worshippers of the maiden Muses?

—ERASMUS, *Colloquies*

> All Pictures thats Panted with Sense & with Thought
> Are Painted by Madmen as sure as a Groat
> For the Greater the Fool in the Pencil more blest,
> And when they are drunk they always pant best.
> —BLAKE, "ALL PICTURES"

Of course, you're a rummy. But you're no more of a rummy than Joyce is and most good writers are.

—ERNEST HEMINGWAY TO F. SCOTT FITZGERALD

Spiritual intoxication often takes the form of artistic inspiration, which may be as abstract as "poetic furor" or as literal as a bottle of booze.[1] In Honoré de Balzac's tale "Gambara," the composer of the title can only write or play beautiful music when he is drunk; otherwise, his compositions are "a jumble of discordant sounds, randomly made, as though intended to destroy the ear of the least sensitive of listeners" (2.38).[2] Byam Warner, the hero of Gertrude Atherton's novel *The Gorgeous Isle,* is a West Indian poet of the highest order—"the legitimate successor of Byron and Shelley, to say nothing of Keats." He "had never written a line of serious work except under the influence of brandy" (54, 115). His wife comes to realize that his poetic power is tied to his addiction, that she cannot have the angelic poet without the drunken brute. At the end of the novel, she enables

99

him in his writing and his drinking by leaving a decanter of brandy on his table. Drunk on wine, Maurice Utrillo "painted the most exquisite pictures of Paris, with subtle nuances in white, greys and greens": his relatives would leave him a bottle of wine and a new canvas, returning later to fetch an empty bottle, a drunk artist, and a fine painting (Sandblom 53; see also Rose 94–95).[3]

The meaning of intoxication in Balzac's tale, Atherton's novel, and Utrillo's life is not clear: does the drink induce artistic inspiration, or are these people alcoholics as well as artists? Does the first story belong to an early regime of convivial intoxication that shades into a later one as intoxication grows medically dark in the nineteenth century, or has the aesthetic proposition always been a cover story for the artists' dependencies? This confusion infects the language of criticism, so that Miriam Allen deFord writes of the alcoholic poet Ernest Dowson, "From thirty years of weakness and agony he distilled a few drops of the true liquor of genius" (198), and Arthur Symons of Dante Gabriel Rossetti, that in "the fire and imagination of Rossetti's genius there is intensity—of will, of conception, of spiritual intoxication, 'of large draughts of intellectual day,' and of 'thirsts of love'" (11). From the perspective of the present the subject matter of this chapter may be nothing more than addicts protecting their supply by telling bright lies about it.

Although I give pride of place to alcohol, narcotic and psychedelic drugs also figure in the chapter, although not the minor drugs, like tea—

> The Muses's friend, tea does our fancy aid,
> Repress those vapours which the head invade
> (Waller 222);

coffee—"*Voltaire* and *Buffon* were great coffee-drinkers, and perhaps drew thence, one, the admirable clearness of thought that is in all his works, the other, the fervent harmony of his style. It is evident that certain passages . . . were written in a state of extreme cerebral exaltation" (Brillat-Savarin 80); or tobacco—as Tennyson said, "I take my pipe and the muse descends in the fume" (Fausset 95).

Early on, Western culture declared intoxication to be a proper foundation for the creation of art—a logical move where the same god oversaw both wine and drama. Reasonable explanations have been offered for this conjunction: A. E. Housman "suggested that the effect of beer was to deaden the brain and to release the poetry that lay buried deep in the nervous system" (Press 83). A psychiatrist, Donald Goodwin, listed the many ways intoxication and creativity can go together:

> Writing is a form of exhibitionism; alcohol lowers inhibitions and prompts exhibitionism in many people. Writing requires an interest in people; alcohol increases sociability and makes people more interesting. Writing involves fantasy; alcohol promotes fantasy. Writing requires self-confidence; alcohol bolsters confidence. Writing is lonely work; alcohol assuages loneliness. (1988, 47–48)[4]

This proposition had an acknowledged place in aesthetic thought through the eighteenth century. During the Romantic period in England and France, the doctrine turned on itself and, more often than not, was taken to mean that only artists who had been forsaken by true spiritual intoxication sought the false inspiration of alcohol and drugs (the "bastard Bacchus" of Coleridge and the artificial paradise of Baudelaire). As a compromise formation, in nineteenth-century Germany intoxicatory inspiration was internalized and became known as "Dionysianism." By the next century the link between intoxication and creativity could not be tolerated by official culture, and the advocates of artificial inspiration (Symbolist poets, avant-garde artists, bebop musicians, Beat poets, etc.) became more and more marginalized.

Certain myths account for the origin of poetry in intoxication. The Indo-Iranian *haoma* inspired both warriors and poets with its hallucinatory properties. In the Norse *Snorra Edda,* the god Bragi replies to Aegir's question "whence originated that art you call poetry?" not, as we might expect today, with an account of the creative process "but of the making and winning of the mead which is poetry in a quite concrete sense" (Stephens 259). The mead was the blood of the giant Kvasir mixed with honey— "Whoever drank of this received the gift of inspiration, and could compose poetry and utter words of wisdom"—and Odin acquired it for men (Davidson 1964, 40). In Celtic mythology, the young Taliesin is reborn as a great poet after tasting a brew from the cauldron of his mother, Ceridwen (Matthews 47).

Art may have been the product of intoxication from the beginning: some anthropologists believe that rock art might be the fruit of hallucinogenic drug states. A crucial text in this body of commentary, J. D. Williams and T. A. Dowson's 1988 article "The Signs of All Times: Entoptic Phenomena in Upper Palaeolithic Art," was summarized as follows by two of its respondents:

> The central premise in this innovative paper is that the order governing prehistoric art is derived from the functioning of the human nervous system in altered states . . . that drug-induced phosphenes [luminous sensations that appear in the visual field independent of an external light source] were the visual sources of inspiration for almost their entire design repertoire. (218, 229)[5]

"Without hallucinogenous substances," the performance artist Jean-Jacques Lebel has written, "pre-Columbian art in Mexico and the art of New Guinea would never have been what they are" (45). People who argue that drugs and drink in the practice of modern art are a kind of parodic reduction are not considering how this practice echoes the origin of poetry in shamanism.

J. C. Bramble chronicles the great debate between the "water drinkers" and the "wine drinkers" in the Hellenistic period, between the school of Callimachus and his Dionysiac opponents—a debate continued in Augustan Rome by Ovid, Propertius, and Horace (48–49). This was the first battle of the books—between the "clear, quiet, derivative, and fine" water drinkers and the "mighty-thundering, original, and ecstatic" drinkers of wine (Donohue 42). Horace wrote the classic statement of the influence of intoxication on creativity in his nineteenth epistle: "O learned Maecenas, if you believe old Cratinus, no verses which are written by water-drinkers can please, or be long lived. . . . Homer, by his excessive praises of wine, is convicted as a booser; father Ennius himself never sallied forth to sing of arms unless in drink" (245–46).[6] By the time this trope reached Rabelais, the genealogy had been expanded to include Aeschylus and Cato:

> Wait a little, till I've swallowed a draught from this bottle. It is my true and only Helicon, my one Pegasus spring, my sole enthusiasm. . . . Ennius wrote as he drank, drank as he wrote. Aeschylus, if you put any trust in Plutarch's *Symposiacs,* used to drink as he composed, to compose as he drank. Homer

never wrote on an empty stomach, Cato never wrote except after drinking. So do not say that I am not following the example of good and praiseworthy men. (284)[7]

In addition to the authors mentioned by Horace and Rabelais, early classical writers associated with what I will call the Horatian aesthetic are Archilochus—"I know how to lead the dithyramb, the lovely song of Lord Dionysus, when my brain is thunderstruck with wine"—and, of course, Anacreon, who has already received a chapter to himself (Bing 21). That chapter locates poetry in the Greek symposium, institutionalizing the connection between creativity and drinking.

The Horatian aesthetic moved along the high road of carnivalesque literature in the work of writers like Erasmus and Rabelais. Erasmus claimed that "the consecration of poets" to Bacchus "is intended, I suspect, to signify that wine both arouses invention and ministers to eloquence, two things very suitable to a poet. This is why poems written by water-drinkers are insipid" (1965, 597), and Alice Berry writes that Rabelais "emphatically associates literary creation with the great god of wine who seizes him in joyful rapture and causes words to pour forth without conscious premeditation or art" (88). Among the various identities Rabelais assumes when introducing himself to the reader, the most persistent is "the tipsy poet writing (or rather speaking) his book at a tavern table and, following the Horatian *topos,* working more by the scent of wine than by the light of an oil lamp" (Jeanneret 128).

In the Renaissance, according to John O'Brien, "'bien parler' requires 'bien boire'; intoxication is necessary for a properly eloquent productivity" (204–5). English writers like Robert Herrick and Ben Jonson and French ones like Pierre Ronsard championed this aesthetic. Jonson is said to have written over the door of the Apollo Tavern:

He the half of life abuses
That sits watering with the muses.
Those dull girls no good can mean us;
Wine, it is the milk of Venus
And the poet's horse accounted
Ply it, and you all are mounted.
(372)

Herrick heaped extravagant praise on his favorite drink, sack:

> 'Tis thou, alone, who with thy Mistick Fan,
> Work'st more than Wisdome, Art, or Nature can . . .
> 'Tis not *Apollo* can, or those thrice three
> *Castalian* Sisters, sing, if wanting thee.
> *Horace, Anacreon* both had lost their fame,
> Had'st thou not fill'd them with thy fire and flame.
> (45)

Ronsard "happily depicted himself as a reveller, a *poeta vinosus,*" a drunken poet (Jeanneret 122–26).

In the Renaissance, as earlier in classical antiquity, the Horatian aesthetic was also promulgated through theories of spiritual inspiration. Marsilio Ficino felt that when poets are "inebriated by a certain new draft of nectar and by an immeasurable joy, they are, as it were, in a bacchic frenzy," and the Pléiade poets invoked a Platonic doctrine of divine drunkenness (*fureur divine*) (Wind 64). This notion of poetic ecstasy was first broached in the fourth century BC by the philosopher Democritus, who claimed that the finest poems were composed "with inspiration and a holy breath" and denied that anyone could be a great poet *"sine furore"* (Dodds 82). "Furor poeticus" entered Renaissance discourse with the recovery of Plato's *Phaedrus,* a dialogue in which Plato laid out his theory of the four furors, or furies. The third, governed by Bacchus, was poetic: a "form of possession or madness, of which the Muses are the source. This seizes a tender, virgin soul and stimulates it to rapt passionate expression, especially in lyric poetry" (492).

Edgar Wind claims the connection between inspiration and intoxication is accidental: because Plato happened to mention nectar as nourishment for the inspired soul, Proclus and Hermias and their Renaissance followers felt, "incorrectly," that the divine madness in the *Phaedrus* could be equated with a doctrine of spiritual intoxication in Plotinus (61). But a compacted form of this equation can be found in Plato's *Ion:*

> For the epic poets, all the good ones, have their excellence, not from art, but
> are inspired, possessed, and thus they utter all these admirable poems. So is
> it also with the good lyric poets; as the worshiping Corybantes are not in

their senses when they dance, so the lyric poets are not in their senses when they make those lovely lyric poems. No, when once they launch into harmony and rhythm, they are seized with the Bacchic transport, and are possessed—as the bacchants, when possessed, draw milk and honey from the rivers. (220)[8]

Nevertheless, the official position is that intoxication can sometimes be a useful metaphor for inspiration, but no more. E. R. Dodds, however, suggests the opposite: "I should myself guess it [the doctrine of poetic inspiration] to be a by-product of the Dionysiac movement with its emphasis on the value of abnormal mental states, not merely as avenues to knowledge, but for their own sake" (82). Inspiration, on the contrary, might be a generalization from an original intoxication, now doomed, like Freud's seduction theory, to survive only in the guise of metaphor.

Eventually the equivalence between the two powers slackened, and they became alternative modes of art, although, confusingly, inspiration would continue to be figured as an intoxication. Charles Lamb could still describe the natural intoxication of the poet as follows:

your poet-born hath an internal wine, richer than lippara or canaries, yet uncrushed from any grapes of earth, unpressed in mortal winepresses. . . . It is denominated indifferently, wit, conceit, invention, inspiration, but its most royal and comprehensive name is *fancy*. . . . Its cellars are in the brain, whence your true poet deriveth intoxication at will;

but Coleridge and Baudelaire would impose an impassable gulf between inspiration and intoxication, with the former as true, the latter debased, currency (Taylor 1999, 83–84). On the other hand, the Renaissance scholar Julius Caesar Scaliger did not see much difference between the two ways of making poetry; for him, these two principles accounted for the pantheon of poets and, between them, produced the highest art:

Of these divinely possessed ones, two classes are to be recognized. The one class are those to whom the divine power comes from above, with no mental effort on their part except the simple invocation. Hesiod classed himself in this category, and Homer is placed there by universal consent. The other class is aroused by the fumes of unmixed wine, which draws out the instruments of the mind, the spirits themselves, from the material parts of the body. Horace said that Ennius was such a poet, and such we consider Horace himself. Tradition says the same of Alcaeus and Aristophanes. (15)[9]

Drugs played such a large part in the profession and practice of English Romantic art that some critics theorize Romanticism as a drug aesthetic, reading the period through Thomas De Quincey's *Confessions of an English Opium-Eater* rather than William Wordsworth's *Prelude*.[10] Echoing Horace's binary, Julian North sets up an opposition between a marginal De Quinceyan aesthetic based on drugs and a dominant Wordsworthian aesthetic based on nature and water.[11] More traditional readings of English literary history, however, find the De Quinceyan aesthetic, nourished in France by Théophile Gautier, Baudelaire, Joris-Karl Huysmans, and others, returning to dominate English letters later, in the period of the Decadence (North 116, 114; Cooke 30).[12]

Josephine McDonagh points out that criticism has generally acknowledged addiction to be "a defining interest of Romantic writing" (116). Clifford Siskin takes this notion further and suggests that Romanticism was always structurally narcotic no matter what its surface concerns might have been: it was neither Wordsworthian nor De Quinceyan but Coleridgean. According to Siskin, the Romantic period was the moment when "two disciplines, medicine and literature . . . grounded their claims to professional status in a tale of lyrical development," which "transformed the drug user into a patient requiring a doctor, and the writer into a genius requiring a critic" (183). Consequently, our critical accounts of the period are "unavoidably dependent upon a discourse of addiction," which includes a "catalog of characteristic Romantic behaviors: to explore mind, to undergo epiphany, to alter vision, to dream dreams, to intensify imagination, to heighten depression, to suffer ecstasy, to fragment experience, to burn out— to flower lyrically and then wither" (181). It is no coincidence, Siskin adds, "that one of those who has most brilliantly fed that habit [M. H. Abrams], began his career with a book about opium usage." Abrams's strategy was to turn Romantic Imagination into something that worked as powerfully and clearly as a drug (183).[13]

Robert Burns, who is often held up as a type of Romantic genius, was certainly a poet in the Horatian tradition, as he admits in "Scotch Drink":

O *Whiskey!* soul o' plays an' pranks!
Accept a *Bardie*'s gratefu' thanks!
When wanting thee, what tuneless cranks
Are my poor Verses!
Thou comes—they rattle i' their ranks
At ither's arses.
(142)

Burns was also a drunk, and he was surrounded by other equally heavy-
drinking Scottish writers, like Robert Fergusson, James Hogg, and John
Wilson.[14] In opposition to the drug aesthetic of De Quincey and Coleridge,
Anya Taylor, in her recent study *Bacchus in Romantic England: Writers and
Drink, 1780–1830,* attempts to center a Romantic drink aesthetic on Burns:

> The admiration of these young Romantic poets for a pleasure seeker, the cre-
> ator of the famous drunkard "Tam O'Shanter" and of drinking songs about
> whisky and willing Caledonian women, signals a new ideal of the poet: a
> rude and earthy rustic, worn by farming a hard land and ruined by the
> rich; a revolutionary democrat expressing Jacobin sympathies; a spontaneous
> artist; an outspoken wastrel in a Pharisaical age; a reincarnation of Diony-
> sus, Pantagruel, and Falstaff. The convivial, passionate Burns was the type
> of the Romantic artist, in part because he was a drunk. (37)

Lord Byron expresses the difference between Burns and Wordsworth as
a difference between whiskey and water or tea: "I doubt if either of them
[Wordsworth or Southey] ever got drunk, and I am of the old creed of
Homer the wine-bibber. Indeed I think you [Hogg] and Burns have derived
a great advantage from this, that being poets, and drinkers of wine, you have
had a new potation to rely upon. Your whisky has made you original"
(Taylor 1999, 57).

In *Romantic Genius: The Prehistory of a Homosexual Role,* Andrew Elfenbein reads that emergent type of special individual as a screen for the homosexual. It is equally possible (and profitable) to read the genius as a covert
addict. In the work of Eve Sedgwick, the alcoholic and the homosexual are
structural twins at least: "The two new taxonomies of the addict and the
homosexual condense many of the same issues for late nineteenth-century

culture" (1990, 172). Benjamin De Casseres declared that "all men at a certain point of intoxication are geniuses," and, in Billy Wilder's *Lost Weekend,* the alcoholic writer Don Birnam spins a grandiose fantasy of the relative losses and profits from his disease:

> It shrinks my liver, doesn't it, Nat? It pickles my kidneys. Yes. But what does it do to my mind? It tosses the sandbags overboard so the balloon can soar. Suddenly . . . I'm one of the great ones. I'm Michelangelo molding the beard of Moses. I'm Van Gogh, painting pure sunlight. I'm Horowitz playing the Emperor Concerto. (De Casseres 59)

Gautier's praise of the Renaissance poet (and drinker) Antoine Girard de Saint-Amant is wrapped in the folds of a rhetoric that looks upon genius and intoxication with an equal regard:

> It would be a mistake to suppose, however, that Saint-Amant is a vulgar drunkard who drinks for the sake of drink. Not at all; he is a drunkard after the fashion of Hoffmann,—a poetic drunkard, who thoroughly understands an orgy and knows what fire may flash from the clinking of the glasses of two clever men. He understands that genius is but the intoxication of reason, and he gets drunk as often as he can. . . . The inspiring beam reaches him much more brilliant and richly colored through the rosy paunch of a wine flagon; his metaphor springs forth more boldly when it accompanies the cork of the bottle. (2.132)

In a dialogue between Tasso and his familiar genie by Giacomo Leopardi, the poet implores the genie to tell him "when despair overtakes me, where can I find you?" "'*In qualche liquore generoso*' is the answer—in some generous liquor—in drunkenness and oblivion" (Festa-McCormick 201).

An identification between the genius and the alcoholic surely informs the romantic cult of the male artist with its permissive code of behavior for men of genius. Wordsworth's *Letter to a Friend of Burns* acknowledges that the poet has a dispensation from ordinary norms of behavior: "Permit me to remind you that it is the privilege of poetic genius to catch . . . a spirit of pleasure wherever it can be found. . . . The poet, trusting to primary instincts, luxuriates among the felicities of love and wine" (124). Like the alcoholic, the genius (the poet Dylan Thomas or the painter Francis

Bacon, say) is a creature of excess and, during his two or three centuries, has been admired for the intemperance that drove and often ended his life. The genius, so the popular mythology goes, is driven by desire for a fame that can only be enhanced by the fact that he lives and dies miserably. For Edgar Allan Poe, all geniuses turn to artificial excitement; all geniuses are or become addicts:

> The earnest longing for artificial excitement, which, unhappily, has characterized too many eminent men, may thus be regarded as a psychal want, or necessity,—an effort to regain the lost,—a struggle of the soul to assume the position which, under other circumstances, would have been its due. (14.190)

The pathology of genius belongs to a long-standing controversy over the ethical status of art, whether holy or demonic, healthy or sick, or, as Coleridge and Lamb parsed it out of Horace, calm or irritable ("the touchy race of poets" of Horace's second epistle) (Coleridge 16). If genius is a pathology, addiction has always been one of its prominent conditions.

In France, the latter half of the nineteenth century has long been seen as an artistic drug culture. Emanuel J. Mickel makes drug experience central to the artistry of Gautier, Baudelaire, and Nerval. Others have drawn the names of Germaine de Staël, Charles Nodier, Eugène Sue, Alfred de Musset, Alexandre Dumas père, and Alfred Jarry into this project. Baudelaire translated the opium addict Poe; Musset and Baudelaire translated or travestied the opium eater De Quincey; Gautier, Baudelaire, and Balzac took part in Joseph Moreau de Tours's "Club des haschischin"; and Gautier and Baudelaire wrote essays on the relationship of drugs and creativity.

The concept of the poet as "voyant," as the recipient of an otherworldly vision resulting from drugs, moves from Baudelaire and Gautier through Arthur Rimbaud to André Breton (Balakian 97–98). After reading what Baudelaire had written about the "almost supernatural" states of soul that drugs could induce, the sixteen-year-old Rimbaud talked excitedly to a friend about the poet's duty to keep his sensations alert, even if it meant using stimulants (Hayman 32).

By contrast, German Romanticism gave itself over to a Dionysianism that was intoxication without drink or drugs—an internal force, a "soul mood." Albert Henrichs writes that the German Romantic philosophers and writers "removed Dionysus from the external space he had occupied since the Renaissance and relocated him in a newly found inner space, that of man's own self. . . . Dionysus became the 'Dionysian,' and the god of wine became a metaphor for a sustained state of higher intoxication" (1984a, 218). Stefan Zweig termed this new, demonic art of the nineteenth century "Rausch-kunst" (intoxicated art) (Hepworth 12).

Reading backward from Nietzsche's *Birth of Tragedy,* this shift seems a familiar story now: while Johann Winckelmann, Goethe, and Friedrich Schiller had been attracted by the serenity and control of Greek culture, it was the wild "Dionysiac" quality of Hellenism that fascinated writers of the later nineteenth century. Goethe represented this power in the Bromius (Dionysus) of his "Wanderer's Sturmlied" and equated it with the poetic "genius of the century":

> Thou art, what inward fire
> to Pindar was
> (1902, 7.203)

According to Max Baeumer, who has written most fully on the subject, qualities of this Greek god were generalized in psychological terms by Max Müller, aestheticized philosophically by Friedrich Schelling, and, finally, made by Nietzsche into a substantive, "the Dionysian" (182). The poetry of Friedrich Hölderlin and Novalis (Friedrich von Hardenberg) celebrated the second coming of the god of wine, summoned by his "holy priests" (the inspired poets) "in enthusiasm and Bacchic intoxication" (170–71). Another genealogy is offered by E. M. Butler: "Dionysus, who came late into Greece, came late into Germany too. Heine ushered him in and then left it to Friedrich Nietzsche to see that he got his rights" (Baeumer 300).

In a detective novel by Reginald Hill, *Arms and the Women,* Ellie Pascoe engages a familiar narrative fiction as she considers why she wants to be a writer:

> She wanted to be a writer because a writer could do anything, go anywhere, answer any question. Here was a world of profit and delight to equal that which tempted Faustus. . . . Maybe as with Faustus the price to be paid was your soul. . . . For she had tasted the sweet poison and knew that more than pipes of opium or lines of coke, when you drank the waters of Hippocrene, all that was actual . . . presently departed from you and left you falling down through the clouds to land lightly on the world of your own creation. (260)

What better way to explore, prepare for, and signal the changing valence
of creative intoxication in the late nineteenth century than to express it
as a pact with the devil? The Faustian pact can be read as a figure for the
second stage in the Horatian aesthetic before it descends into the finality
of addiction. As in the mythology of the genius, art is transgressive and
self-destructive, but well worth it. Thinking of Charlie Parker and Dylan
Thomas, Lawrence Lipton asks, "Would you settle for their final end if
you could perform what they performed—would you make such a bargain?" (19). The outstanding transcription of this version of creativity is,
of course, Thomas Mann's *Dr. Faustus,* where the mechanism of inspiration
is the disease of syphilis raging through the body of the composer, Adrian
Leverkühn. In 1905 Mann planned a work that revolved around the figure
of the syphilitic artist: the poison, he writes, "works as intoxication, stimulant, inspiration; he is filled with ecstatic enthusiasms and creates works
of genius" (Bergsten 56).

Baudelaire had found that music, particularly Wagner's *Tannhäuser,* provided him with the "vertiginous concepts of opium" (Brombert 57). Nietzsche also sensed an "intoxicating quality" in the new music of Richard
Wagner, and this had led him to his rediscovery of the Dionysiac (Hatfield
7). It is in Wagner's work that poetry, music, and theater enter into what
Theodor Adorno called an "intoxicating brew": "Wagnerian music drama
floods the senses and fuses them as a 'consoling phantasmagoria'" (Buck-
Morss 1992, 24). With Wagner, however, the meaning of the Dionysian
moves to a new cultural location: "The musical prelude to *Tristan and Isolde*
expresses one single emotion, endless insatiable longing. This longing is
the longing of addiction" (Leonard 59).

Ewa Lajer-Burcharth reads Edouard Manet's "Absinthe Drinker" as a
transition between two aesthetics. In the later, "early modernist," the
Romantic emphasis on imagination is "vernacularized in the attributes of
intoxication: the glass and the bottle" (22). One of the salient texts of
modernity, this painting was submitted to the Salon of 1859: it is the painting of a "bum—unrepentantly plastered on absinthe"; it dangerously confused the high culture of art with the urban depths represented by the *chif-
fonier,* or rag picker; it hinted at lower-class anger; and, finally, it displayed
a drinker who drank for no other reason than to get drunk (Conrad 16).
In the modern period, the Horatian metaphor acquires a new intensity, as
in André Breton's "First Manifesto of Surrealism": "Everything leads us to
believe that it [Surrealism] acts on the mind in the manner of narcotics;

like them it creates a state of need and can lead man to terrible revolts" (Balakian 99).[15] Such aggressive intoxication easily modulates into addiction. Alina Clej identifies artistic modernism with addiction because of its "cultivation of sublime excesses and distance . . . the practice of shock and simulation, [and] the use of quotation and literary montage to create an illusory effect of the self" (v).

Drink- and drug-induced states are sturdy enough pegs on which to hang the differences of modernist style and technique. Where did those distortions in representation come from? Deriding modern painting as the product of drink was a familiar oppositional trope, going back to Gustave Courbet and the Impressionists (Karmel 125). "Some of the strangeness of *Finnegans Wake*," Matthew Hodgart surmises, "may be attributed to its being written at night while Joyce was drunk" (38–39). Sue Vice measures Malcolm Lowry's avant-gardism by his alcoholism: he re-created the condition of the alcoholic in the shape of the narrative: chronology is uncertain; utterances issue from disembodied voices; there are surrealist-inspired descriptions of surroundings and events. Alcohol is the reason and the excuse for it all: the fantastic (hallucinations), the exotic (verbal games), the narrative trajectory (the Consul's erratic movements), and character (the Consul's jealousy and outspokenness) (1992, 131).[16]

John W. Crowley believes there is a correlation between the ideology of modernism and the incidence of alcoholism among modern writers. Phrases like the "modern temper" or "modernist despair" draw on the new worldview of the alcoholic, the nihilistic worldview of Nietzsche played out as the "white logic" of Jack London's *John Barleycorn*. The addict is deluded, and one of his great delusions is the belief that he sees through the soothing phantasmagoria of civilized life into the abyss of a meaningless reality. In Djuna Barnes's *Nightwood*, Matthew O'Connor declares that drunkenness is not an evasion but a way of "bearding despair, of coming face to skull with the fundamental misery and inescapable emptiness of the human condition" (Crowley 127).

Wolfgang Isernhagen even sees modernism setting up the drug culture of the 1960s, modernism flowing into postmodernism: "One might begin by asking why drugs acquired such cultural significance in the 1960s and 1970s at all. In my view this is because there already existed a well-established cultural tradition—that of aesthetic Modernism." Both systems repudiated the limitations of conventional reality and denied the primacy

of the modes of perception that constituted it. Western civilization had
designated the dream as not real, banned drugs, and isolated madness. Aesthetic modernists, "listening well to Freud and Jung, tended to centralize
the dream as an approach to the real, to experiment with drugs, and to
explore madness" (122).

Drinking and alcoholism certainly dominated American modernity, as
so many commentators have declared.[17] Goodwin speculates that if we
"compile a list of well-known American writers of the past century, quite
possibly one third to one half could be considered alcoholic" (1970, 86).
The concentration is particularly dramatic among the American Nobel
Prize winners (Sinclair Lewis, William Faulkner, Ernest Hemingway, and
John Steinbeck). In his study *The White Logic: Alcoholism and Gender in
American Modernist Fiction,* Crowley isolated a structural paradigm in American modernist fiction that he calls the "drunk narrative" (e.g., *The Sun Also
Rises, Tender Is the Night, Appointment in Samarra, Nightwood*) in which
alcoholism and literary modernism emerged together in a dialectical relationship that produced "both a portrait of the modernist as an alcoholic
and a portrait of the alcoholic as a modernist" (18). And in his book *Coming Home Again,* Geoffrey S. Proehl shows how pervasive and significant
drink and drunkenness have been in twentieth-century American drama,
both as subject matter and aesthetic.[18]

American literary histories open a space for intoxication and creativity in
chapters titled "Revolt against the Village" or "The Expatriate Experience."
This gestating period of twentieth-century American art began with a desire
for more open space for artistic and social engagement than the United
States had to offer in the early twentieth century (and it coincided with the
drying up of liquor in America). Ever since its invention in Henri Murger's
Scènes de la vie de bohème, Bohemia has revolved around the café and drinking (Graña xv, xvii, 268).[19] Even if the drink and drugs did not flow directly
into the art, they were important components of the artist's self-image and,
hence, of creative life. Finally, writes Scott Donaldson, "and this seems to *me*
the most critical causal factor, writers drink because they are expected to"—
it comes with the territory (316). For much of the twentieth century, the
American writer "was expected to drink and suspected if he didn't"; "drinking heavily was admired as a sign of manliness, and of that refusal of re-
spectability that seemed necessary to creative work": "It has come to seem
a natural accompaniment of the literary life—of its loneliness, its creative

aspirations and its frenzies, its 'specialness,' its hazards in a society where values are constantly put in money terms" (Wakefield 1992, 324; Kazin 44).

American popular music of the twentieth century always kept close company with states of intoxication. In American cultural mythology, jazz had its golden moment of drink and drug inspiration before the Second World War, in tune with the alcoholic excesses of Buddy Bolden, Jelly Roll Morton, King Oliver, and many others.[20] With the coming of bebop, drugs went hard, and their use came to be seen as debilitating. Cultural attitudes about drugs and creativity orbit around the figure of Charlie Parker, the great jazz composer and improviser who is now compared to Johann Sebastian Bach and Wolfgang Amadeus Mozart. He is cast as the musician most in love with drugs.

Moving from literature to popular music, we cross a culture divide that has an effect either on use or on the reporting of use. The pop-rock musician David Crosby casually admitted that he had been taking LSD since 1964 and had learned to play guitar on speed: "I don't know any good guitar players who haven't taken speed. . . . I play most of the time high and I always write high" (Shapiro 1988, 143). Among black jazz musicians, at least, the social and emotional logic of narcotics was powerful: the clubs they played in were owned by men who also trafficked in drugs, or the musicians often arrived for work in a state of exhaustion and were expected to be instantly cheerful, and so on (Winick 1961, 55).[21] "It's not so much to *play*. It's to *stand* it, to be able to make it at all," Sonny tells his brother in the James Baldwin story "Sonny's Blues" (856).

The "counterculture" of the late 1950s and 1960s was unabashedly drug-driven, whether its product was Beat poetry; the postmodern novels of Thomas Pynchon, Ken Kesey, or William Burroughs; rock and roll music (including a specific genre known as "acid rock"); the psychedelic art of concert and dance posters and underground comix; or happenings, "acid tests," and psychedelic light shows. Jon Lomberg wrote that artists like Robert Crumb, Victor Moscoso, or Rick Griffin "were creating trip-inspired work that combined Art Nouveau, photography, highly decorative (and distorted) scripts, and mystical images to advertise rock groups whose music dealt with the same experience" (84–85). The Beatles's *Sgt. Pepper's Lonely Hearts Club Band,* Crumb's *Head Comix,* and Thomas Pynchon's *Gravity's Rainbow* have psychedelic experience bound up in their style and content" "In its most banal version, Kesey's work is first of all the attempt to reenact a new psychic state, to recreate the unprecedented experience of the LSD trip, an 'altered state of consciousness' produced by an advanced technology of psychotropic drugs unknown before the 1950s" (Whelan 68).

Rock musicians "smoked dope at least in part because they were emulating the black jazz musicians of the preceding generation—cultural arbiters of hipness—who insisted that getting stoned made the music better" (Farber 174). Nevertheless, Harold Shapiro argues in *Waiting for the Man: The Story of Drugs and Popular Music,* his study of American popular music and drugs, "LSD did create a new environment for rock to develop; it had a significant impact on already creative and talented minds and it is highly probable that without it the best of sixties rock music would not have emerged. . . . [With LSD] Hendrix wrote some of the most powerful rock of all time" (148). Timothy Leary asked his readers to name one "rock group that doesn't have in its repertoire hymns to LSD and marijuana" (Shapiro 174). The Beatles expressed their awareness of a drug lineage on the *Sgt. Pepper* cover with portraits of Poe, Burroughs, Aldous Huxley, Aleister Crowley, and Lenny Bruce.

What followed the sixties was the war on drugs and its terrorizing of the American imagination.[22]

The propriety of intoxication as a foundation for creativity was as stubbornly contested as it had been asserted—either denied outright or read as the sign of degeneration of artistic power. Until recently, biographers and critics worked to contain the lives of their dissolute subjects in order to prevent the life from contaminating the valorized objects of culture. Anya Taylor uses the example of Richard Brinsley Sheridan to show this process at work: "Men watch the drunkard debase himself; they are entertained, shocked, and dazzled; but they hide their risky hero's dual nature from the outside world in a public, decorous, coded language" (1999, 196). Those who noticed bad habits in public usually did so to "prove" that Coleridge or Hemingway were not really addicts and alcoholics or, if they were, that their addiction had nothing to do with their art. The arguments often fastened on a quite ambiguous "zero degree" of creativity: these writers never produced anything of value when they were high.

In spite of the testimony of Horace, Rabelais, and others, the official aesthetic for the fine arts stipulates that while creative states may resemble states of intoxication, artists may not make art out of their alcoholic or narcotic imaginaries. Creating art may not "really" be an intoxication any more than it may be a dream. Jacques Derrida explains: "The drug addict as such produces nothing, nothing true or real. . . . A poem ought to be the product of *real* work, even if the traces of that work should be washed away. It is always non-work that is stigmatized"—art that comes too easily undermines our devotion (8, 12). Actually, traditional aesthetic discourse, with its wild cards like "inspiration" and "genius," wants art to be both work and nonwork, to a mutually impossible degree.

A countertradition had existed from the beginning: Ovid stated that "Bacchus, lord of the vine, is the enemy of art" (Toussaint-Samat 271). In an epigram in the *Greek Anthology*, Diogenes Laertius asked Arcesilaus, "Why did you drink so much wine, and so unsparingly as to slip out of your senses? I am not so sorry for you because you died as because you did violence to the Muses by using immoderate cups" (2.63). Intoxication is the last thing that John Milton wants associated with creativity in *Paradise Lost*, as he calls on his muse Urania to

> drive far off the barbarous dissonance
> Of Bacchus and his revellers.
> (777)

In revenge for an imaginary slight at the hands of the Brownings, Julia Ward Howe repudiated Elizabeth Barrett's narcotic inspiration (without, however, being finally able to label it false):

> I shrink before the nameless draught
> That helps to such unearthly things,
> And if a drug could lift so high
> I would not trust its treacherous wings.
> (Markus 278)[23]

In an article on E. T. A. Hoffmann's tales, Gautier expressed skepticism about the value of alcohol for the writer:

> I do not deny that Hoffmann did smoke a great deal, that he did occasionally get fuddled on German beer or Rhine wine . . . but that sort of thing happens to everybody and has very little to do with his talent. . . . Neither

wine nor tobacco imparts genius, a great man when drunk lurches from side
to side just like anybody else, and because one tumbles into the gutter it does
not follow that one will be exalted to the skies. I do not believe that any man
ever wrote decently after parting with his brains and his reason, and I fancy
that the wildest and most vehement tirades have been composed in the company of a carafe of water. (12.239)[24]

The authors most engaged in an intoxicatory aesthetic were also given
to moments of denial; even "Anacreon," Horace, and Jonson resisted the
notion of artificially supplemented creativity:

Thou pretendest, *Trayt'erous Wine,*
To be the *Muses* friend and *Mine.*
With *Love* and *Wit* thou dost begin,
False Fires, alas, to draw us in.
Which, if our course we by them keep,
Misguide to *Madness,* or to *Sleep.*
(Davidson 1915, 61)

Ever since Bacchus enlisted the brain-sick poets among the Satyrs and the
Fauns, the sweet muses have usually smelt of wine in the morning. (Horace
245)

Then would I promise here to give
Verse, that should thee and me outlive.
But since the wine hath steeped my brain,
I only can the paper stain.
(Jonson 220)

Why should it matter what authors do as a prelude to the production
of art? Some chop wood, some chew gum, some sharpen pencils—Schiller
kept rotting apples in his desk because their scent stimulated reverie, while
Henry Fuseli ate "raw meat in the evening in order to have splendid dreams
which he then transformed into fantastic visionary images" (Sandblom 52).
Some drank: Addison was said to have "composed his verse while walking
up and down a long gallery with a bottle of wine placed at each end. He
continued to walk to and fro until he had finished the composition and

the bottles" (Press 83); and "Bird used to line up eight doubles of whiskey and down them before he hit a note on the job" (Lightfoot 53). What other circumstances have been used to disqualify creativity? About what other state of mind would we tie ourselves in knots worrying whether it is the artist or the state that does the imagining?

In his essay "The Poet," Ralph Waldo Emerson seems to subscribe to a Horatian aesthetic:

> The poet knows that he speaks adequately then only when he speaks some-
> what wildly. . . . or as the ancients were wont to express themselves, not with
> intellect alone, but with the intellect inebriated by nectar. . . . This is the
> reason why bards love wine, mead, narcotics, coffee, tea, opium, the fumes
> of sandalwood and tobacco, or whatever other procurers of animal exhila-
> ration. All men avail themselves of such means as they can, to add this extra-
> ordinary power to their normal powers—

but as the paragraph goes on it becomes clear that, unlike the passages from Scaliger, Gautier, and George Santáyana quoted earlier, the difference be-tween poetical and literal intoxication makes all the difference for Emer-son. He continues: "But never can any advantage be taken of nature by a trick. The spirit of the world, the great calm presence of the Creator, comes not forth to the simple sorceries of opium or of wine" (316–17). The nine-teenth century witnessed a major campaign to disqualify these "sorceries."

With the professionalization of culture in that century, artists became capital whose value could be diminished by association with certain forms of excess: the genius was a treasure to be exploited but also a potential (even, likely) site of immorality. The classic Horatian trope now threatened the integrity and marketability of the new "author" and, hence, the work of art.

Biography worked to contain the pathology, and eventually a new crit-icism severed the connection between the life of the author and the life of the work. In 1830 William Goodell identified the problem with contem-porary biography and history:

> *Why* is it that history and biography have lost their interest and charms? . . .
> Why has the inspiration of the poet degenerated into the vagaries of de-
> rangement? Lord Byron will answer. He confessed that he wrote under the

influence of distilled spirits. Here the disgusting secret is developed. Authors
drink and write: readers drink and admire. (Rorabaugh 199–200)

Seventy-three years later Edmund Gosse declared that the "one horren-
dous fact about his subject which a biographer should under no circumstances reveal is his addiction to drink" (O'Connor 40–41). And in 1988
Joyce Carol Oates attacked David Roberts's study of Jean Stafford for a too
thorough exploration of the poet's life—an extreme state of biography that
she called "pathography" (Dardis 1994, 197–98).[25]
    In much commentary on the life and work of Utrillo, writers marvel at
how separate the two are. "It is as if," Garo Antreasian writes, "Utrillo as
a man and Utrillo as a painter were separate entities" (15); "Whatever disorder, impulsiveness or dissolution may prevail in his life, none of these
have ever penetrated his work" (Edmond Jaloux in Fortunescu II); "in
contrast to the artist's miserable biography, the inner story of the artist, as
visually expressed through these paintings, is not a story of despair, but
conversely it is a story of transcendent happiness told by Utrillo himself"
(Utrillo's White Period n.p.); and "For generations we shall marvel at this
strange antithesis: Utrillo, a sickly drug-addicted and feeble-minded creature, produced not only the least morbid of all paintings, but even built
up an art beaming with health, freshness and ever-renewing youthfulness"
(Maurice Raynal in Fortunescu 13).[26]
    Working from the other direction, New Critics used tools like the "bio-
graphical fallacy," "intentional fallacy," and "persona" as wedges to separate
the drink in the work from the drink in the author. Ovid had distinguished
between the author and his persona in the *Tristia:* "Believe me, my character is different from my poetry: my life is decent, my Muse sportive. A great
part of my *oeuvre* is untruthful fiction, allowing itself indulgences not permitted to its author" (Russell 293). Even earlier, Athenaeus had made a
similar "eloquent apologia" for Anacreon:

But Anacreon, who made all his poetry depend upon the subject of intoxication . . . is maligned for having given himself over in his poetry to laxity
and luxury, although most people do not know that he was sober while engaged in composing, and that, being an upright man, he merely pretends to
be drunk. (4.443–44)

"Athenaeus' sensible explanation," Patricia Rosenmeyer comments, "was ignored for the sake of a vivid and consistent picture of Anacreon as a hedonist" (20). But isn't it more likely that someone so preoccupied with drinking in his art would also be preoccupied with drinking in his life? William Hazlitt replied to Wordsworth's letter on Burns, saying that the Scots poet could not have described the "indulgence" of Tam O' Shanter "if he himself had not 'drunk full ofter of the tun than of the well'" (Cafarelli 137). In the sonnet "Suum Cuique," Rémy Belleau suggests that each artist should sing his "virtue":

> For those who are in love, let them their loves go sing . . .
> Those who affect the arts shall praise to science bring . . .
> Those who love wine of wine and drunkenness shall treat.
> (Payne 44)

The New Critics programmatically excluded information about authors from their criticism. T. S. Eliot stated in his essay "Tradition and the Individual Talent" that "the more perfect the artist the more completely separate in him will be the man who suffers and the mind which creates" (7–8). "There were two Dons," Helen tells her writer-fiancé in *The Lost Weekend*. "You told me so yourself. Don the drunk, and Don the writer." Mark Spilka anchored the intentional fallacy in a significantly different way from other New Critics—not in the indeterminacy of self-knowledge but in the badness of artists: "As everyone knows, authors are suspicious figures, victims of inspiration, drugs, drink, neurosis, vanity, and self-deception; they are fallible, that is, and critics have rightly questioned their pronouncements of intention" (286). I suggest that New Criticism took the work of art away from authors because of their bad characters, although the pathological basis for persona theory was generally hidden. In a small way, however, it was admitted: "Interested critics . . . have used the persona as a device to insulate writers from their own meanings: violent or distasteful expressions in the work of Pope or Swift can be attributed to the persona, this bit of casuistry serving to protect the integrity of the author and the impersonality of the work" (Irwin Ehrenpreis in Elliott 14).

A common litany in the twentieth century is that the artist never worked while drunk, however much he or she drank otherwise. Gabriel García Márquez: "Bad readers have asked me if I was drugged when I wrote some of my works. But that illustrates that they don't know anything about literature or drugs. To be a good writer you have to be absolutely lucid at every moment of writing, and in good health. I'm very much against the romantic concept of writing" (in Plimpton 329). Gary Snyder admitted that he has had "probably more than my share of psilocybin, peyote. . . . And I don't recall having ever written anything that was particularly useful to me while under the influence of any of those" (78). Stephen King says that he never wrote anything "worth a dime" under the influence of pot or hallucinogens and considers alcohol an "extremely benign poison" (Goodwin 1988, 180).

If the author did write while drinking, then, as Snyder and King assert, what they wrote in that condition was relatively worthless. George Bernard Shaw claimed that "alcohol knocks off the last inch of efficiency which, in all really fine work, makes the distinction between first rate and second rate" (Tek Chand 6). A Swedish author, Marika Stjernstedt, who turned to drink at a time of stress, claimed she had no difficulty identifying later the parts she had written under the influence of alcohol, because they were so obviously inferior (Sandblom 52).[27]

The list of disclaimers is extensive. Fitzgerald wrote, "As a matter of fact I have never written a line of any kind while I was under the glow of so much as a single cocktail"; Eugene O'Neill: "I never try to write a line when I'm not strictly on the wagon. I don't think anything worth reading was ever written by anyone who was drunk or even half-drunk when he wrote it"; Ring Lardner: "No one, ever, wrote anything as well after even one drink as he would have done without it" (Rothenberg 116; Sheaffer 323; Donaldson 317). Denunciation of the Horatian aesthetic comes mainly from a master list of known artist drunks. "'Don't you know it's fatal for a young writer to start drinking brandy?' Ford Madox Ford asks Hemingway, and Hemingway does know—'My training was never to drink after dinner nor before I wrote nor while I was writing'" (Beegel 16). Faulkner, as Márquez notes, "had a reputation of being a drunkard, but in every interview that he gave he said that it was impossible to write one line when drunk" (in Plimpton 329). William Styron declared, "I've never written a line in my life while I'd had a drink," and Raymond Carver said that "nothing good" came of mixing drink and writing: "I never wrote so much as a line that was worth a nickel when I was under the influence of alcohol" (Forseth 1985, 585; Dardis 1989, 44). Is this alcoholic denial talking? You bet it is. The disclaimer, when it comes from a heavy drinker, is more likely to be part of an alcoholic alibi system than a statement of fact. Can an alcoholic make such a promise about any other aspect of life?[28]

Sometimes the link between intoxication and creativity is set aside in the name of common sense, the argument being that no one who produced such good work or so much of it could have done so while drinking heavily: "It is not probable that had Anacreon been greatly addicted to profligacy and excesses," Judson Davidson states, "he would ever have attained to such a high position in the republic of letters" (39); Vincent Van Gogh, who was troubled by rumors that Adolphe Monticelli died of absinthe consumption, declared, "When I look at his work, I can't think it possible that a man who was flabby with drink could have done that" (Conrad 61); and Douglas Day muses that if Malcolm Lowry "had been as possessed, drunken, or demented as critics have said, how for one thing could he have produced so large a body of work in such a short time?" (356). Andrew Dakers feels that "it should be sufficient to rebut the view that Burns was a drunk to state that he wrote fifty-two immortal poems in the first six years of his poetic life, while supporting himself and his family as an overworked farmer" (51). But Burns *was* a drunk. To Hamilton Basso's rational outcry that the large body of Faulkner's work "could not have been produced by a crock," Tom Dardis answers, "But it was" (1989, 37). The nasty bias behind such attitudes may be glimpsed in A. E. Dyson's remark: "Drugs might be compatible with intelligent filth like the novels of William Burroughs, but never with the creation of a novel like *Edwin Drood*" (156).

This is a stunning indication of how completely the Horatian aesthetic has been turned around. It is also a stunning indication of how stereotypes drive the ideological imagination: drunks are more often perfectionist workers than indolent drones, more likely to produce art out of their sickness than their health. Even if the truth of this chapter were only an alcoholic truth, it would still contravene the way that alcoholism is supposed to work. Marcus Grant comments on this in his 1981 survey of studies on alcohol and creativity:

> It has remained one of the tantalizing anomalies of the alcoholism field that whilst the trend in occupational program development has been towards emphasizing the loss of efficiency that accompanies excessive alcohol consumption, it has been difficult to ignore the impressive list of writers (and,

to a lesser extent, painters and composers) who have achieved considerable popular artistic success at the same time as drinking very heavily indeed. (88)

Dyson's sneer rests on the assumption that true art is real work and that intoxication, as Derrida reports, produces art without work. For Baudelaire, drug truths are a false substitute for those sublime art truths that should only be available as a consequence of striving.[29] Even in the official aesthetic tradition, however, there are two allowable shortcuts, and these are precisely the constructs I have put in question here, *genius* and *inspiration*.

The bottom line in saving the author is to claim that he or she may have been a writer who drank but never a drunk who wrote—as if this marked an extremely important distinction—and, since certain authors must drink, that they wrote "in spite of" alcohol, not because of it. This is a replay of the Romantic medical-hedonist opposition, so important in the early history of addiction study: a distinction between taking drugs because they were medically prescribed and taking drugs because you liked the way they made you feel.

If biography and New Criticism worked to deny that the drink in the life was also in the work, another wide range of interpretive techniques was put in place to deny that the drink in the work was actually drink. Commentaries on O'Neill's *Iceman Cometh* and Lowry's *Under the Volcano* feature many of these strategies. The first is a play by an alcoholic writer set in a skid-row tavern where most of the characters are acute alcoholics. The second is a novel about the last day in the life of a former British consul who is drinking himself to death by a British writer who, according to Goodwin, "was an alcoholic who drank almost every day of his life . . . and whose alcoholism permeates his work to an extent unparalleled in literature" (1988, 138–39). Nevertheless, criticism regularly gives us formulations like these:

> Although drunkenness is the main theme of Lowry's book, "the drunkenness of Geoffrey Firmin," as a critic puts it, "is the correlative of the drunkenness of the world as seen by both Dostoevsky and Hesse, a world reeling down the corridors of disaster filled with the sins of both commission, and, particularly, omission, a world which had apparently condemned itself to impotence in the dark night presided over by palpable evil." (Daniel Dodson in Dorosz 16–17)

Under the Volcano is "no more about drinking," Stephen Spender said, "than *King Lear* is about senility" (Hill 1974, 151).

Why aren't these vast, inflated symbolic constructions of meaning read as a function of alcoholism working through a codependent commentator, since we know the alcoholism was there and that alcoholism inflates meaning in that way? What is at stake here seems to mark a fault line between literature and something far less valuable: Spender warned that if the disintegration of the Consul as an alcoholic "takes over," *Under the Volcano* cannot succeed: "It is the artistic problem of the novel to make the Consul stand for *more* than a justification—or even, an apology—for the lot of the addict, more than a figment of extended autobiography" (Smith 1978, 32).

Although a recovering alcoholic himself, Jason Robards, who played Hickey in the 1956 New York revival of *Iceman,* was upset by a suggestion that the play is actually about alcoholism, so he had to be told that there are "many ideas and issues in the play which place O'Neill's work on a grander, broader scale"; this apparently satisfied him (Garvey 22).[30]

In both families and texts, secrets are often reformulated superficially as jokes. Some years ago, a student of mine saw the joke under his nose in the title of a Poe tale, "MS Found in a Bottle." The title has no anchor in the work, and reading it in reference to intoxication tells us in a sly way where the tale comes from. In answer to the blanket denial expressed by the formula *a heavy drinker, perhaps, but he never wrote while drunk,* there is much testimony to the contrary. Much documented "good" work has come out of alcohol and drugs: by Wilkie Collins—"That this tightly plotted and controlled novel *[The Moonstone]* could have been written in such conditions finally disposes of the theory that opium necessarily prevents the writer from doing his work"; by Modigliani—"No matter how much he drank and drugged he worked, and seemingly worked better, under the influence"; by Faulkner—he "drank while he wrote right from the start"; by Kesey—"The discovery of the Chief [Broom] was the missing link in the novel. . . . a gift from the Muse, he'd come to Kesey in the midst of a peyote haze"; and by Paul Scott—his biographer, Hilary Spurling, "fails to note how extraordinary it is that *The Raj Quartet* is apparently the only extended masterpiece to have been written by an author in something like a state of continuous intoxication" (Hayter 1968, 259; Douglas 104; Dardis 1989, 43; Stevens 227; Gilmore 1992, 21).

The British novelist Arthur Calder-Marshall said of Lowry that "he regarded drinking as an essential part of the creative act" (Hill 1974, 44). Of his friend Joseph Roth, Hermann Kersten wrote that he "was one of the most prodigious drinkers of his time": "Working hours not spent in his hotel room were spent at some coffeehouse table . . . plying himself with the alcohol without which he could not write in the end" (Mornin 80). Francis Bacon would be back in the studio a couple of hours after a night spent drinking, "wrestling with a new image. 'I often like working with a hangover' was all he would say about this unusual performance, 'because my mind is crackling with energy and I can think clearly'" (Peppiatt 1996, 161).[31]

The opposite of *never wrote while drunk* is *never wrote while sober,* and Henry Nevinson claims that this was popularly believed of Lionel Johnson (192). August Strindberg thought that "because of his abstinence from alcohol, he was losing all his strength, and feared that he might fold up like an old rag" (Jaspers 31). Of certain artists it was believed that their talent waned after they sobered up: Richard Aldington has "argued that Swinburne's power to make poetry ceased when Watts-Dunton bore him off to a bourgeois and sober existence" (Bartlett 34). After his marriage at the age of 53, at the peak of his career, Utrillo stopped drinking and "was satisfied, until his death at the age of 72, with copying postcards" (Sournia 1994, 59).[32] Other artists, like Richard Brinsley Sheridan, Athol Fugard, and Vincent Van Gogh, felt they could not produce art at all without drink (Sournia 1990, 88; Hershman 164).

Henry Steele Commager argues that in his nineteenth epistle, Horace is "satirizing a popular attitude, not endorsing it" (30). From the beginning the Horatian aesthetic had been regarded by cynical readers as a ploy to disarm suspicion of an author's heavy drinking, to protect an alcoholic author's dependency on drink. With the coming of addiction, "science" dismissed the Horatian aesthetic as a pathetic alibi. Eventually an understanding grew that artists have an affinity for intoxicating substances. Abraham Lincoln declared that "there seems ever to have been a proneness in the brilliant and in the warm-blooded, to fall into this vice. The demon of intemperance ever seems to have delighted in sucking the blood of genius and of generosity" (Tek Chand 141–42). Harriet Martineau wrote in her autobiography that a clergyman who "knew the literary world of his time so thoroughly that there was probably no author of any mark then living in

England, with whom he was not more or less acquainted," told her there was no author or authoress who was free from the habit of taking some pernicious stimulant; either strong green tea, or strong coffee at night, or wine or spirits of laudanum. The amount of opium taken to relieve the wear and tear of authorship was, he said, greater than most people had any conception of: and *all* literary workers took something (Hayter 1980, 37).

Edmund Wilson read the Romantic artist through the Greek tragic character Philoctetes: a victim of a disease that renders him abhorrent to society, but also master of an art that everyone must respect and sometimes needs. Toward the end of the nineteenth century, the metaphoric implications of Romantic theory became scientific fact, as Cesare Lombroso, in his *Man of Genius* (1891), and Max Nordau, in *Degeneration* (1892), argued that genius was pathological and identified some of the many artists who had also been addicts. Within the context of late-nineteenth-century degeneration theory, neurasthenia and dipsomania studies, and temperance discourse, it became a fact of substantial record that many artists were heavy or problem drinkers. Truman Capote put it simply, "I don't know a single writer . . . who isn't an alcoholic" (Forseth 585).[33]

The presence of alcoholic subject matter in the work had long been read as proof of the author's personal habits—to repeat Horace, "Homer, by his excessive praise of wine, is convicted as a booser" (245). "By construing all praise of wine as a confession that the author wrote only when drunk," Commager writes, "they might mount any poet upon the same Pegasus. Archilochus, Anacreon, Alcaeus, and Aristophanes were soon conscripted, while Sophocles' praise of Aeschylus . . . was similarly vulgarized" (28). This was what the New Criticism had been reacting to.

Even if, to take the extreme case, all artists are addicts, may not the addiction function, willy nilly, as an aesthetic? Drink may be the condition for creativity because of desire or necessity, because it is, finally, where life has put the artist if he or she is to do any writing at all. However the author wrote, it was the only way he or she could have written. Lawrence Lipton says that "Coleridge needed opium and Wordsworth needed Nature. Nature would not have written *Kubla Khan* for Coleridge and opium would not have written the *Intimations of Immortality* for Wordsworth" (19). Coleridge's "mere bane, the drugs to which he resorted as a relief from suffering," John M. Robertson wrote, "is rather by reason of its first magical effects, *the special source of his literary immortality*" (Lowes 418).

One cannot simply peel the addiction from the artist, as so much naive commentary implies through its language. Dardis and others write as if drink or drugs invade the artistic sensibility, impeding or destroying it, as a disease germ invades an otherwise healthy host—"Gas and sleeping pills kill poets; drink and drugs kill poets more slowly, but on the way to killing the poet they kill the poems" (Hall 29)—and they wish that the drink had not been there so that the artist could have written more or better.[34]

Claire Lyu argues that in *Le Poème du hachisch,* Baudelaire's prose piece on the artificial paradise of drugs, he is quite insistent about distinguishing his poetic voice from the voice of intoxication and his writing about intoxication from the experience of intoxicants. Nevertheless, helplessly, "The text constantly oscillates between the desire and the attempt to keep poetry and hashish separate, on the one hand, and the difficulties and the failure in marking and maintaining the difference between these two, on the other" (698–700).

Some commentators compromise, seeing a reversal of effects of substance use over time: "The kindling of creative power that alcohol can ignite must then be dearly paid for later, when the glow is covered by ashes"; or, "if it be true that opium killed the poet in Coleridge, it is also no less true that opium developed and elicited the poet in him" (Sandblom 53; Smith 1975, 21). The formula that governs the alcoholic biographies in Dardis's *Thirsty Muse* is that "creativity diminished ever more sharply as they continued to drink." As it works out in this otherwise valuable study, however, the model of vanishing talent seems arbitrary or subject to great variation. Take the case of Hemingway: in the writing of *To Have and Have Not* in late 1937, we are told that "there is a marked difference between the superb opening chapters (the earlier magazine material) and the remaining two thirds of the novel"; and

although he had twenty-four years of life ahead, he published only three books in that time, each either flawed in design or weakened by a prose that increasingly tended to be on the edge of self-parody. . . . his decline as a writer is clear, and a great share in it must surely be attributed to alcohol, which is notorious for dissolving a writer's capacity to make the finer distinctions that the creation of a work of art requires. (177, 178, 184)

But in the unedited version of *Garden of Eden* (1947), Hemingway is still capable of "describing locales with unmatched power," and, of course, *The*

Old Man and the Sea (1951) won him the Nobel Prize ("The fantastic triumph of the book included its being hailed by people of taste such as Bernard Berenson and Cyril Connolly, who compared it to Flaubert's 'A Simple Heart'") (185, 191). And there was still another anomaly to come in 1957, *A Moveable Feast*.

When Dardis turns to Faulkner and Fitzgerald, the rules seem to relax even more, and the terrain is dotted with exceptions, puzzles, mysteries, and miracles:

> But since the time of De Quincey and Baudelaire, we have grown to know that such rules are not inflexible. There *are* exceptions and Faulkner is clearly one of them. . . . How he was able to write such a succession of amazing books under these circumstances is a tantalizing puzzle. . . . During this period he underwent hemorrhages and several hospitalizations for drinking, not to mention dozens of hangovers, but was capable of writing one of the great American novels *[Absalom, Absalom]*. His ability to write with such power under such killing circumstances is little short of miraculous." (44, 48, 65–66)

His treatment of Fitzgerald continues the theme of the miracle: "Considering the circumstances under which the book *[Tender Is the Night]* finally came forth after eight years in the making, it is miraculously good despite its many faults," and "Miraculously, the *Esquire* pieces demonstrated that even after hitting bottom with the Philippe stories, he was still capable of writing with the power and authority of the past" (123, 132). Dardis is certainly correct about the fiction of this period being damaged by the alcoholism of its authors, yet the period his book covers remains one of the two great flowerings of American fiction.

Various relationships can exist between writing and drinking. London drank so he could write:

> a new and most diabolical complication arose. The work refused to be done without drinking. . . . My brain could not think the proper thoughts because continually it was obsessed with the one thought that across the room in the liquor cabinet stood John Barleycorn. When, in despair, I took my drink, at once my brain loosened up and began to roll off the thousand words. (300–301)

O'Neill functioned well as a playwright while an active alcoholic, but wrote even better after achieving a measure of sobriety, except that then he could not bring work to a close. "What they failed, or chose to fail, to comprehend was that Bird plays brilliantly on heroin because he was dependent on it, that was the only time he felt well enough to play normally—i.e. better than anyone else. He wasn't playing better because of heroin; he was just playing normally because he didn't feel sick" (Shapiro 1988, 67). Binge drinking after finishing one work and before beginning the next is a common pattern among artists. That makes a different kind of sense out of the truism, *never wrote while drinking*. O'Neill "never actually drank whilst writing, choosing rather to alternate between drinking binges and writing binges" (Grant 1981, 88). Lewis, as Albert Rothenberg puts it, "drank in order to avoid writing, sobered up in order to write, then drank in order to avoid writing" (117).

Even the disastrous long-term effects of substance abuse are not immutable. Far from ending a career, the last stages of addictive breakdown are sometimes reaestheticized, as in the cases of Utrillo and John Berryman: critics hail the terminal pathology as wondrous new art. Between early and late Utrillo, Philip Sandblom declares that alcohol clearly damaged his work, but then adds that a "continuous change in aesthetic convention is evident from the fact that some of my young friends prefer this late, awkward painting because of its more expressive approach as compared to the artistic refinement of the early version" (54). And Alfred Kazin can write of Berryman's *Dreamsongs:* "Snooty, heartbreaking, maudlin, clearly written under booze, quick to portray every side of the divided self that emerges under booze, these poems are the human heart's rushed shorthand. They are also in Berryman's most maddeningly allusive style" (49). Is there any point at which we can differentiate true art from the pathology of addiction? At the end of Emile Zola's *L'Assommoir,* Gervaise imitates Copeau's dance of death, his extravagant "delirium tremens" dance, to entertain their circle, and the next generation—their daughter Nana—will perform this dance as "art" on the stages of Parisian music halls (411).

Whether or not artists tend to abuse alcohol or drugs, a separate and important question is what drink and drugs (and addiction) do for and to their art. Aesthetic criticism has programmatically avoided this question, although it has been easily asked and answered, with great specificity, about popular musicians. It is absurd to pretend that a life of hard drinking doesn't color the work. Fitzgerald was an alcoholic and a storyteller, and alcoholics tell discernibly different kinds of stories from those told by people who do not suffer from their disease. Alcoholics' stories replicate their personal distortions of the world—and they are particularly appealing.

Complementing Donald Goodwin's list of the ways in which intoxication and creativity fit one another is a second set from Torsten Norlander: alcohol reduces anxiety, helps the writer study other people, can reduce inhibitions when one is blocked, helps one relax after a period of writing, and, he adds, good ideas may occur during "the good hangover" (3). As drink poetry ceaselessly sings, drink banishes care. Rothenberg lists as the cardinal issue "the need to use alcohol to cope with the anxiety that is generated by the creative process itself. . . . writers and other artists are highly irritable during intense periods of work or for some time afterward" (129). Alcohol and drugs ease the anxiety of composition and performance, and, in the case of jazz, simultaneous composition and performance.

According to some testimony, intoxication focuses the mind and gives it staying power, as Robert Stone has said: cocaine "certainly supplies you with a great deal of energy, so you can do a lot of sustained work. It keeps you from wandering off, concentrates the mind" (Hughes 1999, 175). Musicians talk of their "peak experiences" as an intoxication: Sinead O'Connor says, "It feels like being drunk, it's like an out-of-body experience"; Branford Marsalis, "High, you feel high" (Boyd 50–54).

After his first use of marijuana, Mezz Mezzrow declared,

> The first thing I noticed was that I began to hear my saxophone as though it was inside my head. . . . Then I began to feel the vibrations of the reed much more pronounced against my lips and my head buzzed like a loudspeaker. I found I was slurring much better and putting just the right feeling into my phrases. I was really coming on. All the notes came easing out of my horn like they'd already been made up . . . so all I had to do was blow a little and send them on their way, one right after the other, never missing, never behind time, all without an ounce of effort. . . . it was all made to order and suddenly there wasn't a sour note or a discord in the world that could bother me. (Shapiro 1988, 31–32)[35]

Finally, and most contentiously, the altered states of intoxication allow access to an alternative reality (or new perspectives on familiar reality). The

Finnish writer Christer Kihlman maintains that "without alcohol I would not have been able to write a single book. With the help of alcohol I've become conscious of the forms of reality, of its surface and contours. But alcohol has also opened up the bars of my consciousness to the difficult knowledge of the very contents of reality" (Koski-Jännes 123). For William Styron, "drugs liberated his pencil and gave him access to surrealistic visions and to deep levels of his subconscious mind" (West 292–93). And Walter Benjamin found that

> under the gaze of the hashish smoker the object transformed itself so that the very details of its surface appeared in changing configurations: "the first rush loosens and entices things out of their familiar world; the second places them very quickly into a . . . new one." The drug experience was especially significant for Benjamin's secularized theory of the "aura" of objects. Emanating from the surface of the phenomena and revealing their inner essence, this aura became visible within the "image-zone" of drugs, and could be reproduced on the artist's canvas. (Buck-Morss 1977, 127)

Might one take the Horatian aesthetic so far as to eliminate the author completely and claim that it was the drink or drugs that wrote the work? Given the "deadly mix" of chloral hydrate and whiskey in Dante Gabriel Rossetti's life, Stanley Weintraub wonders, "as in any case of drug addiction," how much of the art is genius "and how much is beyond the control of the individual." He also wonders what this does to the "aesthetic inferences of critics with respect to the work, when the work has clearly gone beyond the control of the artist" (132).

Sophocles applied this extreme alcohol trope to the works of Aeschylus and concluded that "wine . . . not Aeschylus, was the author of his tragedies," and De Quincey addresses opium as if it were a primary creator: "Thou buildest upon the bosom of darkness, out of the fantastic imagery of the brain, cities and temples, beyond the art of Phidias and Praxiteles. . . . oh, just, subtle, and mighty opium!" (Scaliger 15; De Quincey 83). Timothy Leary insisted on the creative potential of hallucinogens regardless of individual talent:

> More than 100 psilocybin sessions run in a maximum-security prison demonstrated that creative vision and mystical illumination are a function of

the cortex when it is temporarily relieved of word and ego games. . . . Creativity is not a function of lucky heritage or elite training. There are more visions in the cortex of each of us than in all the museums and libraries of the world. (59)

And Byron commented that "Imagination and Invention" were common qualities and that "an Irish peasant with a little whiskey in his head will imagine and invent more than would furnish forth a modern poem" (Kitson 12).

Western criticism did not insist on the agency of genius to account for one of the world's great works of literature: it knew that *The Thousand and One Nights* had been written by drugs. D. W. Cheever believed that it was Fitz Hugh Ludlow, the "American De Quincy," who first pointed out "the probability that the peculiar imaginative turn of the *Arabian Nights* was due to the influence of a narcotic":

> While we all have admitted the wonderful and unflagging charm of these unequalled stories, and have been at a loss to account for the existence and mysterious anonymousness of so rare an author, no other theory has been advanced of their origin so plausible as that of a narcotic influence. (Cheever 380–82)

By like reasoning, all Eastern literature was treated as drug created: Bayard Taylor, for example, wrote that "in the gorgeous fancies of the Arabian Nights, in the glow and luxury of all Oriental poetry, I now recognize more or less of the agency of hashish" (1854, 405).

The *Arabian Nights* could be abandoned to drugs, but Coleridge's "Kubla Khan" could not, because English literature hung in the balance. "Kubla Khan" is the great staging ground for anxieties over the Horatian aesthetic. What was at stake was poetry and criticism themselves, poetry because "Kubla Khan" was regarded as the ultimate lyric poem, and criticism because if the poem were written by opium, then criticism should be rendered speechless. As a consequence of this tension, Coleridge's poem oscillated between being a precious work of the artistic imagination and the mere transcription of the opium reverie or dream it was originally announced to be: "Enough that in the summer of 1798, under influence of an 'anodyne' now definitely known to have been opium, he fell asleep while reading in *Purchas his Pilgrimage*, and in that state composed a poem 'in which all the images rose up before him as *things*'" (Abrams 1934, 46).

Since 1953, the controversy surrounding "Kubla Khan" has usually been presented as a spent case, finally decided against opium with the publication of Elizabeth Schneider's *Coleridge, Opium, and Kubla Khan,* which, as Paul Youngquist puts it, saved the poem "from all unseemly pharmacological taint" and taught us once and for all that drugs cannot produce the art effects that Coleridge and De Quincey claimed for them (887). Schneider's case was apparently so forcefully put that M. K. Abrams silently recanted his first book on the influence of opium on romantic poetry.[36] But when has a comparable issue in literary criticism and theory ever been so agreeably closed before? Outside the quiet precincts of Coleridge studies, no attention was paid to this determination. Surrealism and the psychedelic art of the 1960s raised the issue as if it had never been satisfactorily settled in the negative.

On the other hand, what the drink and the drugs write, if they are granted creative power, is, sad to say, simply themselves. In the 1960s, according to cultural commentators like Spiro Agnew, drugs wrote rock songs that whispered "drugs" (Orman 6). Another way of reading the addict in the work is to read the work as an allegory of intoxication. Sir Walter Scott wrote *The Bride of Lammermoor* while he was taking laudanum for cramps. After it was published, he could not remember one thing about it, but Hayter notices that the "difference between the strong-hearted unglamorous Jeanie Deans, heroine of Scott's previous novel, and the lovely but feeble Lucy Ashton . . . whose neurotic fear and anxiety prepare the way for her outbreak of insanity is almost an allegory" for normal and opium-influenced imagination (Hayter 1968, 293). Walter Pater saw William Morris's poetry as representing "two different operations of the senses . . . the early poems as opium dreams, the later as the recovery of the senses from such unnatural dreaming" (Clements 104).[37]

In 1926 Emile Legouis, a Sorbonne professor of English literature, read the Shakespeare canon as a fabric written by drink. He began by noticing that drink plays through all of Shakespeare's dramas from the early comedies to the mature tragedies, although "you scarcely find a trace of it in the solemnity of ancient or modern tragedy" otherwise (127). "It now remains for the man with a fixed idea to see whether the whole evolution of the Shakespearean drama might not be plausibly accounted for from the Bacchic point of view. . . . Nothing would indeed be easier" (130–31).

The comedies and tragedies split for Legouis as intoxication and addiction. As for the tragedies, while

different explanations can of course be offered for the wildness and disequi-
librium apparent in all. . . . still it remains to say why such contrary passions
should in all cases assume much the same form of wild derangement. . . . impulsiveness, irrepressible vehemence, want of self-possession and self-control
in words and deeds, lack of balance, sudden shiftings of determination, bitter
melancholy fits, a tendency to outrageous railing and cursing. . . . Man who
formerly was a creature of reason and will is now upset, irascible, with nerves
strained to the breaking-point, with fits of disproportionate anger. (130)

Or why excessive drink should be the constant accompaniment of these
various forms of imbalance. Legouis finds a comparable derangement only
in the plays of Christopher Marlowe, and there it is overtly linked to
alcoholism:

When Marlowe's ranting heroes made their appearance on the stage, his rival
Nashe had at once denounced them as the products of an imagination over-
cloyed "with a more than drunken resolution." The clever satirist John Hall
had followed suit, accounting for the thundering threats of a Tamberlaine
by "the drink-drowned spright of the author." (130)

Drink and drugs are found to reproduce their own features as imagery,
mood, and style. The notion of a "drunken style" was quite acceptable in
the context of classic literary studies: "Men's style is the counterpart of their
lives. . . . you'll find his [Maecenas's] eloquence that of a drunken man,
tangled, rambling, and full of eccentricity" (Seneca 1932, 225–26, 261).
Lombroso felt that

the great writers who have been under the dominion of alcohol, have a style
peculiar to themselves, whose characteristics are a deliberate eroticism, and
an inequality which is rather grotesque than beautiful, owing to too unre-
strained fancy, frequent imprecations and abrupt transitions from the deepest
melancholy to obscene gaiety, and a marked preference for such subjects as
madness, drink, and the gloomiest scenes of death. (325)

Alfred Kazin reads Faulkner's "insensately long sentences" as "the abandon
that so often comes to a drinker as the 'connections that make up anxiety'
are broken off" and goes on to quote Donald Newlove: "Faulkner's ruinous

pose as a master of Latinate diction is the direct result of alcoholic harden-
ing of the ego" (48). Paul Desmond was once asked how he developed his
tart lyrical style, and he replied, "I think I had it in the back of my mind
that I wanted to sound like a dry martini" (Conrad 10).[38]

Virginia Woolf observed that opium permeated De Quincey's "English
Mail-Coach" and produced as its proper literary symptoms, "the opening
out and deepening down of space, the hallucinatory expansion of sound,
the sense of involuntary movements of sinking down, the removal from
experience as if cut off from others and imprisoned in another dimension"
(Lilienfeld 210). Abrams praised John Livingston Lowes for identifying "the
extraordinary mutations of space" as the most characteristic effect of "Kubla
Khan," an effect that "we know is the mark of opium," and noted further
that George Crabbe utilizes the illusion of flight in his poetry, "an authenti-
cated characteristic of narcotic experience" (Abrams 1934, 47, 16). Kingsley
Amis felt that the peculiar styles of Poe and Dostoyevsky are "metaphori-
cal illuminations of the world of the hangover" (90). Similar equations
have been provided for artists with extreme visions or styles, such as John
Martin, Monticelli, Van Gogh, and Pablo Picasso: Picasso's blue and green,
for example, have been identified as the colors of absinthe, and "the lan-
guid magic and beauty of Picasso's work between 1904–1906 can be attributed in part to the 'black blood of the poppy'" (Conrad 76; Panter et al.
266).[39]

One can also, it seems, fine-tune the Horatian aesthetic to produce a
menu for artistic production. In his letter to Charles Diodati, Milton aligns
the water and wine of my opening with different artistic genres or modes:
"Grand banquets are quite all right for elegiac poets, and they can get drunk
on old wine as often as they like. But the poet who writes about wars . . .
let this poet live frugally. . . . and may he drink soberly from a pure spring"
(118). At the beginning of *Les paradis artificiels*, Baudelaire recalls a moment
from Hoffmann's *Kreisleriana:* the advice given to the conscientious composer to drink a fine Burgundy to write an opera, Rhine wine for religious
music, and "fiery wines" for Italian canzone (Griffin 60).

In the field of popular music, Charles Winick aligns early jazz, swing,
and bebop with alcohol, marijuana, and heroin respectively, finding that the
musical styles reproduce the effects of the drugs (1961, 57). In his exploration
of what he calls the "polypharmacy of rock," Shapiro finds that "neither
rock 'n' roll, nor the mod or garage bands of the 60s, nor punk in the 70s,

can be legitimately considered outside the context of amphetamines. The same applies to West Coast rock and acid and to marijuana and reggae," while heroin "served the symbolic, functional, psychological and social needs of the cool, aloof, hipster jazz musician" (1988, 64, 99, 115).

Entire systems of art have been understood to be psychotropic or psychedelic. In his travel book *Bali and Angkor*, Geoffrey Gorer hypothesizes a relationship between drugs and iconographic style in the art of the peoples of Angkor Wat in Cambodia and the Aztecs in Central America.

> The question of drugs is particularly pertinent as far as Angkor is concerned, for I am morally certain that the Khmer was an opium-soaked community. . . . Opium is, however, absolutely necessary for the comprehension of their art (which has the strange combination of being extremely sensual and completely sexless). . . . I have only seen Aztec carvings in a few museums and photos, not nearly enough to enable me to do more than suggest that Aztec art is a mescaline-tinted vision. I think, however, there is something to be said for this proposal; the peculiar Aztec composition, with the whole field of vision filled so that there is no empty space, the continual repetition of pattern-movement and the sudden changes without transitions all occur in the visions produced by mescaline; and the discomfort, the insistence on death and decay are allied with the psychological effects of that drug, which was undoubtedly used in Mexican religious ritual. (179–80)[40]

Theories of reception are similarly drug dependent: Havelock Ellis wrote that many of Wordsworth's most memorable poems cannot be "appreciated in their full significance by one who has never been under the influence of mescal" (1975, 188), and Baudelaire felt that if "all plays were listened to in this fashion [i.e., having taken hashish], they would gain much new beauty—even the plays of Racine" (96). Allen Ginsberg claimed that he "first discovered how to see Klee's *Magic Squares* as the painter intended them (as optically 3-dimensional space structures)" while high on marijuana (Solomon 1966, 196), and Nicholas Bromell, in his recent study *Tomorrow Never Knows*, argues that within the aesthetic of rock, "getting stoned and listening to music as if it mattered" should be considered as a unitary experience (3). The Grateful Dead "arrived stoned, played stoned and their fiercely loyal fans, 'Deadheads,' were stoned along with them. Acid stretched the length of the concerts to legendary proportions. . . . Indeed, some of their sixties material is almost unlistenable unless one is in an altered state of consciousness" (Shapiro 1988, 142).

Marie Bonaparte set Poe up as an artist who danced to the tune of three mood-altering substances, alcohol, opium, and ink: "For Poe had another 'drug' at his call, to keep his strange, unstable, hag-ridden nature from ending in madness or crime—a drug out of reach of most men. This was the ink, with which he eternalized on paper, in his fine, careful hand, the fearsome but comforting 'imagos' which at times gave him respite from grief" (89). The Horatian trope may finally configure the far more profound fact that art and intoxication are twin systems.[41] Ben Jonson rhymed

I drink as I would write,
In flowing measure, filled with flame and spright.
(349)

U.S. Sen. James Buckley denounced record company advertising that told listeners to "turn yourself on with a diamond needle" because it used drug code words to sell a product (Orman 13). Poetry has long been thought to be a drug, because, Pindar wrote, it causes men to forget their pain (Steiner 20). The Horatian aesthetic flows through the text as literary metaphor, especially in Rabelais where reading is an intoxicating activity: "Every honest boozer, every decent gouty gentleman, everyone who is dry, may come to this barrel of mine. . . . If they wish, and the wine is to the taste of their worshipful worships, let them drink frankly, freely, and boldly" (286). For Sir Philip Sidney, the poet intoxicates the reader:

Nowe therein of all Sciences . . . is our Poet the Monarch. For he dooth not only show the way, but giveth so sweete a prospect into the way, as will intice any man to enter into it. Nay, he dooth as if your journey should lye through a fayre Vineyard, at the first give you a cluster of Grapes: that full of that taste, you may long to pass further. (206)

And Beethoven is reputed to have said that the "world doesn't know that music is the wine which inspires one to new generative processes, and I am the Bacchus who presses out his glorious wine for mankind and makes them spiritually drunken" (Sullivan 1960, 3).[42]

Even the conventional language of art hints at this forbidden story; it casually expresses how beauty coerces desire through a vocabulary of involuntary attraction: "From *Macbeth* to *Dorian Gray*, literature has literalized its effects through a syntax of casting spells and charms" (Ronell 130). This is particularly true of music, which is for Baudelaire "directly evocative of the tormenting and delicious elation of artificial paradises" (Brombert 57). What most people seek in music, Igor Stravinsky wrote, is "une drogue, un *doping*" (176).

chapter 8

Carnival, Creativity, and the Sublimation of Drunkenness

From dawn onwards
Each drank.
It was the feast of Bacchus.
—ARCHILOCHUS

We have seen that the connection between intoxication and creativity appears regularly in the history of the arts. Yet this connection is also elided, so that the "intoxication" of Friedrich Nietzsche's *Birth of Tragedy* finally comes to mean almost everything but the intoxication of drink and drugs. One of the great modern sites of creativity is the reconstituted "carnival" of Mikhail Bakhtin, where popular play is artistic in itself but also feeds the individual artistry of a François Rabelais and the novel that follows. Mood-altering substances are left out of the mix that produces this event, with the result that Bakhtin and his commentators cannot offer any explanation for that festive institution beyond itself.

Western culture has tended to ignore the material base of experience, but one can still discover its vagrant traces. In this final chapter I explore how a far-reaching aesthetic project of the late nineteenth and twentieth centuries—the Dionysian aesthetic of Nietzsche and the carnival aesthetic of Bakhtin and others—is unable to suppress its connection to intoxication as a remarkable fact of social life.

The Birth of Tragedy celebrates intoxication as the driving force of Western creativity, and it is the foundation text of the carnival aesthetic. Peter Stallybrass and Allon White propose this sequence: "For both Michel Foucault . . . and for Mikhail Bakhtin in his seminal study *Rabelais and His World,* the Nietzschean study of history leads to the ideal of carnival" (6).[1] The nature of Nietzsche's Dionysian energy "is brought home to us most intimately by the analogy of intoxication," but this intoxication *(rausch)* is both literal and metaphoric: "Under the influence of the narcotic potion hymned by all primitive men and peoples, or in the powerful approach of spring, joyfully penetrating the whole of nature, those Dionysiac urges are awakened" (Nietzsche 17).

For Nietzsche, culture is divided between the two ideals of Apollonian and Dionysian, the separate worlds of dream and intoxication (33). Dionysus, however, was the more powerful cultural force: Apollo played a role in Greek tragedy subordinate to that of Dionysus, "the god of wild flute music, of wine and intoxication" (Wimsatt and Brooks 562). At times Dionysian and Apollonian are not equivalent, but opposite, principles, the true versus the false, a deep versus a superficial ideal: "The muses of the arts of 'illusion' paled before an art that, in its intoxication, spoke the truth" (Nietzsche 46).

Bakhtin's festive aesthetic ranges from the literal intoxication of "carnival" to the metaphoric intoxication of the "carnivalesque." It is driven neither by individual genius nor by the imagination, and, eventually, a hybrid figure like "the dialogic imagination" arises to fill the authorial gap. For Bakhtin this is the relevant aesthetic: it allows him to recover a valuable literary tradition that accounts for the Renaissance, the rise of the novel, and the postmodern present.[2] As Gary Shapiro suggests, this festive aesthetic may also be regarded as the aesthetic unconscious, since aesthetics, a "recent invention," "is built on the exclusion of laughter, the festive, and the grotesque" (49–50). Balancing Bakhtin's notion of "carnivalization" in a negative way is a modernist counteraesthetic: the "narcotization" of mass art. If literature was theoretically intoxicated, mass culture was perceived to be drugged. These two movements in the history of modernity enable us to rename the split between art and pop culture as intoxication and addiction (alcohol and drugs).

From a present-day perspective, the concept of intoxication that mobilizes this chapter (and this book) may seem utopian—that is also a basic charge leveled against Bakhtin's notion of carnival—but the contours of drunkenness explored here should be regarded as the expression of a cultural imaginary, a self-indulgent historical narrative in which the valence of intoxication is said to change radically in the late nineteenth century from Rabelaisian ecstasy to the sodden depression of Edgar Degas's "Absinthe-drinker" or Zola's "L'Assommoir."

If art is like the social institution of carnival for Bakhtin, then it was modeled on an event that can be explained only by the transformative presence of mood-altering substances. Herodotus told of a journey to Bubastis where, on the new moon festival "all Egypt gets drunk with wine, and when more wine is drunk than during all the rest of the year," and at the Babylonian festival of Sacaea, "men, dressed in the Scythian garb, pass day and night drinking and playing wantonly with one another, and also with the women who drink with them" (Lutz 2; Bourboulis 16).

There is ample testimony to the fact that drunkenness was not only permitted at grand festive occasions; it was obligatory, the order of the day. According to Tibullus,

Let wine make a festival of today; on a feast day there's no reason
to blush at being drunk and mismanaging one's crazy steps (98)

And in Lucian's "Saturnalia," Cronos announces a "festive season, when 'tis lawful to be drunken, and slaves have license to revile their lords" (4.110).[3] E. S. Drower tells us that it was a blessing to be drunk on the Jewish festival of Purim: Jews are supposed to drink "until they can no longer distinguish 'Blessed be Mordecai' from 'Cursed be Haman'" (11). Edmund Spenser wanted every guest drunk on the day when he married his Elizabeth:

Poure out the wine without restraint or stay,
Poure not by cups, but by the belly full,
Poure out to all that wull,
And sprinkle all the postes and wals with wine,
That they may sweat and drunken be withall,
Crowne ye god Bacchus with a coronall,
And Hymen also crowne with wreathes of vine.
(444)

In 1700 Thomas Brown saw carnival as the institutionalization of intoxication:

However the Names and Appellations of such . . . drunken Ceremonies may differ . . . all the polite Governments of *Europe* . . . have their Carnavals; the drunken *Mahometan* his Days of Excess before the *Biram;* the *Protestants and Lutherans* their Holy-days; and this Reverent City, what the Learned call their *Act.* These are Times dedicated to Drinking, and all the irregularities that attend the Wanton Fumes inspired by the God of Wine. (Watson 16)

Samuel Johnson defined drink as carnivalesque in his dictionary: "That ale is *festical,* appears from its sense in composition; as, among others, in the words Leet-ale, Lamb-ale, Whiston-ale, Clerk-ale, and Church-ale" (Wilson 1969, 25). Carnival also means "getting drunk" within the economics of traditional society where "alcohol was not readily available except on rare celebratory occasions; the pattern was thus one of sporadic heavy consumption" (Barrows 10).

By the time of the Reformation this would be turned around and the masses would be accused of turning innocent feasts into drunken orgies, in denunciatory tracts like Phillip Stubbes's *Anatomy of Abuses in England* (1583). But it continued to be a pattern in European society through the nineteenth century—from France (in the 1830s at the *Mi-Carême* "when, made anonymous by costumes and masks or dominos, everyone relaxed moral restraints, and plunged into a mad citywide bacchanal") to Russia ("In the carnival before Lent, they give themselves over to all manner of debauchery and luxury, and in the last week they drink as if they were never to drink more") (Samuel Collins in Gasperetti 168; R. Miller 42).

Nevertheless, most accounts of carnival do not specify what is causing the explosive states designated by terms like *festivity, license,* or *freedom,* but instead seem content to describe carnival in terms of its effects, as, for example, "a reign of confusion where boisterous anarchy appears to prevail.... During carnival time, riotous behavior, obscene gestures, and abusive language singularly inappropriate in daily life are not only tolerated but seen as 'normal'" (Stewart 144). We are meant to believe that these moods and behaviors are produced by and for the holiday occasion, that they are the result of a sui generic force, a "festive uplift." States of being like festive uplift or natural euphoria stand as unexamined, even tautological, causes of carnival, occupying roughly the same relationship to carnival intoxication as "furor" does to poetic intoxication. Circumventing a distinction between material and sublime causes, Erasmus's "Folly" likens festive uplift to both drink and divinity: "I no sooner stepped up to speak to this full assembly than all your faces put on a kind of new and unwonted pleasantness. So suddenly have you cleared your brows, and with so frolic and hearty a laughter given me your applause, that in truth . . . [you] seem to me no less than Homer's gods drunk with nectar and nepenthe" (1958, 7).

Carnival is unthinkable without mood alteration, and no other component of the carnival mix explains the quality of transformation better than drink. Scenes like the following, from a thirteenth-century feast of fools, can hardly be attributed to spontaneous festive uplift:

> After the mass was ended, the people broke into all sorts of riotous behavior in the church, leaping, dancing, and exhibiting themselves in indecent postures, and some went as far as to strip themselves naked, and in this condition they were drawn through the streets with tubs full of ordure and filth, which they threw about at the mob. (Wright 1875, 209)

Wine was the cause of all the Bacchanalian behavior that Livy observed: "When wine had inflamed their minds, and night and the mingling of males with females, youth with age, had destroyed every sentiment of modesty, all varieties of corruption first began to be practised, since each one had at hand the pleasure answering to that to which his nature was more inclined" (McGinty 15–16).

If drink does not drive carnival, carnival drives drink in Pieter Bruegel's painting "The Battle of Carnival and Lent," where the personification of carnival rides a wine barrel instead of a horse. In one text for such allegorical combats, "'Lent, Princess of Fasting and Penitence,' exhorts 'Carnival, Emperor of the Drunkards and Gluttons,' not to forget his soul over the feasting and drinking" (Swarzenski 2). Bakhtin tells us that, in the seventeenth century, one "of the most popular figures of comic folklore was Gros Guillaume": "He was girt with two belts: one under his chest, the other under his belly, so that his body resembled a wine barrel" (292). Shakespeare's Falstaff is also a Carnival "barrell": a tremendous "bolting-hutch of beastliness" and a "bombard of sack" (Marshall 27).

In an attack on carnival by the late-fifteenth-century British poet John Skelton—

> In the rites of *Bacchus,* not only the priests, but all the people, men, women, and children, having their faces smeared with the lees of wine, and being half-drunk, ran about the fields, and through the woods, in a most horrible fit of distraction, howling like wild beasts, and frisking from place to place with such

ridiculous and immodest gesticulations, as nothing but the strong possession of some demon could have prompted them to—

Skelton, by the end of his sentence, has forgotten the perfectly appropriate motive power for the behavior with which he began (Stock 181). Bruegel's "Land of Cockaigne" is the pictorial equivalent of Bakhtin's view of carnival: there is food but no drink. In Pieter Baltens's "Land of Cockaigne," however, a painting often alleged as Bruegel's source, a jug tied to the branch of a tree pours its liquor down on one of the sleeping men. The opening of Victor Hugo's *Nôtre-Dame de Paris* gives the most ample treatment of carnival in nineteenth-century literature with its extended presentation of a late-fifteenth-century Feast of Fools. Although Hugo summarizes all the causes of the crowd's unrest, he never mentions drink.

For Bakhtin and contemporary writers on carnival and the carnivalesque, drinking and intoxication have been erased from the scene. Katerina Clark and Michael Holquist casually mention that the drunken aspect of carnival was deliberately suppressed by Bakhtin, who desired to "concentrate primarily on the eating and elide the drinking because of his originary thesis that carnival is a descendant of the aftermath of the hunt" (301).

The cultural record shows that the connection between carnival, drink, and intoxication has been consistently broken. Examples of this suppression in recent studies would include Monica Rector's extensive piece on South American carnival and Emmanuel Le Roy Ladurie's *Carnival in Romans,* both of which present scenes of political riot without any mention of intoxication. Robert Stam's *Subversive Pleasures: Bakhtin, Cultural Criticism, and Film,* a book about carnival past and present, contains barely a passing reference to intoxicants. Stam writes, for example, that "in the United States the sixties were the privileged era of carnivalized politics, when demonstrations incorporated colorful elements of music, dance, costume and guerrilla theater," but there is no mention of the centrality of drugs to that period (136). Stam does not even think that alcohol and drugs need to be listed as proximate causes: "Behind Bakhtin and Nietzsche is a collective rite whose folk origins antedate Christianity, a rite in which mask-wearing revelers become 'possessed' and transform themselves (whether through costume, attitude, or musical frenzy) into blissful alterity" (89).

Drink is invariably missing from twentieth-century inventories of carnival: "On such days," Bakhtin writes, "there is greater abundance in everything: food, dress, decorations," or, to quote a later writer, "Rabelais places an emphasis on feasting and elimination, sexuality and death," and these establish the chronotope of carnival (Bakhtin 276; Kershner 16). Julia Kristeva describes carnival as "the holiday of food and excrement" (115); Peter Burke claims there were three major themes in carnival: food, sex, and violence (186). The central icon of carnival for Bakhtin and others, the grotesque body, eats enormously, farts, shits, and gives birth, but there is little to suggest that it drinks or takes drugs and acts out the extravaganzas of intoxication. According to David Lodge, the grotesque body is a "body defined by the organs of self-transgression, the bowels and the phallus, mouth and anus, a body perpetually in the process of becoming, eating and defecating, copulating, giving birth and dying at the same time through the displacements and condensations of carnival and dream" (40).

Bakhtin's carnival may not be the one contemporary theory wants, since it is such a sublimated event, and certain critics have charged Bakhtin with robbing carnival of its dark potency and rendering it a sanitized utopia: "In Carnival he sees only the joy of parody, not the danger of irresponsibility and violence" (Emerson and Morson 57). Similarly, Renate Lachmann claims that Bakhtin's folk carnival allowed "for neither frenzy nor ecstasy" and must be contrasted with those of Florens Christian Rang and Hans Peter Duerr (127). As she notes, for Rang it is the will to frenzy that is of central importance in carnival, and his emphasis on murder and atrocity—"every despicable act, every murder, every form of excess that licentiousness and lunacy have dared to dream"—strikes a tone incompatible with Bakhtin's conception (127). There have also been extensive political and feminist revisions of Bakhtin's model on the grounds, for example, that carnival was often manipulated by political factions as a cover for organized violence against such groups as women or Jews. Bakhtin's critics darken his carnival even if they do not drunken it.

Drink is also elided in statements that include it without naming it: "Bacchanalia were the festivities held by the Greeks and Romans to pay homage to Bacchus and Dionysus. They came to be associated with libertinism, feast, banquet, and orgy" (Rector 39). The secondary cultural structures that Rector lists connote sex and food, although all four can also faintly be seen to be fueled by drink. Dominick La Capra similarly observes that Bakhtin's grotesque body "enjoys food and sex; it is always eating, drinking, defecating, or copulating either literally or figuratively" (299). In this formulation the initial mention of food gets repeated as eating and defecating, and sex as copulating, but drinking has no control term in the sentence (except for food): it is an outlaw term sneaked in after the fact. In a fifteenth-century account of carnival violence and folly, drink is an afterthought: "Burghers run around with whips and farmer's clothes. They run into people's houses, catching women in the corners. They bump into others and knock them off their feet as if they were felling trees. They knock you over with their breath, too, stinking of malt" (Kinser 11). The same anticlimactic rhythm occurs in a twentieth-century account of English fairs: "The smell of roast-pig was everywhere. And no doubt there was ale enough to wash it down" (Addison 53).[4]

When drink appears in Bakhtin, it is confined in the phrase "food and drink," or variants like "appetite and thirst" and "excrement and urine" (22, 147). The phrase "food and drink" expresses a false symmetry and disrupts social experience even further when the reference is to strong drink, for then drink is no longer a pleasant accompaniment to dining but a much fiercer substance, a pleasure that can drive food from the festive place altogether.[5]

The main strategy for making drink invisible, however, is to allegorize and sublimate it, to make it the sign of an ideal nonalcoholic essence. C. J. Jung's letter to Bill W., co-founder of Alcoholics Anonymous, is a patent model of sublimation. The craving of a former patient for alcohol, Jung wrote, was "the equivalent on a low level of the spiritual thirst of our being for wholeness. . . . Alcohol in Latin is *spiritus,* and you use the same word for the highest religious experience as well as for the most depraving poison" (Raphael 133).

Bakhtin insists that for Rabelais drink stands for truth as in the maxim *in vino veritas:* "And the tirade concludes with an invitation to drink, which in Rabelaisian imagery means to be in communion with truth. . . . Diogenes at the siege of Corinth . . . transforms his tub into a barrel filled with wine, Rabelais' favorite image of gay and free truth" (175–79). With such interpretations, Bakhtin betrays his stated desire to be true to the body and instead locks it into an official hierarchy. Most statements in Rabelais's own work, however, resist sublimation and read very much like stubborn accounts of people drinking: "Therefore they did nothing but pour wine down his throat with a funnel. . . . As a consequence, each man in the army began to tipple, to ply the pot and swill it down. In fact, they drank so much and so much that they fell asleep like hogs, in disorderly fashion all about the camp" (258).[6]

The distinctive markers of carnivalesque art are less likely to be intoxication and drunkenness than the trope of the world upside down, destructive laughter, feasting, or the image of the grotesque body. This line of reference merely displaces the problem of intoxication, since the "World Upside Down," for example, was "a common name for English taverns and inns" (Jonassen 10). Insofar as the antonym of laughter in these formulations is "sobriety," laughter is also a code word for intoxication. In George Meredith's treatise on comedy, intoxication becomes an oxymoron—like the drink in Alexander Pope's "Essay on Criticism," which sobers when drunk largely: "But the laughter directed by the Comic Spirit is a harmless wine, conducing to sobriety in the degree that it enlivens" (50).

Although culture has determined that alcohol be available to signify only as something else, that is also its salvation, allowing the forbidden substance to seep back into writing in the form of slips, puns, and metaphor. Consider Roger Sales's statement of the ambivalent relationship between carnival and official authority: "There were two reasons why the fizzy, dizzy carnival spirit did not necessarily undermine authority. First of all, it was licensed or sanctioned by the authorities themselves. They removed the stopper to stop the bottle being smashed altogether" (Stallybrass 13). Drink finally surfaces toward the end of *Rabelais and His World* as a totalizing metaphor, entering through Bakhtin's criticism of what he saw as faulty understanding of Rabelaisian comedy. Criticizing later attempts to reduce Rabelais's anarchic laughter to satire, specifically Heinrich Schneegans's *History of Grotesque Satire,* Bakhtin writes:

> Schneegans is forced to admit that even with considerable effort it is impossible to find the satirical orientation in all of Rabelais' exaggeration. He explains this by the very nature of exaggeration, which always tends to transgress its own limits; the author of grotesque is carried away, is "drunk" with hyperbole, at times forgetting the true role of exaggeration and losing his grasp on satire. (307)

The notion of the literature of grotesque realism as a drunken literature must come from a more opaque level of signification for Bakhtin to accept it. The word *drunkenness* as the term for this central quality of culture remains in his text.

Drink is a strong presence in almost every work of carnivalesque art cited by Bakhtin. Bakhtin's two great authors, Rabelais and Dostoyevsky, neatly express the duality—the euphoria and the misery—of drinking.[7] The work that Bakhtin put at the center of literary culture, Rabelais's *Histories of Gargantua and Pantagruel,* represents, among other things, a high moment of drunkenness: "Bakhtin reminds us that Rabelais, too, begins his great medieval carnival with the image of a drinker: 'Gargantua was born shouting "Drink, drink, drink!"'" (Mierau 321). Pantagruel's name "in Rabelais' burlesque etymology means 'the all-thirsting one,'" and the narrator of *Gargantua* "brings the entire narrative under the sign of the bottle and drink"; it is "a lesson in how and how not to drink" (Winandy 9).

In Rabelais's book, drinking is the privileged context for both producing and properly consuming art:

> Every honest boozer, every decent gouty gentleman, everyone who is dry, may come to this barrel of mine, but need drink only if he wishes. If they wish, and the wine is to the taste of their worshipful worships, let them drink frankly, freely, and boldly without stint or payment. Such is my statute; and have no fear that the wine will give out, as it did at the marriage at Cana in Galilee. As much as you draw out at the tap, I will pour in at the bung. (286)

The book ends, in the prologue to book 5, by stating that "therefore, my dear boozers, I advise you in good time to lay up a fair store of them [his books]. . . . When the chance comes you must not only shell them, but gulp them down as an opiate cordial and absorb them into your systems" (605).

Dostoyevsky was the child of an alcoholic (although this is disputed) and an addict himself. According to Caryl Emerson and Gary Saul Morson, the shape of addiction is written into the qualities of his fiction: the roller-coaster emotions, the sudden shifts from abasement to aggression, "the explosive mixture of intense insult with self-assertive pride," secrets and scandal (258). The three stories that Bakhtin cites in his study of Dostoyevsky as particularly carnivalesque are "Bobok," "A Gentle Spirit," and "An Unpleasant Predicament." The first and the third open with drunkenness; "Bobok" begins with an allegation of perpetual drunkenness: "Semyon Ardalyonovitch said to me all of a sudden the day before yesterday: 'Why, will you ever be sober, Ivan Ivanovitch? Tell me that, pray'" (507). In "An Unpleasant Predicament," the narrator has been drinking all day with three of his colleagues in the imperial bureaucracy, and he conceives the intention of graciously visiting the wedding of a subordinate (399–462).

Apart from the works mentioned by Bakhtin, strong drink is central to most other carnivalesque art in Western culture. The plays of Hans Sachs of Nuremberg, for example, generally start with the characters coming from a scene of drinking and end with them going back to one. "The Stolen Bacon" begins:

> Ohhhh. Oh my head. Oh whatta headache. I can barely stand on my own two feet. The whole night drinking. Hic. No wonder I staggered home. All that sausage makes me so thirsty I drink all the more. Oh-well. At carnival time everybody drinks, gets happy, and like me—gets a little foggy in the head. (40)

It ends:

> Why get all steamed up and just hurt myself. I give up on you. Here, take this money and go over to the tavern and fetch us some wine. We might as well drink up the money I made at the market. Come on let's sit down and drink our wine. Let's forget this hullabaloo and hassle and bring on some good times—so says Hans Sachs. (53)

Following Bakhtin, certain Anglo-Saxon carnivalesque critics like Northrop Frye or C. L. Barber detoxify the tradition, appropriating riotous and orgiastic ceremonies like the Roman Saturnalia without allowing any of their indecorous meanings to slip over into art, so that, for them, the imagination is never drunk. Nevertheless, in the case of Barber, the key texts in his *Shakespeare's Festive Comedy* are Erasmus's *Praise of Folly,* Thomas Nashe's *Summer's Last Will and Testament,* and the tavern scenes in *Henry IV,* parts 1 and 2.

Erasmus's Folly is an alcoholic baby, begotten by Plutus in his "full strength and pride of youth . . . at such a time when he had been well heated with nectar, of which he had, at one of the banquets of the gods, taken a dose extraordinary." Folly's inheritance is allegorically doubled in his upbringing: "I was suckled by two jolly nymphs, to wit, Drunkenness, the daughter of Bacchus, and Ignorance, of Pan," and the festive uplift that he promises is very like intoxication: "But how much larger and more present is the benefit you receive by me, since, as it were with a perpetual drunkenness I fill your minds with mirth, fancies and jollities, and that too without any trouble?" (13–14, 77).

Falstaff is the epitome of drunkenness: "One of the first associations that come to mind at the mention of Falstaff," Roderick Marshall writes, "is his devotion to sack, his unremitting intoxication." Marshall takes Falstaff back through a lineage of mighty drinkers like the Slavic Ilya, the Chinese Eight Immortals of the Wine-cup, the Indian Ganesha, and the Greek Silenus (121). From Nashe's *Summer's Last Will and Testament,* Barber features the Bacchus episode (even though most commentators do not regard it as central), because he wants to find an analogue to Falstaff in Nashe's Bacchus ("god fatback . . . god barrellbelly"), "a prince of tavern mates," of whom Will Summers asks: "What is flesh and blood without his liquor. . . . How many tuns of wine hast in thy paunch?" (Barber 27, 71).

In addition to the works of Rabelais and Erasmus, the major carnivalesque works in the Western tradition are Euripides' *Bacchae* and Shakespeare's *Midsummer Night's Dream,* and both are preoccupied with intoxication and its effects. In the Shakespeare comedy everything that Bakhtin posits of carnival (the world upside down, the dethroning of the official king for the space of the holiday) is literally driven by drink, the "liquor" of the "juice," a magical liquid that releases sexual inhibitions and unleashes violent feelings. The play stages an answer to the question asked by Duerr (i.e., what were the witches' salves and ointments): the holiday transformation is motivated by an extremely potent mood- and reality-altering drink, but the material substance, the literal of the experience, is immediately forgotten by the participants and invisible to those who look back at it.

By way of documenting the persistence of carnival intoxication, I want to take a final look at the European tradition reflected in the New World. Classic American fiction stages the origin of European America as a drunken carnival: in Washington Irving's "Rip Van Winkle," conventionally regarded as the instituting work of a truly "American" literature, which features a drinking party, and in Nathaniel Hawthorne's "May-Pole of Merrymount," which reprises a battle between Carnival and Lent for control of future American civilization. Yet, unlike Bruegel or Rabelais, the mood of these and other American fictions is far from joyous: Irving presents a grim picture of play and drink, and the possibility of a carnival-like Merrymount in America so frightens Hawthorne that he counters that possibility with a temperance fable. These tales respond to the savage pace of drinking in the early United States, as recorded by W. J. Rorabaugh in his study of American drinking, *The Alcoholic Republic: An American Tradition.*

In the wilderness outside his village, Rip meets a carnival crew wearing ancient costumes and playing at ninepins. They possess grotesque bodies: "Their visages, too, were peculiar. One had a large head, broad face and small piggish eyes. The face of another seemed to consist entirely of nose" (34). They also drink liquor, and in fact, drink is the first sign of a sacred presence in those mountains. Rip sees a little man who "bore on his shoulder a stout keg that seemed full of liquor, and made signs for Rip to approach and assist him with the load" (33).

Nevertheless, denial of festivity marks the tale: "What seemed particularly odd to Rip was, that though these folks were evidently amusing themselves, yet they maintained the gravest faces, the most mysterious silence, and were, withal, the most melancholy party of pleasure he had ever witnessed" (34). They are drinking and partying in a stony and lackluster manner. Rip's response to this disparity is to become very drunk: "One taste provoked another, and he reiterated his visits to the flagon so often that at length his senses were overpowered, his eyes swam in his head—his head gradually declined and he fell into a deep sleep" (35). For the others there is drinking but no intoxication.

Rip had been described earlier as a bon vivant and "naturally a thirsty soul" (34–35). The "foremost man at all country frolics," he "was one of those happy mortals of foolish, well oiled dispositions, who take the world easy . . . and would rather starve on a penny than work for a pound" (30, 31). Rip's commitment to pleasure disturbs his marriage, but marital discord is blamed only on the wife, not on Rip's drinking: she "kept continually dinning in his ears about his idleness, his carelessness and the ruin he was bringing on his family. Morning noon and night her tongue was incessantly going" (31). Rip's response to the situation at home is to spend as little time there as possible. Instead he frequents the local tavern and thinks of himself as "driven from home" (31). His magical drinking in the woods is a displacement of the ordinary drinking in the village; the potent draught belongs more to village life than to the wilderness. Like the American that he is, Rip drinks quickly in order to produce oblivion, and he suffers radically alienating social effects.

Hawthorne's art has an unexpected carnivalesque aspect. This festive strain includes "The May-Pole of Merrymount" (a tale about whether America will be wet or dry); "My Kinsman, Major Molineux" and "Young Goodman Brown," which interpret the American Revolution (or something very like it) and a witches' sabbath as carnival; and the beginning of *The Marble Faun* and the end of *The Blithedale Romance,* which are given over to literal carnivals. Hawthorne's American carnival usually has dark and forbidding features. In "May-Pole," he writes, "Had a wanderer, bewildered in the melancholy forest, heard their mirth, and stolen a half-affrighted glance, he might have fancied them the crew of Comus, some already transformed to brutes, some midway between man and beast, and the others rioting in the flow of tipsey jollity that foreran the change" (9.56).

In *The Blithedale Romance,* as Miles Coverdale is returning from town to the Blithedale colony after the harvest has been gathered and a holiday declared, liquor and intoxication pervade the world around him: "The atmosphere had a spirit and sparkle in it. Each breath was like a sip of ethereal wine, tempered, as I said, with a crystal lump of ice" (3.204). Before showing himself to his colleagues he climbs into his personal retreat, a grape arbor. Unlike his first visit there, this is a very wet episode, a hymn to Bacchus (the coming of wine to America):

> The grapes, which I had watched throughout the summer, now dangled around me in abundant clusters of the deepest purple, deliciously sweet to the taste, and, though wild, yet free from that ungentle flavor which distinguishes nearly all our native and uncultivated grapes. Methought a wine might be pressed out of them, possessing a passionate zest, and endowed with a new kind of intoxicating quality, attended with such bacchanalian ecstasies as the tamer grapes of Madeira, France and the Rhine, are inadequate to produce. And I longed to quaff a great goblet of it that moment! (3.208)

Hawthorne's America stages a much wilder festival than the Old World could show, and the need for carnival transformation is urgent.[8]

The intoxication that makes carnival possible ranges from the intense drinking of the festive participants to a spirit like Nietzsche's elemental, transcendental, and metaphoric *rausch*. However, the history and theory of intoxication and addiction are just beginning to be written. Many more inflections and local histories will become visible; those that already exist will find a more systematic articulation: for example, John Walker's "soft" contrast between the bacchanals of Titian and Rubens; Rubens, he says, "changes the emphasis, sees the scene described differently, treats it as a Northerner would. Wine ceases to be an inspiration of poetry; instead it becomes a source of ecstatic abandon" (89).

At the outset of this chapter, I referred to an aesthetic driven not by individual genius or the imagination but rather by intoxication. Yet the choice need not be *either* intoxication *or* imagination, if we understand that both terms are porous and problematic enough in themselves and do not serve understanding easily. The terms have a long history of overlap, even interchangeability: in Ralph Waldo Emerson's essay "The Poet," for example, poets write poems because they are "intoxicated by the imagination" (276), and intoxication both displaces and replaces the imagination in the modern period (see Clej).

Mikhail Bakhtin had a vision of popular play and fabrication that, at one remove from the scene of art production, was as easy as getting drunk. Bakhtin's vision of carnival and carnivalesque art was more of a quaint narrative than a coherent program. There is a severe, possibly a fatal, gap between the two elements. Nevertheless, in the former, the aesthetics of intoxication finds metaphoric support in existing accounts of carnival alongside an ostentatious denial of intoxication, and, in the latter, it is reconstructed in the self-reflexive notations of carnivalesque art.

Notes

INTRODUCTION

1. Although I often treat intoxication and addiction as corresponding conditions, they are also asymmetrical: for example, intoxication is an effect of drinking, addiction both is and is not. One contribution of Alcoholics Anonymous was to announce that alcoholism is not homologous with drunkenness; an alcoholic is an alcoholic drunk or sober.

2. Eve Sedgwick suggests this, treating alcoholism as parallel to homosexuality: "Something changed. Under the taxonomic pressure of the newly ramified and pervasive medical-juridical authority of the late nineteenth century, and in the context of changing class and imperial relations, what had been a question of acts crystallized into a question of identities" (1993, 131).

3. The main cultural difference between drugs and alcohol is that there is usually no division between intoxication and addiction imposed on the former, whereas, for alcohol, getting high and getting hooked are very different, often opposite, processes. In obedience to this conflict of categories, I sometimes refer to drugs as drink's opposite but more often deploy drink as a term that includes both. How to arrange and group the full range of psychoactive substances is a pretty problem that I more or less beg. Splitting alcoholic drink and certain drugs off from the full range of psychoactive commodities is a common practice. In the German title of his study of "substances ingested or inhaled by humans to produce a pleasurable effect," Wolfgang Schivelbusch can refer to them all under the heading of *Genussmittel*, "articles of enjoyment," but the subtitle of the English translation requires the three words *spices, stimulants,* and *intoxicants* (xiii).

4. There are excellent individual studies of the classical symposium and the place of drink in Greek religion and society by historians like Marcel Detienne or François Lissarrague.

5. Addiction is also invisible (like invisible writing) because the signs that identify it only appear in the absence of the drug, in the withdrawal.

6. A comparable psychotic insistence on the grandeur of the lowly and insignificant is played out in carnival and in literary forms like mock epic.

1. THE MYSTERIES OF INTOXICATION

1. Elizabeth Judd asks us to consider the possibility that "millions of years ago the accidental consumption of hallucinogens by our ape ancestors provided the first spark of consciousness that demarcated human beings from the other animals" by stimulating "brain lateralization, bipedalism, and increased manual dexterity" (9). Terence McKenna believes that the "intake of psilocybin by primates living in the African grasslands prior to the last Ice Age may have led to the origins of human language itself" (Drury 144). Drink is constitutive of the human in other ways as well. H. W. Janson refers to a Hebrew tradition according to which the forbidden fruit was the grape (243).

2. Théophile Gautier wrote that God "has granted to us alone the triple and glorious privilege of drinking when without thirst" (in Graña 264). David Courtwright puts this another way: "In evolutionary terms, *accidental* intoxication may be valuable: it warns an organism not to go near the plant again. *Seeking* intoxication, let alone profiting from it, is paradoxical. It seemingly defies the logic of natural selection" (91). Edmund Waller, however, turns this around so that the path of excess is also the path of reason:

Let brutes and vegetals, that cannot think,
So far as drought and nature urges, drink;
A more indulgent mistress guides our sprites,
Reason, that dares beyond our appetites . . .
And with divinity rewards excess.
(89)

3. Omar in Elwell-Sutton 158; Ward in Watson 54.

4. Homer in McNutt 40; Goliardic verses in Symonds 169. In one of many "accidental fermentation" narratives, an anecdote in James Malcolm's *History of Persia,* the meaning of intoxication shifts from poisonous to wonderful. Jamshid, the legendary king of Persia, put some grapes in a jar and left for a hunt. On his return, he was astonished to find they had fermented, and he wrote "poison" on the container. An unhappy court lady tried to commit suicide by drinking the liquid, but intoxication and then sleep restored her to a healthy state of mind. As a result, the qualities of the wine become celebrated, and the brew was called "'Zahri Khush,' the Agreeable Poison" (Bicknell 8). In another Jamshid tale, the poisonous juice was given to a murderer who, after his second cup, "began to make merry and sing and dance about. . . . 'Give me one more drink,' he shouted, 'Then you can do what you like with me.'" The next day he told his jailers: "I don't know what it was I drank, but it was delicious. . . . The first glass I had some trouble swallowing, because it tasted acid, but when it had settled in my stomach I found I wanted to have another. When I drank

the second glass I felt lively and merry. All my shyness disappeared, and the world seemed a wonderful place to live in" (Arberry 1958, 86–88). With the Greek Icarius, the story goes the other way: Dionysus taught him how to prepare wine for the delight of society. The shepherds he invited to drink, however, did not mix the wine with water, and they "grew so drunk that they saw everything double, believed themselves bewitched," and killed their host (Graves 1.262).

5. "But can such a small—such a trifling—alteration as the slight intoxication produced by the moderate use of wine or tobacco produce important consequences? . . . 'but it surely cannot have any serious consequences if a man merely comes slightly under the influence of hops or tobacco,' is what is usually said. It seems to people that a slight stupefaction, a little darkening of the judgement, cannot have any important influence. But to think so is like supposing that it may harm a watch to be struck against a stone, but that a little dirt introduced into it cannot be harmful" (Tolstoy 63). A contemporary sociologist, Salvatore Lucia, continues to beg the question: "Drinking alcoholic beverages in moderation is drinking in such amounts and with such frequency and on such occasions as to present no threat to the health, to the welfare, and to the functioning of the individual. Such a definition of moderation, of course, precludes intoxication, and certainly precludes repeated intoxication. . . . but the fact that they do not become intoxicated does not signify or mean that the smaller amount of alcohol which they drink is without any effect on their feeling or on their behavior. They may experience . . . diminished tension or anxiety, and change of mood" (110–11). Why isn't this intoxication?

6. Seneca wants to include a selective intoxication within civilization as a safety valve: "At times we ought to reach the point even of intoxication, not drowning ourselves in drink, yet succumbing to it; for it washes away troubles, and stirs the mind from its very depths and heals its sorrow just as it does certain ills of the body" (1929, 283).

7. For Anacreon, Horace, and other classic authors, narratives of centaurs expressed this wildness of intoxication, e.g., the legends of both Eurytus and Pholus. The first led to the drunken mass rape at the wedding of Pirithöus, king of the Lapiths (Ovid 1958, 291–301). While he was entertaining Hercules, Pholus opened a jar of wine that had been left with him by Dionysus: "Now when the jar had been opened and the sweet odor of the wine, because of its great age and strength, came to the Centaurs dwelling near there, it came to pass that they were driven mad," and "they rushed to Pholus' cave armed with rocks, tree-trunks and torches and Heracles battled with them" (Diodorus Siculus 381; Grimal 370).

8. McDonell in Crawley 79; T. Andrews 2; O'Brien 1992, 3. The Greek Dionysus has been identified with various other divinities: the Anatolian Sabazius, the Arabian Adoneus and Dusares, the Aryan Haoma or Soma, the Celtic Braciaca and Goibniu, the Egyptian Osiris or Antaeus, the Flemish Gambrinus, the Gaulish Sucellus, the Indian Siva, the Welsh Seithenyn ap Seithi, and the Yoruba Ogenki (Stanislawski 435; Raben 29; Kerenyi 257; Davis 4; T. Andrews 32–33; Lutz 114; Toussaint-Samat 274; O'Flaherty 81; Butler 1985, 61; Zabus 215). Ausonius wrote, "The sons of Ogyges call me Bacchus, Egyptians think me Osiris, Mysians name me Phanaces, Indians regard me

as Dionysus, Roman rites make me Liber, the Arab races think me Adoneus, Lucaniacus the Universal God" (187). The equivalent god in British culture is John Barleycorn (see Marchant 346). There is also a category of wine hero, like Jamshid, Prometheus, or Tantalus. The latter two offended the gods by stealing their nectar and ambrosia and giving them to mortals (Steadman 35).

9. Athenaeus included another version by Epicharmus, a fifth-century writer of comedy: "After a sacrifice, a feast . . . after the feast, drinking. . . . after drinking comes mockery, after mockery filthy insult, after insult a law-suit, after the lawsuit a verdict, after the verdict shackles, the stocks, and a fine" (1.157–9).

10. For how long and involved the ritual of toasting could be, see Barnabe Riche, *The Irish Hubbub* (1619) and Richard Brathwaite, *The Law of Drinking* (1617). Toasting is the way the absent women get back into the drinking situation. A good example of this is the drinking song from Richard Brinsley Sheridan's *School for Scandal:*

> Here's to the maiden of bashful fifteen;
> Here's to the widow of fifty;
> Here's to the flaunting, extravagant quean,
> And here's to the housewife that's thrifty.
> Let the toast pass—
> Drink to the lass—
> I'll warrant she'll prove an excuse for the glass,
> etc.
> (265)

Pierre Ronsard's Corydon invites Rémy Belleau to praise his mistress by drinking "as many glassfuls as she has letters in her name" (Jeanneret 126).

11. In its second mode, intoxication is characterized by a host of physical symptoms. These include red faces, red noses, and red cheeks—

> Come, sit we by the fireside
> And roundly drink we here,
> Till that we see our cheeks all dyed
> And noses tanned with beer;—

seeing double; and lack of motor control, as in Hesiod's lines: "Wine bindeth feet and hands together and tongue and wits with fetters unspeakable," and Plato's a "man in his cups does but sprawl and fumble all ways at once; his body is as crazy as his mind" (Robert Herrick in Koken 64; Hesiod 94; Plato 1961, 1352).

2. DRINK POETRY

1. McVicker 29; Shaw 17.

2. Waddell 1929, 339; Silver 315; Colford 142; J. M. Sullivan 89. Of Tao Ch'ien, a "renowned commentator went so far as to suggest that not a single one of his poems was unrelated to wine" (Shilin 48).

3. Brewer's *Reader's Handbook* lists Anacreon Moore; Francesco Albano, the Anacreon of Painters; Bertrand Barère de Vieuzac, the Anacreon of the Guillotine; the Abbé Guillaume Amfrye de Chaulieu, the Anacreon of the Temple; Walter Mapes, the Anacreon of the Twelfth Century; Pontus de Tyard, the French Anacreon; Paul Fleming, the German Anacreon; Hafiz, the Persian Anacreon; Alexander Scott, the Scotch Anacreon; and Giovanni Meli, the Sicilian Anacreon (40). Edward Phillips declared that Brome wrote in "so Jovial a strain, that among the Sons of Mirth & *Bacchus . . .* his name cannot chuse but be immortal, and in this respect he may well be stil'd the *English Anacreon*"—an epithet he shares with Abraham Cowley (Doyle 193; Brome 18). These phrases are ambiguous because this name can signify a preoccupation with either love or drinking.

4. As exceptions to this generalization, I would instance particularly the works of Braden 1978; Harb; Mason; and Anya Taylor. Tom Moore quotes Toderini on the learning of the Turks: "In the delicate bard of Schiras [Hafiz] we find the kindred spirit of Anacreon: some of his gazelles, or songs, possess all the character of our poet" (8). Joseph van Purgthall-Hammer, an eminent German Persian scholar, compared Hafiz to Anacreon and Catullus, while Edward William Lane said of Abu Nuwas that he was the Rochester or Piron of his age (Strich 136; Ingrams iii).

5. In his study of Hafiz and Goethe, Henri Broms takes on Ahmad Kasravi, who says of Western admirers of Hafiz that "they wish to keep the East in the state of lassitude expressed by him, they have imperialistic motives for wanting his outlook to survive. . . . The Divan of Hafiz is more useful to them than an army of a million men" (10). Broms finds such a perspective absurd.

6. The *Carmina Anacreontea* consists of sixty poems by many poets, and it spans "almost six hundred years, from late Hellenistic or early Roman times to the Byzantine era" (Rosenmeyer 1992, 3).

7. Fulvio Orsini tried to publicize the error in 1568, and in 1732 a Dutch scholar, Jan Cornelis de Pauw, rejected the authenticity of the *Anacreontea* in a book on the subject.

8. Decker xvi–xvii; Brown 67 (see also Dashti 155).

9. Greek and Persian drink poetry, at least, is homosexual in its erotic dynamics involving a passionate address to a young male cupbearer, as mythologized in the Greek figure of Ganymede:

Drink not strong wine save at the slender darling's hand;
Each like to other in all gifts the spirit grace:
For wine can never gladden toper's heart and soul,
Unless the cup-boy show a bright and sparkling face.
(Abu Nuwas in Ingrams 30)

10. Drinking songs are standard items in English drama from the Renaissance through the Restoration as well as in the European opera and operetta traditions. Nineteenth-century temperance writers certainly thought drink was a dominating subject for poetry: "Edward Hitchcock, temperance advocate and professor of chemistry

at Amherst College, lamented the fact that 'the distinguished poets of ancient and modern times, have devoted their most captivating numbers to the praise of Bacchus'" and, in 1828, the Scottish physician Robert Macnish wrote that "the pleasures of drinking constituted one of the most fertile themes of the poetry of liquor-producing countries" (Warner 27, 237).

11. Ode 39 in Davidson 1915, 113 and Burns 115. One trope that inhabits the dark side of drinking is the denial that there ever was euphoria or that it lasted long.

12. Rossi in Lissarrague 1990, 124; Murray 1983, 264.

13. Chinese drink poetry is an exception to the generalizations about euphoria and sympotic conviviality. If the drinking is done in company, it is generally with one old friend, but most often it is solitary and the feeling-tone is pleasantly sad. The convivial event has taken many institutional forms over the centuries: the Greek symposium or the Roman *convivium;* their Chinese, Arabic, Persian, and Japanese equivalents; the medieval and early modern tavern; the Parisian cabaret or café; and the French Caveau, English drinking club, and Anacreontic society. Painting also devotes itself to the sympotic context of drinking in early modern bacchanals, kermisses, and merry companies.

14. John Clare in Maynard 51; Thomas Dekker in Marchant 266; Martin Parker in Maynard 33; Carey 248.

15. Waller 90; Calverley 27.

16. This is the original and enduring motif that drink carries in poetry: in Homer—"In wine, Menelaus, the gods devised the best remedy for mortal men to dissipate care" (Athenaeus 1.155); Alcaeus—"Wine's the duller-of-grief the son of Zeus and Semele / gave to men" (Martin 1972, 51); Euripides—"For filled with that good gift, suffering mankind forgets its grief" (1960a, 280); the *Old Testament* (as paraphrased by Burns)—

> *Gie him strong* Drink *until he wink,*
> *That's sinking in despair;*
> *'liquor guid, to fire his bluid,*
> *That's prest wi' grief an' care.*
>
> *There let him bowse an' deep carouse,*
> *Wi' bumpers flowing o'er,*
> *Till he forgets his loves or debts,*
> *An' minds his griefs no more* (173);

Otimo ne Tabito—

> Rather than worry
> Without result,
> One should put down
> A cup of rough sake (Bownas 32);

and Hafiz—

> But if the beggar's wise, he'll tell you this:
> Not tears of men—tears of the grape we need.
> (Streit 40)

17. Kenko, in fourteenth-century Japan, wrote that "liquor makes you forget your unhappiness, we are told, but when a man is drunk he may remember even his past griefs and weep over them" (152).

18. An intermediate trope would be "learning in a bottle," as in Alexander Brome's "Companion":

What need we take care for *Platonical* rules?
Or the precepts of *Aristotle?*
They that think to find learning in books are but fools,
True Philosophy lies in the bottle
(131);

or Tom Brown: "The same Divinity encourages the Youth of this University. . . . they find Rhetorick, Divinity, Physick, Philosophy, Law and all other Sciences in a Bottle" (Watson 17).

19. Many traditional carpe diem poems work through love rather than intoxication, but love also provides a "hit" of euphoria (in one of his four thousand books, Didymus the grammarian investigated "whether Anacreon was addicted more to lust or to liquor"), and there must be some kind of euphoric reward for the logic of carpe diem to operate: all carpe diem floats on forms of intoxication, not just *bibe diem* (Seneca in Campbell 1932, 23). As carpe diem is taught through Andrew Marvell's "To His Coy Mistress," the genre only advertises love's intensities, but the love and the drink of lyric poetry are interinvolved (the drink makes the love possible, the drink makes the love indispensable).

20. "Confronted with a cosmic disorder," Raymond Anselement writes, "the carousing speakers [in Brome's poetry] often propose their own universe. Drink-flushed faces become stars or heavens, and the circular motion of the round and the tipsy spinning of the head vie with the movements of the planets," as in his "Companion":

We'l drink till our cheeks are as starred as the skies,
Let the pale-colored students flowt us,
And our noses, like Comets, set fire on our eyes,
Till we bear the whole heavens about us.
(Anselement 43; Brome 131)

21. Congreve 350; Sedley in Hutchison 89–90. Here is the early-nineteenth-century Russian poet Nikolai Yazykov:

And love, well, what of love? 'Tis aye
Too cold if Bacchus be not nigh,
But with him—something too unruly!
She plays the role of double-dealer . . .
Just fill my glass up to the brim:
But not to pledge thy health, O Lila!

But as for Bacchus, O my friends,
How sweet our life when he attends,
No here-today-and-gone-tomorrow:
Today, the next day, he is ours!
(Myers 78)

22. The opposition between "Anacreon" and Omar replicates the division between alcohol and drugs in cultural mythology, whereby the former produces a positive pleasure, while the latter merely numbs pain.

23. Giangrande 106; Burnett 132. Sometimes the honors are rolled even further back: not Alcaeus but Archilochus of Paros (mid-seventh century BC): "Alcaeus has pride of place in this chapter [on drinking poetry], but Archilochus had provided a precedent for drinking-songs written in boisterous tone" (Campbell 1983, 34). Anacreon, even in his reduced role as the poet of the duality of drinking, takes a second place to Theognis of Megara (first half of the sixth century BC): "The cautionary tone is more commonly heard in Theognis's poetry. He counsels moderation again and again. . . . 'I am neither sober nor too drunk. The man who goes beyond due measure in drinking is no longer master of his tongue or his wits; his speech is foolish, a disgrace to sober men, and there is nothing that he is ashamed to do when he is drunk: he was sensible once, now he is a simpleton'" (Campbell 1983, 43–44).

24. In English Cavalier poetry, on the other hand, drinking was fighting, and from the depth of the tavern, one drank at one's enemies, as in Thomas Jordan's "A Chirping Cup":

It is the right way our foes to confound,
We'll bang the Rogues,
Hang the Rogues,
For *Charles* his glory,
And that will end the story.
(Sullivan 1981, 72)

25. Humphrey Trevelyan blames "Anacreon" for "an utterly false picture of Greek life, according to which the Greeks spend their days, and especially their nights, reclining flower-wreathed around the convivial board, in endless flirtation with easy-kissing girls" from which Johann Winckelmann and, even more, Friedrich Nietzsche, would rescue Western civilization (10).

26. "Anacreon"'s alcoholic legend seems to work particularly through statuary: an epigram by Leonidas of Tarentum on a statue of Anacreon declares the subject to be drunk as he accompanies himself on the lyre—"Stricken by wine he has lost one of his two shoes, but keeps a wrinkled foot in the other"—while Pausanias describes the posture on another statue as of a man singing while drunk (P. Rosenmeyer 23, 25; Campbell 1988, 2.33). Virtually every poet mentioned in this chapter has been accused of heavy drinking. Drink poetry, it would seem, is the genre on which persona theory flounders.

27. If the aged lover is a woman, as in Martial or Théophile de Viau, however, the spectacle is ridiculous or horrifying.

28. Also according to Warde, early modern Anacreontic movements should be read as critiques of reigning artistic, philosophical, and social trends. German anacreontism, for example, "was anti-baroque, anti-didactic, anti-rhetorical, anti-rationalistic, and anti-platonic [and emancipated German poetry] from bombast and obscurantism, moral didacticism, sectarian fervor, and philosophical abstraction. . . . Anacreonticism recommended itself because its simple clarity of form and expression contrasted so strongly with the rhetorical pathos of the baroque" (54, 61, 53). There was a similar revolt led by Abu Nuwas against the classical Arabic ode; a "transition from ode to lyric clearly took place during the thirteenth century. . . . with Sadi the lyric is firmly established as a medium for conveying human, carnal passion" (Arberry 1958, 207).

29. Herrick had produced excellent imitations of "Anacreon" earlier, in 1648, and Cowley translated some of the odes in 1656. These last were highly regarded by the Romantics who (like Hunt and Tom Moore) could themselves only produce jingly adaptations:

Often fit we round our brows,
One and all, the rosy boughs,
And with genial laughs carouse.
Love himself the golden-tressed,
Bacchus blithe, and Venus blessed,
Come from heaven to join our cheer,
So completely does appear
Comus, youth's restorer, here.
(Hunt 1923, 391)

30. Janet Levarie claims that English Anacreontic poetry also turned away from an original hedonism: "It is amusing that, accepting the theme of pleasure, the English shy away from the figure of the old man singing drunkenly and calling for his girls. Youth may choose such a life for a while, but the old man ought finally to be soberer and 'manage wisely.' The English speak of moderate drinking—a cup of good wine and a friend at the table. The Italians, like Anacreon, enjoy the madness of the drunkard. . . . The English desire for order and measure cuts off the energy of the god. The pagan gods are not mixed with the Christian nor seriously allowed any power" (230, 232).

31. Mason 105; Miner 110; Dundas 156; Revard 605.

32. It may also be possible to explain a long-standing lyric riddle through this opposition between "Anacreon" and Pindar: the inexplicable presence at the end of Elizabethan sonnet sequences by Edmund Spenser, Thomas Lodge, Samuel Daniel, and Shakespeare of a few playful Anacreontic verses (see Levarie, Miola).

33. "The Cup" uses the same motif of replacement: Vulcan is asked to put aside the manufacture of armor in order to make a goblet; it is to be decorated not with heroes or constellations but with vines and Bacchus: in John Oldham's translation:

I'll have no Battles on my Plate,
Lest sight of them should Brawls create,
Lest that provoke to Quarrels too,
Which Wine it self enough can do.
(Levarie 226; Oldham 217)

In a famous letter to Charles Diodati, John Milton opposed epic to Anacreontic poetry as water to wine: "But why complain that banquet and bottle frighten poetry away? Song loves Bacchus, and Bacchus loves songs. Ovid sent back poems from the land of the Coralli, but they did not have banquets or cultivate the vine there, so the poems were no good, and every page smells of the wine he has been drinking. The Roman lute-player was drunk with four-year-old wine when he sang his sweet songs about Glycera and about Chloe with her golden hair. So grand banquets are quite all right for elegiac poets, and they can get drunk on old wine as often as they like. But the poet who writes about wars, and about a heaven ruled over by a Jove who has out-grown his boyhood, about heroes who stick to their duty and princes who are half gods . . . let this poet live frugally, like the philosopher from Samos, and let herbs pro-vide his harmless diet. Let a bowl of beech-wood, filled with clear water, stand by him, and may he drink soberly from a pure spring" (118).

34. Goethe, however, later rejected the pretty Hellenism of "Anacreon" for Hafiz.

35. An engraving by James Gillray in William Henry Irving's *John Gay's London,* facing page 336, shows the "Anacreonticks in Full Song": all are drinking and smoking and appear to be quite drunk. There is a punch bowl on the table and an overturned glass, while the floor is littered with spent pipes and empty bottles.

36. There was also an earlier fall, the redemption of which was, ironically, the Romantic drinking song: the seventeenth-century Cavalier drinking songs and the drinking songs of Lord Rochester are written as a fall because of the "growing coarseness of Anacreontic poetry in England from the late seventeenth-century onwards" (Thor-mahlen 17; see also Damrosch). The drinking songs of Burns are read as the recovery.

3. DOUBLE DIONYSUS

1. "The imagery on the vases generally highlights this function of Dionysus who, elsewhere in Greek culture, is not solely the god of wine," Lissarrague writes; "on the vases, however, he is almost always portrayed near a vine, holding his drinking vase" (1990, 18).

2. Homer in Eddy 101; Rosenmeyer 1992, 261; Chaucer 181.

3. Euripides 1960a, 204; Baudelaire in Detienne 1; Otto 147.

4. Winnington-Ingram in Sale 81; Vernant 204; Segal 18; Dodds 77.

5. Sheila McNally insists that the pairing of maenads and satyrs is fully present in the plastic art of antiquity: "From the beginning of recognizably Dionysiac scenes the dominant theme is the mixed satyr-maenad band, sometimes alone, sometimes with Dionysos, Dionysos and Ariadne, or Hephaistos." In literature, however, she writes, "the mixed band is not mentioned until much later, and is never significant" (109–10).

6. The "maenads were women who received their ecstasy naturally from the god himself, the komasts were males who acquired their altered state artificially from the god's gift of wine" (Hoffman 111). "Males clearly worshipped Dionysus too, but in different ways: above all through drinking parties, which probably included singing and possibly some dancing, but not outdoor dancing of the Maenadic variety" (Nussbaum xxxii).

7. Thornton Wilder wrote a modern satyr play to accompany his translation of *Alcestis*. Titled "The Drunken Sisters," it told of Apollo getting the three Fates drunk and tricking them into sparing Admetus's life.

8. This separation is undermined in other ways as well, according to Xavier Riu: In *Ion*, Euripides implies that men participated in the maenadic ceremonies. In *The Bacchae*, "he shows quite clearly what happens to a man who goes up the mountain as a maenad; yet in the same *Bacchae* he states that Cadmus and Tiresias go to the mountains dressed as maenads" (175).

9. Evidence from antiquity that seeing double was a sign of drunkenness can be found in Ovid 1990, 148; Petronius 70; and Strato in *Greek Anthology*, 4.383–4.

10. The play equivocates three times between ecstatic religion and intoxication: first, where Pentheus says, "Reports reached me of some strange mischief here, stories of our women leaving home to frisk in mock ecstasies among the thickets on the mountain, dancing in honor of the latest divinity, a certain Dionysus, whoever he may be! In their midst stand bowls brimming with wine. And then, one by one, the women wander off to hidden nooks where they serve the lusts of men" (201–2); second, where he tells Cadmus, "Only your age restrains me now from sending you to prison with those Bacchic women for importing here to Thebes these filthy mysteries. . . . When once you see the glint of wine shining at the feasts of women, then you may be sure the festival is rotten" (203); and third, where he answers Dionysus, who has asked him if he would like to see the women's revels, "Of course I'd be sorry to see them drunk" (228).

11. Pentheus parallels another mythic character, Lycurgus, whom Dionysus also punished with intoxication and its consequences. King of the Edonians, Lycurgus insulted the god as he came West with his bacchants. The bacchants were imprisoned, but Dionysus found asylum with Thetis, who hid him beneath the sea. Afterward, Dionysus maddened Lycurgus as he was pruning a vine, so that he turned the axe from the vine stock to his own son, Dryas. Lycurgus was eventually drawn and quartered by his subjects (Apollodorus 62). In the legend as related by Hyginus, "Lycurgus drove Dionysus out of his kingdom, calling his divinity into question. Then after drinking wine he tried to rape his own mother. . . . To stop a recurrence of such disgraceful behavior he tried to uproot all the vines, but Dionysus made him mad and he killed his wife and son. Then Dionysus exposed him to the panthers on Mount Rhodope" (Grimal 264).

12. See Grube 415; O'Brien-Moore 140; Padel 81; Rosenmeyer 1968, 151; Vernant 395; Winnington-Ingram 53.

13. Compare this with a parallel confusion in classical scholarship: "Scholars used to think of him as a foreign god who became naturalized in Greece, but the truth is

the opposite: he is a Greek god who came to be seen as foreign" (Woodruff xiii). According to Sarah Peirce, the opposition of maenadism and wine discussed earlier corresponds to the distinction between an "eastern and Aegean Dionysus associated with wine, fertility, satyrs, spring and the spring festival of the Anthesteria" as opposed to a "Boeotian Dionysus associated with Thracian ecstatic cults, maenads, winter and winter festivals such as the Lenaia" (68).

14. Also, "filled with that good gift, suffering mankind forgets its grief; from it comes sleep, with it oblivion of the troubles of the day. There is no other medicine for misery" (204); "These blessings he gave: laughter to the flute and the losing of cares and the wine-bowl casts its sleep on feasters crowned with ivy" (208); and "he who gave to mortal men the gift of lovely wine by which our suffering is stopped. And if there is no god of wine, there is no love, nor other pleasures left to men" (225). Segal would object to the assertion of duality as a great simplification: "To pose an alternative of praise or blame, attraction or horror, is to dissolve that mysterious and perhaps ultimately unformulable coexistence of opposites that is the essence of Dionysus and of the realm of mythic and symbolic representation to which the Dionysiac stands so close, in music, mask, and drama. What Euripides gives us in the *Bacchae* is not a choice between one side or another, but an experience, an experience that involves the doublings, ambiguities, crossing of opposites into one another that form the essence of Dionysus himself" (20). This may be true, but there is also a script of dualism, of good and bad effects that belongs to wine and its congeners.

4. SOCRATES UNDRUNK

1. See also Plato 1951, 12; Neumann 33; Plochmann 328; Morgan 86; Hyland 120.

2. The "two elements [poetry and philosophy] are welded together with such consummate art that to dissect them is likely to destroy the perfect balance of the whole" (Plato 1951, 9).

3. All citations to *The Symposium* in this chapter refer to the Walter Hamilton translation.

4. One occasionally glimpses another Socrates, for example, the philosopher of Aristophanes' *Clouds,* whom the tradition refuses to recognize, or the following Socrates from Diogenes Laertius: "Frequently, owing to his vehemence in argument, men set upon him with their fists or tore his hair out; and . . . for the most part he was despised and laughed at, yet bore all this ill patiently" (151).

5. Apollodorus's friend upbraids him for the extravagance of his delusions about philosophy: "As far as I can see you believe that, but for Socrates, everybody in the world is wretched" (35).

6. See also Nikolchina 243 and Nye 198.

7. Glaucon to Apollodorus: "Don't make fun of me . . . tell me when this party happened" (34). Eryximachus to Aristophanes: "If you preface what you have to say by making us laugh, you will force me to be on the watch for jokes in your speech, which might otherwise run its course in peace" (58). Aristophanes to the company: "I

know that Eryximachus is anxious to make fun of my speech, but he is not to suppose that in saying this I am pointing at Pausanias and Agathon" (64–65). Aristophanes to Eryximachus: "Remember my request, and don't make fun of it" (65). Agathon to Phaedrus: "There is my speech, Phaedrus, a decent compound of playfulness and gravity, and let it be dedicated to the god as the best medley that I can contrive" (72). Socrates to Alcibiades: "What have you in mind? Are you going to make fun of me by a mock-panegyric? Or what?" (99). Alcibiades to the company: "He will perhaps think that I mean to make fun of him, but my object . . . is truth, not ridicule" (100).

8. Since "the symposiarch must not be drunk," Joel Relihan wonders, "Plutarch is hard put to explain Alcibiades' behavior in what must still be the model symposion/symposium" (232).

9. See also Sider 47 and Morgan 94.

10. For Socrates as Eros, see Bacon 424 and Rosen 232. For Alcibiades as Dionysus, see Rosen 287 and Anderson 13.

11. See Plato 1951, 121 and Phillips 270.

12. Guy Michael Hedreen cites a fragment of Pindar as the "earliest surviving reference" to a "wise silen," but the reference, which is cited by Pausanias, doesn't support his contention (177).

13. According to Lissarrague, a "remarkable transformation" in Greek vase painting occurs in the years 440–30 BC: "It is no longer a nymph or a maenad, but a satyr of a new type, an elderly one, who receives the child," Dionysus. These new satyrs must be wise, Lissarrague contends, because they are aged and because they have been chosen as Dionysus's nurse: "In vase imagery, the idea of a wisdom belonging to satyrs is not self-evident and appears only late, when a paternal figure of the satyr is developed that contrasts with the puerile character of the younger of his fellows." Lissarrague then goes on to undermine his contention, admitting that the pictorial narrative (the self-evident proof of wisdom) says just the opposite: "On the vases, it is the moment of Silenus' capture that is retained; Silenus, caught by means of a fountain of wine, is a victim of his own inebriation: strange sort of wisdom indeed. . . . The wisdom, it seems, is more like a fool's bargain" (1993, 216–18).

14. Before Nietzsche, Erasmus and Rabelais made much of Plato's image of a wise Silenus. Erasmus is very taken by it, and he takes it most ideally. It was "Erasmus' favorite symbol for the disparity between appearance and reality," is "mentioned in the *Colloquies* and the *Enchiridion*," and is a "major rhetorical figure in *The Praise of Folly*" (Baines 45). In the *Sileni Alcibiadis* (1515), Silenus has become unrecognizably generalized as an image of the divine presence in the heart of even the ugliest of us. But even Erasmus's Silenus is both wise and foolish: "The subject of these statuettes is taken from that ridiculous old Silenus, the schoolmaster of Bacchus, whom the poets call the jester of the gods (they have their buffoons like the princes of our time)" (Erasmus in Phillips 269). When the trope descends to Rabelais, it is still used to construe Socrates' ideality or divinity, but it has shifted from a statue to a box and what is inside is no longer a little figure of the gods but drugs: "But inside these boxes were kept rare drugs, such as balm, ambergris,

caradamum, musk, civet, mineral essences, and other precious things"—although this is immediately sublimated: "But had you opened that box, you would have found inside a heavenly and priceless drug: a superhuman understanding, miraculous virtue, invincible courage, unrivalled sobriety, unfailing contentment, etc." (37).

15. Walter Kaiser and Alice Goodman repeat Plato's move, making an odd, disruptive comparison between the Socrates of the *Symposium* and a seemingly unlike figure—in their case Shakespeare's Falstaff ("At first glance there would not seem to be the remotest resemblance between the wise fool of Athens and the fat fool of Eastcheap"). Like Plato they go on to justify this comparison philosophically and never even mention that both are heavy drinkers (Kaiser in Goodman 97).

16. The comic playwright Eupolis left us the following fragment:

Socrates was next; he ran through a Stesichorus
Leider recital—and went off with the decanter.

The scholiast to Aristophanes' *Clouds* claims that although Eupolis "does not often introduce Socrates, he hits him off better than Aristophanes in the whole of the *Clouds*" (Ferguson 173).

17. For the first see also Osborne, for the second Ellis 1989, 60. It is generally agreed that Alcibiades was not involved in this offense but in another with which it was regularly confused, the mocking celebration of the mysteries in private houses.

18. See also Dover liv. But Socrates' death is also blamed on Aristophanes: "According to Plato, when Socrates stood upon his trial, twenty-four years after the *Clouds*, he felt his most serious danger to be the general misunderstanding and prejudice caused in the mind of the Court by 'his old accusers,' who had persuaded them [the Court] in their childhood or youth that 'there was a person called Socrates, a wise man, a meditator on the things above us, and a researcher into all the secrets beneath the earth, who made the worse cause into the better'" (Murray 1933, 97).

5. "OUT, LOATH'D MED'CINE! O HATED POTION, HENCE!"

1. Here is William Faulkner on the effects of drink: "When I have one martini I feel bigger, wiser, taller. When I have a second, I feel superlative. When I have more there's no holding me" (Blotner 2.1487).

2. One narrative wrinkle in the Alexander legends has the magical waters withheld by a younger man from an older who "needs" it more (Devereux 89). This motif also occurs in the tales by Shelley and Balzac and in Harrison Ainsworth, *The Elixir of Life*. In Shelley's "Mortal Immortal," the apprentice accidentally drinks a potion brewed by his master, Cornelius Agrippa, for himself. And in Balzac's "Elixir of Life," the saving potion is withheld by Don Juan from his dying father.

3. Edgar Allan Poe's cousin Neilson attested that "he passed by a *single indulgence*, from a condition of perfect sobriety to one bordering on the madness usually occasioned by long continued intoxication" (Robertson 121). The mythology of the single

glass of liquor that is written into Poe's life and works of fiction, like "The Angel of the Odd" or *The Narrative of Arthur Gordon Pym*, reflects a notable feature of alcoholism—the reversal of tolerance, whereby an alcoholic who has been able to drink inordinately without showing signs of intoxication suddenly finds himself weaving and slurring after just one drink (see Bonaparte 87).

4. Hawthorne's interest in elixirs of youth is also reflected at the center of his canon in tales where magic drinks that are primarily poisons confer a form of immortality, tales like "Rappaccini's Daughter" and, by implication, "The Birthmark." At the end of *Septimius Felton* and *The Dolliver Romance,* the elixir of youth proves, like the drink which Giovanni gives to Beatrice as an antidote, to be a deadly poison: "What if he should see the bottle, and secretly put it to his lips and drink a great gulp, and go home and be found dead the next morning?" (Davidson 1949, 125).

5. Regardless of the literal narrative data, criticism generally reads Shakespeare's potion as an inebriant. Jan Kott refers to the "entire action of this hot night" in Shakespeare's play as a "drunken party": Hermia "is ashamed. She does not quite yet realize that day has come. She is still partly overwhelmed by night. She has drunk too much" (1965, 176, 179). Neil Isaacs and Jack Reese write that "intoxication and sexual promiscuity are strongly implied. Some form of intoxicant was an essential ingredient of Dionysian revelry and ecstasy, and Oberon's magic potion . . . clearly produces an inebriated state. . . . Under the influence of the herb, the four lovers and Titania act in a manner suggestive of frenzied promiscuity" (353).

6. A similar secularization of the fountain of youth occurs in George Ade's 1911 poem of that name, which continues the search of Ponce de León for the magical waters, until, in 1907, he visits a Virginia resort:

> And strange to relate, as the cup went around,
> The old boys began to get up and expound . . .
> For would you believe it, though some in that room
> Seemed old and decrepit and marked for the tomb,
> The magical cup took them back to their teens
> By some supernatural method or means;
> Until doctor, professor and lawyer and sage,
> Arrived at a most irresponsible age.
> (72)

7. Sucking, or suckling, is the core of alcoholism in psychoanalytic theory: "As we have repeatedly shown, the predilection to wine, alcohol and drinking, however deeply tinged with later acquired homosexuality, primarily derives from the first nutrient proffered the child—the milk of the mother's breast" (Bonaparte 523).

8. A paragraph in Plutarch's *De Iside et Osiride* informs us that the king-priests "began to drink [wine] . . . at the time of Psammetichus, and before that they did not drink wine or pour it in libation as something acceptable to the gods, but as the blood of those who had once made war against the gods, believing that vines grew from these when they had fallen and mingled with the earth" (1970, 125–27).

9. There is a coherent distribution of narcotics and drink in *Dracula:* upper-class men and women take drugs—mostly sedatives—and lower-class men and women drink alcohol. The working-class male is invariably represented as thirsty for strong drink, and this is always expressed as a euphemism: "The extraordinary state of drouth to which they had been reduced by the dusty nature of their occupation"; my "appreciation of their efforts in a liquid form"—as opposed to drug references that are invariably straight-forward: "I asked Dr. Seward to give me a little opiate of some kind" (156, 227, 260). When the servants are drugged, it is a result of drinking what they thought was wine.

10. According to Colin Manlove, Hyde's "drug is a mere catalyst permitting him to carry the process to the limit: it is, almost, reducible to a mechanism for allowing the full expression of his nature. To this extent the drug itself is quite unimportant" (96). Unlike *A Midsummer Night's Dream,* however, one can't read through the drug; the drug sticks, as Theodore Watts-Dunton says: "A story of astonishing brutality, in which the separation of the two natures of the man's soul is effected not by psycho-logical development, and not by the 'awful alchemy' of the spirit-world beyond the grave, as in all the previous versions, but by the operation of a dose of some supposed new drug" (Geduld 107). So much so that Henry James complained, "I have some difficulty in accepting the business of the powders, which seems to me too explicit and explanatory. The powders constitute the machinery of the transformation, and it will probably have struck many readers that this uncanny process would be more con-ceivable (so far as one may speak of the conceivable in such a case), if the author had not made it so definite" (171). Early readers, however, kept the drug in focus and made it the meaning of the tale: Dr. Clifford Allen notes the influence this possibility had on the public's reception of Stevenson's story: "The suggestion that there might be a drug which would enable the 'good' personality to be separated from the 'bad' . . . was a new and, to most people, a horrible idea. So much excitement did the story cause that sermons were preached about it, and the more timid of the Victorians fervently hoped that the doctors who at that time seemed to be discovering everything would not unearth the mysterious drug which Stevenson made Dr. Jekyll use to free the un-pleasant Mr. Hyde" (Geduld 8). This, apparently, is how Oscar Wilde read the tale: "Even Mr. Robert Louis Stevenson, that delightful master of delicate and fanciful prose, is tainted with this modern vice, for we know positively no other name for it. There is such a thing as robbing a story of its reality by trying to make it too true. . . . the transformation of Dr. Jekyll reads dangerously like an experiment in the *Lancet*" (530).

11. Stevenson goes on to say that Hyde was "not, Great Gods! a mere voluptuary. There is no harm in voluptuaries; and . . . none—no harm whatever in what prurient fools call 'immorality'" (Eigner 150).

12. Oates finds John Jasper, an opium addict in Charles Dickens's *Mystery of Edwin Drood* who "oscillates between 'good' and 'evil' impulses in his personality," to be an antecedent of Stevenson's doctor (607).

13. According to William Veeder, Stevenson makes a slip of the pen when he chooses the bizarre name of "Maw" for Jekyll's chemist: "Orality is stressed through-out the novel in the patriarchs' consumption of wine and in Jekyll's drinking of the

potion. . . . Also like the regressive Jekyll, Utterson is characterized by orality. . . . He seems to stand for another Jekyll-and-Hyde tale which is intoxicatory and benign: 'and when the wine was to his taste, something eminently human beaconed from his eye'" (Veeder and Hirsch 128, 134, 145). Vladimir Nabokov also puts the wine in binary opposition to the potion: "There is a delightful winey taste about this book; in fact, a good deal of old mellow wine is drunk in the story: one recalls the wine that Utterson so comfortably sips. This sparkling and comforting draft is very different from the icy pangs caused by the chameleon liquor, the magic reagent that Jekyll brews in his dusty laboratory" (180).

14. Shakespeare 956; Nashe in Watson 14; Lyly 187.

15. The novella can be read, too, as a parable about the self-immolation of alcoholism. The references to Jekyll's drinking habits and the reminders of Hyde's "brutish, physical insensitivity" point to inebriation. A drunkard is someone who, during a binge, reveals his latent ogre and afterward, in remorseful bouts, is shocked by what his alter ego has done. The vice of drunkenness by degrees assumes control of human character (Davenport-Hines 311).

16. This notion is radically signified in the John Barrymore film on the morning after the transformation. Dr. Jekyll wakes troubled, and we see a huge fantasy spider creep out from beside the bed and crawl into bed with him. It lies on Jekyll, and he transforms into Hyde. In an earlier sequence, the drunken father of a maiden Hyde courts breaks down in d.t.'s, thinking he's covered with red ants.

6. SPIRITUAL INTOXICATION AND THE METAPHORICS OF HEAVEN

1. George Cave writes that drunkenness is the only realm of human experience that can be used to describe the ecstasy of union with God (20), and Annamarie Schimmel claims that "the age-old symbolism of the sacred intoxication . . . better than any other symbol expresses the overwhelming power of the mystical state" (1980, 149). An opposite rhetoric, where "drunk" means locked in the darkness of this world, also has religious circulation, mainly in the discourse of Gnosticism—"He who thus shall know perceives. . . . as one who, having been drunk, has turned from his drunkenness" (Foerster 59). This usage occurs later as well: For Cotton Mather, spiritual drunkenness is evil, taking the form of "Corrupt Doctrines" that "as it were intoxicate & inebriate the Souls of them that do imbibe or embrace them" (Warner 233), and, in 1680, George Hicks lamented "the Poison of Enthusiasm," which is "the Spiritual drunkenness" that makes men feel inspired (Tucker 148).

2. This list includes Philo, Plotinus, and Proclus; Origen, Gregory of Nyssa (the notion of sober intoxication was "particularly important" for him [Screech 1980, 74]), Ambrose, John Chrysostom, Augustine, Gregory the Great, Bernard of Clairvaux, Richard of St. Victor, Jacques de Vitry, Aelfric, Alcuin, Isaac of Ninevah ("the image of drunkenness, which is so often used by Isaac" [Wensinck li–lii]), Bede, and Dionysius the Areopagite; and many later mystical writers like St. Teresa de Avila, St. John of the

Cross, Ramon Lull, Fray Luis de León, Jan van Ruusbroec, Richard Crashaw, Henry Vaughan, Thomas Traherne, and, above all, Mechthild von Magdeburg. For secondary work on the concept of spiritual intoxication, see especially Lewy; also Arbman, Danielou, Louth, Magennis, McGinn, Runia, Screech 1980, and Sterling.

3. Ecstasy: St. Gregory of Nyssa, "Since inebriety of this kind arises from the wine the Lord sets before His guests, through which there arises a going out of the soul towards divine things" (Toal 3.125); Isaac, "And upon the wings of faith . . . [the soul] is lifted up above the circle of the visible world and, as drunk, it is constantly in ecstatic thought of God" (Wensinck 253); St. Teresa, "When experiencing this joy, it [the soul] is so deeply inebriated and absorbed that it seems to be beside itself in a kind of Divine intoxication, knowing not what it is desiring or saying or asking for" (Williams 1963, 91); Jan van Ruusbroec, "Out of this bliss [the descent of God into the heart] comes spiritual drunkenness. Spiritual drunkenness means that man receives more sensible relish and well-being than his heart or his desire can either desire or contain. Spiritual drunkenness brings man to strange and remarkable behavior" (Verdeyen 113). Mystical union: St. John of the Cross: "When memory is united with God, it is left without form or shape. Imagination is lost, and memory is drunk with the highest taste" (de Nicolás 187); St. Bernard, "A love of sufficient ardor is a kind of inebriation; and so it must needs be in order that the soul may have the mad audacity to aspire to the divine union" (Gilson 112). Divine love or grace: Philo: "When grace fills the soul, that soul thereby rejoices and smiles and dances, for it is possessed with a frenzy, so that to many of the unenlightened it may seem to be drunken, crazy and beside itself" (Wolfson 2.49); Isaac, "From time to time he will become drunk by it as by wine; his limbs will relax, his mind will stand still and his heart will follow God as a captive. And so he will be, as I have said, like a man drunk by wine" (Wensinck xliii). God: Dionysius, "[God, like a drunken lover] stands outside of all good things, being the superfullness of all these things" (McGinn 179). Christ: Origen, "But when . . . [the Bride] now reflects upon the teaching that flows forth from the Bridegroom's breasts, she is amazed and marvels: she sees that it is far superior to that with which she had been gladdened as with spiritual wine served to her by the holy fathers and prophets" (1957, 65); R. P. Diego de Estella, "Even, too, like unto Noah, who 'planted a vine and drinking of the wine' in such abundance was inebriated. Thou wert inebriated by the wine of love" (17). The New Testament as the vital words of Christ: Bede, "For truly he consumes the banquet of the table of life but is not filled up, and drinks the cup of salvation but is not made drunk, who has indeed learned the words of Scripture . . . but has not, however, changed his life. . . . he drinks but is not made drunk, who gladly hears the commandments of life but remains inactive and lazy in fulfilling them" (Magennis 1999, 142); Ambrose, the "word of more fervent spirit that inebriates like wine and gladdens the heart of man (Ps 103:15), and also the milky word, pure and clear" (McGinn 208). Holy Ghost: Isaac, the Holy Ghost causes the impulses to be "drowned in a heavy drunkenness and man is no longer in this world" (Wensinck 117).

4. Sober drunkenness can be rationalized to mean an apparent drunkenness, referring to the mistaken reception by Romans and Jews of the ecstasy of the disciples:

"When the Apostles come out of the room in which they have received the gift of speech, and begin preaching in Jerusalem, the general sense of amazement at these uneducated men speaking fluently and in foreign languages receives one particular persuasive explanation: 'These men are full of new wine'" (Campbell 1994, 186). But this is obviously a false gloss.

5. "Therefore the mystic wants that even the *mohtaseb* [market police], the model of sober orthodoxy, should taste this Divine wine which is licit and whose fragrance makes all the saints both visible and invisible" (Schimmel 1980, 150).

6. Athenaeus in Mulroy 130; Trilling 1978, 15, Prior 1.159. Samuel Taylor Coleridge wrote of Newton that he

> Feels his pure breast with rapturous joy possest,
> Inebriate in the holy ecstasy,

and in "The Nightingale," of "tipsy Joy that reels with tossing head" (Cooke 39). In *Prometheus Unbound*, Percy Bysshe Shelley describes an oracular vapor "hurled up" a

> chasm in the realm of Demigorgon,
> Which lonely men drink wandering in their youth,
> And call truth, virtue, love, genius, or joy;
> That maddening wine of life, whose dregs they drain
> To deep intoxication; and uplift,
> Like Maenads who cry loud, Evoe! Evoe!
> The voice which is contagion to the world.
> (340)

One thinks also of the poetry of Emily Dickinson.

7. If we read wine allegorically we understand ecstasy, but if we read Dionysus allegorically we understand wine. Mythographers read the life and exploits of Dionysus to produce a description of drink and its effects. In Francois Pomey's poem *Pantheum mythicum* (1659), the qualities of inebriety are symbolized by Dionysus's nudity, "ivy crown, youthfulness, femininity, maskings, and hilarious mirth" (Allen 237). The sixth-century Latin grammarian Fulgentius had written, "He is also said to ride on tigers, because all intoxication goes with savageness. . . . Dionysus is depicted as a youth, because drunkenness is never mature" (77).

8. "Whether the psychedelic movement would have happened without Dr. Leary," Jay Stevens writes in *Storming Heaven,* by far the best book on this cluster of events, "is a matter of debate, but there can be no question that he defined its public style, churning out pamphlets, books, and records that equated LSD with the discovery of fire and the invention of the wheel" (xv). Leary remembers that "Allen [Ginsberg], the quintessential egalitarian, wanted everyone to have the option of taking mind-expanding drugs. It was the fifth freedom—the right to manage your own nervous system" (Dunaway 370).

9. This does not include a "shadow line" of research conducted by many of the same scientists for the CIA in their search for a mind-control drug (Stevens 79–82).

10. Here is Octavio Paz on the subject: "Religious believers—and those who are upholders of conventional morality—are repelled by the idea of drugs as the key to divine vision, or at least to a certain spiritual peace. Those who react in this way may have failed to realize that drugs are not a substitute for the old supernance powers. The disappearance of the idea of God in the modern world is not due to the appearance of drugs (for drugs have after all been known and used for thousands of years). We might, in fact, say the exact opposite: the use of drugs betrays the fact that man is not a *natural* being; he experiences not only thirst, hunger, dreams, and sexual pleasure, but also a nostalgia for the infinite. . . . Confronted by experiences such as those described by Michaux, we may again ask the question: is pharmacy a substitute for grace, is poetic vision a biochemical reaction?" (77, 85).

11. One thesis of Eliade's book on shamanism is that "narcotics already represents a decadence and that, in default of true ecstatic methods, recourse is taken to narcotics to induce trance" (417). Michael Ripinsky-Naxon calls Eliade's assertions "hapless and unfounded" (132). Peter Furst and many others believe recent evidence supports the view that the use of hallucinogens in shamanism goes back to the Paleolithic and Mesolithic eras, and that, in fact, the substitution of disciplinary practices like yoga for drugs represents a later stage in the development of religion (1972, ix). See also McKenna 144; Reichel-Dolmatoff 12; and Rudgley 41.

12. Braden 1967, 41; Bevan 156; Barnard 582; Metzner 4; Burkert 108; Cheever 378; Duerr 197; Otto 145; Davis 138.

13. Metzner 4; Norman Taylor in Solomon 1966, 10; Arbman 257; Rickels 275; Toussaint-Samat 575; Dols 257. When the revisionist project includes a materialist rereading of Christianity (or Western philosophy), however, warning flags are raised: "Yet while acknowledging the significance of drugs here and elsewhere, we must not get things out of proportion as, for instance, John Allegro so manifestly does in his curious book, *The Sacred Mushroom and the Cross*. We must not fall into the trap of assuming that shamanism and ecstasy can only be produced with the aid of such powerful pharmacological aids" (Lewis 1988, 71). (And Robert Masters and Jean Houston suspect that Gordon Wasson's "mycophobic zeal exceeds his academic rigor when he suggests that Plato came upon his theory of an ideal world of archetypes after having spent a night at the temple of Eleusis drinking a mushroom potion" [1968, 252].)

14. See Hughes 1965, 102 and Quaife passim. It has also been suggested that the Salem outbreak of 1692 was the result of accidental ergot poisoning (Sharpe 10; Quaife 5).

15. The opposition between Islam, on the one hand, and Christianity and Zoroastrianism, on the other, is figured by wine and drinking in Persian poetry, as Jamal al-Din Salman (1300–76) writes:

Saki, the wine he poured into the cup—
that was a fire he kindled in my heart;
that wine's perfume enticed me from the mosque
and clapped me in the Christian hostelry.

The road to mosque our elder too has left
And turned aside into the Magian lane.
(Arberry 1958, 323)

"The resignation that Okura expresses is Buddhist rather than Confucian, and in the following generation Yakamochi, whose clan had continued to fall in status and power, advocates not the Taoist virtues of wine, but the Way of the Buddha" (Brower and Miner 91); "Tabito's poems on sake represent what may be called Taoistic epicureanism" (Brower and Miner 91, 147); the triumph of Taoism over Confucianism was accompanied by a great surge of hedonism: "Why preserve life if you could not enjoy it?" (Fang Dai 17); "the third couplet [of a poem by Lu You] has an unmistakable Daoist flavor, with its 'drunken roaming,' 'complete abandon,' and 'freedom and ecstasy'" (Duke 122). For Judaism as a drink religion, see Drower 11, Nock 2.897; Jastrow 190. Erwin R. Goodenough states that wine was an important part of later Jewish culture, so much so that the golden vine in the Temple "suggested to many gentiles that the Jews were worshipping Dionysus" (6.128).

16. Desmond Seward cites "certain German miniatures from the twelfth to the fifteenth centuries [which] depict Christ in his Passion as a crucified and crowned vine-dresser treading out the grapes, the blood spurting from his wounds to mingle with the grape juice" (32). In one of Crashaw's Latin epigrams, Christ is represented as a wine cask broached by the spear. Crashaw fears that the liquor is too strong to drink (Williams 1963, 96). According to some Hebrew and Christian cosmographies, the fruit of Eden was the grape, not the apple (see Drower 62; Raymond 46). Similarly, Schimmel recounts an Islamic creation myth in which "Man was created, as Rumi says in a mythological image, from the first sip of Divine wine that fell into the dust, whereas Gabriel the Archangel was created from that sip which fell into heaven" (1980, 247). And Omar alludes, in one of his poems, to a "mystical legend, that in the beginning Divine Love, the saki of God the Lover, poured wine for God the Beloved on forty successive mornings, and so created the world" (Arberry 1971, 20).

17. Although Christianity was a wine religion, it had abandoned what Andrew Malcolm calls "a drunken approach to God" by the time of the Protestant reformation (34). Carl Jung had a clear sense of this schism: "The medieval carnivals and *jeux de paume* in the Church were abolished relatively early; consequently the carnival became secularized and with it divine intoxication vanished from the sacred precincts. . . . But intoxication, that most direct and dangerous form of possession, turned away from the gods and enveloped the human world with its exuberance and pathos. The pagan religions met this danger by giving drunken ecstasy a place within their cult. Heraclitus doubtless saw what was at the back of it when he said, "But Hades is that same Dionysos in whose honor they go mad and keep the feast of the wine-vat" (1953, 136).

18. While the alcoholic imagery may have come from earlier religious formations, it was anchored and justified by metaphoric sites in the new gospels. Early Christians,

writes Peter Demetz, "found the literary cues for the interpretations of the pre-Christian images mainly in two passages of the Scripture: first, in Psalm 128 in which . . . a good wife was likened to a fruitful vine, and secondly, in the Gospel of John, xv.1, in which the vine appears as the image of Christ himself" (524). According to Jean Danielou, the biblical discourse of intoxication "is found in connection with Wisdom's banquet (Prov. 9.3), the Canticle (5.2), and the *goodly chalice* of the Psalms (Ps. 22.5)" (34).

19. "When distillation was discovered in Europe in the twelfth century, it was the monks who—for medical purposes—first made *aqua vitae*" and "countless *eaux-de-vie* each with its secret formula (Chartreuse, Benedictine, etc.). . . . Even the first maker of Scotch whisky known to history was a friar" (Seward 16).

20. There are others both pagan and Christian of whom this magic is predicated: Oenotropae, the changers of water into wine, was the name of the three or four daughters of King Anius in Delos because they had received from Dionysus the power of changing water into wine, and anything else they chose into grain and olives (Bell 1982, 276). In Christianity this miracle also belongs to Saints Columbanus, Willibrord, Cuthbert, Machutus, and others, while Saint Brigit changed vats of water into mead (Magennis 1986b, 7–8; Gayre 60).

21. See also St. Teresa in Arbman 81 and Richard Crashaw's "Sancta Maria Dolorum,"

> where the poet must
> drinke, and drinke, and doe his worst,
> To drowne the wantonness of his wild thirst.
> (Williams 1963, 91)

22. Indeterminacy becomes a major figure in the interpretation of Hafiz: so Friedrich Rückert, the German poet and orientalist, described the nature of Hafiz's poetry as evoking "'something metaphysical' when he talks 'about something sensual' and vice versa, so that the secret of its poetry is 'unübersinnlich'—one of Ruckert's many word-coinings meaning something like 'inextricable by thought'" (Bürgel 10).

23. The practice in contemporary Western commentary is to read Hafiz's work materially as *rind* poetry: poetry spoken by a libertine (a character type alleged to be based on the biographical, fictional, and poetic persona of Abu Nuwas) who boasts of his exploits in the tavern and praises the wine that is his only object of devotion; he "prefers honest sin to hypocritical piety and urges his listener to 'seize the day.'" As if "a kind of drunkards' order had been established as a rival to the Sufi Order," "he wickedly puns on the sacred words of the Koran to say that wine is good, very much as the Goliardic squibs of the Middle Ages besmirched the sacred Latin of the Vulgate and the Mass" (Meisami 93; Rypka 268; Draper 10).

24. Consider Rumi's words, "The drunkenness of this world vanishes after one night's slumber, / The drunkenness of the beaker of God accompanies you into the tomb" (Glünz 27).

25. The intoxication in question is somehow not an intoxication, just as, for Wordsworth, taste is not a taste: he speaks disdainfully of "Men . . . who talk of Poetry as a matter of amusement and idle pleasure; who will converse with us as gravely about a

taste for Poetry, as they express it, as if it were a thing as indifferent as a taste for . . . Frontiniac, or Sherry" (Trilling 1965, 61).

7. DRINKING IN STYLE

1. Sometimes of scientific inspiration as well: August Kekulé solved the problem of the benzine molecule by understanding it to be a ring rather than a chain of carbon atoms "when in a fatigue- (or alcohol-) engendered daydream he saw a snake swallow its tail" (Ghiselin 226).

2. There are two formulas for Gambara's genius: in the first he is only a mediocre composer until transformed by intoxication. The second is a Platonic reading of the tale in which the ideal music that he reproduces is so far beyond existing forms that his contemporaries can only hear it as discord. Louise Fiber Luce poses the alternatives: "Is the structure a drink joke (as I think it is) or is he a true artist in an age of frigid formalism," in a "world unready for his genius?" (72). Either way, the sign of inspiration is intoxication.

3. Comparable stories are told of several other *peintres maudits* of the period, particularly Amadeo Modigliani (Picasso said of the Italian painter that he "only had to touch Utrillo to get drunk") (Fifield 90). O. Henry used to boast that he combined a little orange juice with a little scotch, drank to the health of all magazine editors, sharpened his pencil, and began to write; "When the oranges are empty and the flask is dry, a saleable piece of fiction is ready for mailing" (Rothenberg 116).

4. Charles Winick sees the jazz connection as equally logical: "There is no doubt that much that is original and profound in modern jazz has come from musician addicts. . . . Over-simplifying a complex subject, we could say that jazz was primarily a music of protest and alienation, and the musicians who were the most alienated were those who took drugs . . . so that they could function and express these feelings in music" (1961, 66).

5. See the work of Michael Ripinsky-Naxon, Richard Rudgely, G. Reichel-Dolmatoff, Andrew Sherratt, and others.

6. This is an adaptation of Plato's distinction among poets in the *Phaedrus*: "But if any man come to the gates of poetry without the madness of the Muses, persuaded that skill alone will make him a good poet, then shall he and his works . . . be brought to naught by the poetry of madness" (492).

7. Horace projected the origin of the wine-drinking position back on the comic poet Cratinus, as had Nicaenetus before him: "Wine is a swift horse to the poet who would charm, but, drinking water, thou shalt give birth to naught that is clever. This Cratinus said, Dionysus, and breathed the perfume not of one bottle but of all the cask; therefore was he great, loaded with crowns, and his forehead, like thine, was yellow with the ivy" (*Greek Anthology* 5.21). In 423 BC, Cratinus's play, *The Wineflask*, beat Aristophanes' *Clouds* in the City Dionysia in Athens. In his *Peace*, Aristophanes has Hermes ask if Cratinus is still alive. Trygaeus answers: He died "of a swoon. He could not bear the shock of seeing one of his casks full of wine broken" (188).

8. In an article on poetic inspiration in Greek literature, E. N. Tigerstedt quotes another parallel passage from *The Laws:* "There is . . . an ancient saying—constantly repeated by ourselves and endorsed by every one else—that whenever the poet is seated on the Muse's tripod, he is not in his senses, but resembles a fountain, which gives free course to the upward rush of water." He points out that the words about the tripod would remind every Greek reader of the famous tripod of Apollo in Delphi, on which the Pythia sat when the god spoke through her mouth. This was commonly known to depend on narcotic intoxication (164).

9. Speaking of Saint-Amant, Gautier holds to Scaliger's equivalence of the two principles: "There are some men who have the power of separating at will their dream from the reality. . . . Others are compelled to have recourse to factitious means, to wine or opium, in order to put to sleep the prison jailer and to let their fancy rove" (2.132). Writing on Lionel Johnson, George Santayana concluded: "Yet I should be the last to deride the haze in which he lived, on the ground that Bacchus had something to do with it. Bacchus too was a god; and the material occasion of inspiration makes no difference if the spirit is thereby really liberated" (Bartlett 35).

10. Even before this bias was taken literally, Romanticism attracted metaphors of intoxication. F. L. Lucas, for one, speaks of Romantic verse as "the wine of Dionysus" and writes that the "Romantic writer, squeezing 'Joy's grape' against his palate, grows more eloquent, more magical in the music of phrase and imagery" (50, 54). Thomas Mann always equated the Romantic and the Dionysian (Hepworth 26).

11. The alignment of Wordsworth and Coleridge with water and wine also rhymes with the alternate goals they set themselves in modern poetry: poems of ordinary life as opposed to supernatural subjects that give "the interest of novelty by the modifying colors of imagination" (Coleridge 168). Terence McKenna tries to refine this model further: "Opium was a major driving force on the Romantic imagination—Coleridge, De Quincey, Laurence Sterne, and a number of other writers were creating a world of darkened ruins, abandoned priories, black water sucking at desolate shores—clearly a gloss on the opium state. Then around 1820, Byron, Shelley, and others began experimenting with hashish as well. . . . [but it] never made inroads into the English literary imagination the way that opium had" (240).

12. "Just as the bohemians of Paris had found inspiration for their *Club des Hachischins* and drug experimentation in general from the Anglo-Saxon writers, Coleridge, De Quincey and Poe," Peter Haining writes, "so were they in turn to infuse enthusiasm for experimentation among the English 'decadents' of the turn of the century. . . . Initially these young men, led, figuratively speaking, by the poet Arthur Symons, were a pale imitation of the French; they drank laudanum, smoked opium, and ate hashish— particularly in the universities and the favorite cafés and dives of the period. Among their ranks were many familiar names, Oscar Wilde, Aubrey Beardsley, Richard Le Gallienne, Ernest Dowson, Selwyn Image" (174).

13. In this book, Abrams implied that opium made George Crabbe a Romantic: "On two occasions ['Sir Eustace Gray' and 'The World of Dreams'] something happened to Crabbe which 'set the winds of inspiration blowing,'" and freed him from

the restraints of eighteenth-century poetic diction. Opium gave Crabbe's poetry "a simplicity and inevitability," which looked forward to the later "Ancient Mariner" (1934, 21). Kenneth Burke believed that Coleridge's "drug problem" infects the famous distinction between imagination and fancy, "disclosed in his suggestion that the extreme of imagination would be mania and the extreme of fancy would be delirium, which are precisely the two terms for distinguishing between the effects of the drug in its euphoric stage and the stage of 'falling abroad' (his term) that goes with the withdrawal symptoms" (83).

14. In his poem "The King's Birth-Day in Edinburgh," Fergusson begins by calling on the Muse for hard liquor:

> O *Muse,* be kind, and dinna fash us
> To flee awa' beyont Parnassus,
> Nor seek for *Helicon* to wash us,
> That heath'nish spring;
> Wi' Highland whiskey scour our hawses,
> And gar us sing.

"The picture," Alan MacLaine writes, "of Fergusson buying drinks for the Muse and anxiously warning her against accepting the last glass for fear it will make her tipsy . . . is irresistibly funny" (41). It is also precisely what one form of the Horatian aesthetic demands of the intoxicated author.

15. Walter Benjamin wrote in his essay on surrealism: "To win the energies of intoxication for the revolution—this is the project about which Surrealism circles in all its books and enterprises" (189).

16. In a contemporary review, Elizabeth Hardwick praised *Under the Volcano* as "an ambitious and expansive novel and probably for that reason Lowry has made his central character, the Consul, an alcoholic in whose mind the past and present remain undifferentiated" (199). For orthodox criticism such a connection is unthinkable: "The drugs, predominantly hashish . . . taken in pellet form, loosened Modigliani's shyness, but, like his excessive drinking, cannot be said to have influenced his artwork. Perhaps the most appalling case of misrepresentation by a 'biographer' of Modigliani centers around this issue. André Utter maintains that at a social gathering where the drink and drugs were flowing freely, Modigliani 'suddenly gave a yell and, grabbing paper and pencil, began to draw feverishly, shouting that he had found "the Way."' When he had finished he triumphantly produced a study of a woman's head with the swan neck for which he has become famous" (Reischuck 33).

17. See Goodwin; Dardis 1989; Gilmore 1987; Newlove; Wakefield 1992; Crowley; Sinclair 1956; Forseth.

18. Proehl instances *The Iceman Cometh* (1946), *A Streetcar Named Desire* (1947), *A Moon for the Misbegotten* (1947), *The Country Girl* (1950), *Come Back, Little Sheba* (1950), *The Seven-Year Itch* (1952), *Cat on a Hot Tin Roof* (1955), *Long Day's Journey into Night* (1956 [1939–41]), *Look Homeward, Angel* (1957), *A Raisin in the Sun* (1959), *All the Way Home* (1961), *Night of the Iguana* (1961), and *Who's Afraid of Virginia Woolf?* (1966).

19. Ironically, Murger himself first described his bohemian artists as "'water drinkers' or artists too poor and too dedicated to their work to dissolve their problems in alcohol" (Wilson 2000, 1). French artistic modernism was also bred in the cafés of Paris, and the café, understandably, became one of the primary subjects of modern French painting.

20. The marijuana-smoking jazz musician was known as a "viper," a "flamboyant, eccentric, verbally adroit kind of showman along the lines of a Cab Calloway or a Stuff Smith," and his name and nature runs through a jazz repertoire in songs like Louis Armstrong's "Song of the Viper," Sidney Bechet's "Viper Mad," Willie Bryant's "A Viper's Moan," Cab Calloway's "Viper's Drag," Rosetta Howard's "If You're a Viper," Mezz Mezzrow's "Sendin' the Vipers," and Freddie Taylor's "Viper's Dream" (Wiedemann 123).

21. A musician in Charles Winick's survey stated, "We'd get up on the bandstand looking awful. The audience would say, 'Why don't they smile? They look like they can't smile.' I found I could pep myself up more quickly with heroin than with liquor. If you drank feeling that tired, you'd fall on your face" (1959, 246).

22. Obviously the story doesn't end there. If anything, drug use became even more pervasive and ordinary in the "chemical generation."

23. But Milton was also a Horatian: earlier, in his Latin sixth elegy, he writes, "But why complain that banquet and bottle frighten poetry away? Song loves Bacchus, and Bacchus loves songs. . . . Ovid sent back poems from the land of the Coralli, but they did not have banquets or cultivate the vine there, so the poems were no good" (117–18).

24. And the denial at work in regard to Hoffmann works through Hoffmann's denial as well: In the frame for "Serapionsbruder," Hoffmann has Ottmar "dismiss popular notions of drunken poets, whereas true creation demands the utmost lucidity" (Jennings 192).

25. Formulations that deny that the author is a drunk, or claim that he or she is not exactly a drunk or not a drunk like all those other drunks, seem like a parody of T. S. Eliot's sui generic aesthetic emotions. "Drink did not seem to be an uncontrollable habit for Lewis and there is some doubt, at least in the strict medical sense of the term, that he was an alcoholic" (Lundquist 22). Since there is no strict medical sense of the term *alcoholic,* what is being denied here? "Was he an alcoholic?" Constantine Fitzgibbon asked of Dylan Thomas. "I have never been quite sure that I understand the meaning of that fashionable word" (146). Faulknerians take a "different tack," says Dardis: "Yes, he was undeniably an alcoholic, they acknowledge, but they insist that he exercised a degree of control over his drinking unknown to most alcoholics" (1989, 7). Dylan Thomas's biographers exerted a great deal of ingenuity to control his drinking after the fact: "Dylan was not, indeed, an alcoholic. He did not crave drink, only the ease which it brought to his overworking brain and the facile company that relieved his solitude"; they were particularly concerned to suspend the understanding that he died of drink (Sinclair 2000, 78; in general, see Ferris, Tremlett). Biographers also came up with various formulations that allowed readers to guess that the author was an addict without its needing to be said. The biographical issue is still alive; see the

review by Terry Castle of Joan Acocella's *Willa Cather and the Politics of Criticism,* in the *London Review of Books,* December 14, 2000, 15–20.

26. A few critics, however, see Utrillo's life clearly reflected in his work: "Utrillo has revealed a Montmartre burnt out, dying and dead: a world in ashes, seen by the despairing eyes of an artist whose own life lay in ruins" (Slocombe 273).

27. Or the author could only produce short work while drunk. De Quincey believed that "even great literature—'eternal creations'—might still be conceived and carried on during advanced opium addiction, but it would be in 'parts and fractions,' a lyric rather than an epic" (Hayter 1968, 117). Fitzgerald once apologized to his editor for drinking so much when he was writing *Tender Is the Night:* "'A short story,' he explained, 'can be written on a bottle, but for a novel you need the mental speed that enables you to keep the whole pattern in your head'" (Goodwin 1988, 43). Another defensive position announced that intoxication adds no new content to the mind: Alethea Hayter refers to "later authorities" who claim that nothing "is imagined under the influence of opium which could not be imagined equally well by the same mind in a voluntary and conscious rêverie" (1968, 44). Strongly opposed to this is the claim made on behalf of opiates in the nineteenth century and psychedelic drugs in the twentieth that drugs open the mind to a new and higher reality and thus, one presumes, a radically new content. An associated argument, following Poe rather than De Quincey, is that drink and drugs paralyze the constructive powers of the artistic mind. To quote Hayter again: "Baudelaire believed that drugs do . . . affect the literary imagination; but they give only to those who already have much, they give less than they seem to do, and they take away the power to make use of what they give" (1968, 160–61).

28. Alcoholic writers often differentiate themselves from more overt alcoholics, the "drinker's drunk": what Richard Savage was for Samuel Johnson, Richard Brinsley Sheridan for Lord Byron and Tom Moore, Lardner for Fitzgerald, and Fitzgerald for Hemingway.

29. This opposition between true and false work had been figured earlier in the trope of oil versus wine. Rabelais alludes to "a certain imbecile," who "declared that his [Horace's] verses smack rather of wine than of oil," and also declares that there is "an upstart who says as much of my books. But a turd for him! How much more appetizing, alluring, and enticing, how much more heavenly and delicious is the smell of wine than the smell of oil!" (39). After bidding farewell to sack, Robert Herrick announces

what's done by me
Hereafter, shall smell of the Lamp, not thee.
(146)

But the artist, for a complex of reasons, had already become an image of idleness in the nineteenth century. See Audrey Jaffe's excellent reading of Arthur Conan Doyle's "Man with the Twisted Lip" and the many readings of Herman Melville's Bartleby as an artist figure. In Virginia Woolf's *To the Lighthouse,* Mr. and Mrs. Ramsay and Lily perceive the opium addict Mr. Carmichael "as doing the work of a literary artist—not as overcome by opium—while lying about on a lawn chair seeking the exact word" (Lilienfeld 209).

30. In an excellent article on the subject, Art Hill writes, "Perle Epstein's approach is an example of the usual critical approach to the drunkenness theme in *Volcano*. It is seen as pure symbolism; only its figurative meaning is important. The fact that Lowry was literally a drunk, writing about genuine, mind-shattering, cold-sweat, hand-shuddering drunkenness, is apparently thought inconsequential" (46). There are certainly minority voices. Gerald Weales, for example, wrote that O'Neill's work was best when he came closest to his alcoholism—once programmatically and once biographically: "The excellence of his own last plays of which *Iceman Cometh* and *Long Day's Journey into Night* are the finest examples" (353). These two plays seemed to bubble up effortlessly after O'Neill found himself unable to continue work on his great project of a play-cycle titled "A Tale of Possessors Self-Dispossessed" (Gallup 1). Michael Hinden is the only critic I have read who connects the philosophy of disillusionment in *Iceman* with O'Neill's alcoholism.

31. John Cheever used alcohol "to great excess" while he was writing *Wapshot Chronicles, Wapshot Scandal,* and *Bullet Park* (Rothenberg 120). Burroughs claimed that marijuana "is very useful to the artist, activating trains of association that would otherwise be inaccessible, and I owe many of the scenes in *Naked Lunch* directly to the use of cannabis" (Solomon 1964, 172). Jack Kerouac acknowledged that "'Poem 230 from *Mexico City Blues* was written purely on morphine.'. . . He wrote on junk time: one line, wait an hour, write another line, wait another hour"; *On the Road* was written "flat out in one mammoth sitting, was composed on one long amphetamine binge" (Miles 203; Burgess 227). John O'Hara's idea for *Pal Joey* (or parody of that idea) very definitely arose out of drink: I had an idea for a story. I said to my wife I'd go to Philadelphia. Hole up in the Hotel Ben Franklin a couple of days, lock myself in, eat on room service, just work. I get up the next morning and I am dying. On the way to the station, I told the cab to stop at a hotel bar and got a drink or two. I feel what-the-hell. Better take a nap. Then began a real beauty. Just getting stiff and passing out. By Saturday I'd drunk myself sober. At that point remorse set in. I asked 'there must be somebody worse than me.' Then I got it—maybe some nightclub master of ceremonies" (Rothenberg 117).

Francis Bacon's *Crucifixion* triptych was painted under the continuous influence of alcohol: "I was drunk all the time I was painting it," he confessed (Alley 19). Michael Peppiatt wonders "how Bacon did it—how he managed to drink immoderately for some fourteen hours a day, drifting from club to bar, leaving scores of woozily incapacitated in his wake, and then focus on the hazardous process of bringing a new image into existence—remains a mystery. Bacon himself pretended he painted particularly well with a hangover. 'My mind simply crackles with electricity after one of those evenings,' he would announce with disarming simplicity to the dazed and pallid friends who had stayed the course with him. 'I think the drink actually makes me freer,' he sometimes added, rosy-cheeked and cheerful, as if he had consumed pure elixir in the last seedy outposts of the London night" (1999, 25).

32. "One is reminded of another painter of the period, the Norwegian Edvard

Munch, who suffered a nervous breakdown, was hospitalized, recovered, and never touched alcohol again, but also never again created works as poignant as those he had done as a 'psychopath'" (Werner 40).

33. It makes no difference to this argument whether the pathology from which these artists suffered was primary alcoholism or, more likely, a bipolar disorder self-treated with alcohol and drugs to control its depressive cycle (see Holden, Jamison).

34. If art is also pathology, as earlier discussions of genius strongly suggest, how can Dardis and Goodwin suddenly turn around and treat it as great good health threatened by the disease of alcoholism? So many statements simply oppose art and drinking as good and bad behavior, when in fact they are intricately involved in one another. Goodwin even writes of Faulkner: "One last question needs asking: What kind of writer would Faulkner have been if he hadn't been alcoholic? Would he have been a writer at all? The questions are unanswerable. In Faulkner's case . . . writing and drinking were so intertwined that one is justified in thinking that one could not have existed without the other" (1988, 121). Kingsley Amis said that "alcohol in moderate amounts and at fairly leisurely speed is valuable to me—at least I think so. It could be that I could have written better without it . . . but it could also be true that I'd have written far less without it" (Ludwig 168).

35. Bill Evans claimed that "'when things were just right, he could get every molecule in a given place to begin scintillating in a new and higher fashion. . . . This was something he could *see* when it was occurring.' If this sounds like the cocaine talking," Peter Pettinger adds, "nevertheless we may connect such perception with the audacious and noble music being produced—a fitting resolution to two decades of trio artistry at the Vanguard" (276). There was disagreement, of course: John Hammond maintained that dope "played hell with time," and Parker warned young musicians away from drugs: "Any musician who says he is playing better either on tea, the needle, or when he is juiced, is a plain, straight liar. When I get too much to drink, I can't even finger well, let alone play decent ideas. And, in the days when I was on the stuff, I may have *thought* I was playing better, but listening to some of the records now, I know I wasn't" (Shapiro 1988, 33; Priestley 38).

36. When Abrams reviewed Schneider's book in 1955, he claimed not to be entirely convinced by it, but he dropped the subject of opium from his own future discussions of Coleridge. Hayter's 1968 study of drugs and creativity can be understood as an attempt to mediate between Abrams and Schneider. Contemporary critics have been reluctant to accept Schneider's verdict as final, often attempting to hide in the middle as Marshall Suther does in his *Visions of Xanadu*: "One may agree with Miss Schneider in minimizing the influence of opium upon the composition of the poem and still feel that Meyer Abrams has done it no disservice in calling his book on the subject *The Milk of Paradise*" (282).

37. Some critics agree that such an allegorical formula would hold for George Crabbe's "World of Dreams" and "Sir Eustace Gray," Coleridge's "Kubla Khan" and "Ancient Mariner," Francis Thompson's "Hound of Heaven" and "Finis Coronat Opus," and James Thomson's "Insomnia."

38. "Montaigne talks about his style in a chapter [of the *Essays*] ruled by Bacchus

because his style resembles the stumblings of a drunken Bacchus" (Engel 188). Robin Burgess felt that the patterns of *On the Road* reproduced "something of the feel of amphetamine intoxication" (227). Drugs are also believed to provoke stylistic watersheds in the careers of certain artists, like John Lennon (Lomberg 88). Discussing psychedelic painters, Robert Masters writes that "LSD-type experience, as we have noted, can be powerful enough to transform the work of an artist almost totally. It can motivate people to become creatively active and it can alter basic creative process even in an artist whose work patterns have developed over many years and seem firmly established" (119).

39. The psychoanalyst A. A. Brill suggested in 1931 that "Swift's Lilliputians and Giants surely have something to do with the phenomenon of microscopia and macroscopia so frequently observed in alcoholism," and Hayter declared that Elizabeth Barrett Browning's "True Dream" is "almost a case-book list of opium-inspired imagery, with its slimy glittering snakes, its stony faces, its poisonous kisses, its rainbow smoke, its breaths of icy cold" (Brill 374–75; Hayter 1968, 65). J. M. W. Turner was an alcoholic. I don't want this fact to answer for his blurred style, but it should be taken into account: two old boatmen who rowed Turner on sketching excursions on the Thames stated that the artist "always took a bottle of gin with him for inspiration and never gave them any" (Bailey 353).

40. Cannabis is so important to the culture of North Africa that, according to Paul Bowles, it has affected important areas of aesthetics: "Music, literature and even certain aspects of architecture have evolved with *Cannabis*-directed appreciation in mind" (Emboden 227). Among the earlier art forms so interpreted are *rock* art and stained glass and art nouveau, which have been associated with psychedelic drugs, while in the 1960s, new psychedelic species were spawned by the drug culture: rock art (especially acid rock), new wave science fiction, fantastic realism in painting and experimental film, psychedelic posters, light shows and trip festivals, and cinema sci-fi special effects. For drugs as subject matter and style in works by Roger Zelazney, Robert Sheckley, Harlan Ellison, and Samuel Delaney, see Seymour 16. For the "drug time" of Andy Warhol's films, see Tyler 99–101. In Wes Wilson's posters, Cary Million wrote, "the movement of a still object, the clashing complementaries, and the melting or burning words all connect to 'psychedelic' perception" (74). Bob Fried wanted his "posters to convey feelings of dimensional space, like what you feel when you trip on acid. Passing from one reality into another. I wanted to express a kind of space network, rushing, floating, going through time" (in Grushkin 83). Like rock lyrics, the posters are filled with visual and verbal drug puns. In the light shows, the "subjective effects of LSD are recreated artificially with colored lights, concrete pop music, slides of liquid in which tints are injected and stroboscopes (which can induce hysteria in certain subjects in the technically controlled environments of little synthetic paradises)," while Kesey's acid tests were "weird carnivals with videotapes, flashing strobes, live improvised rock and roll by the Grateful Dead, lots of bizarre costumes, and dancing" (Allsop 64; Lee 125).

41. This correspondence is also a sociological truth. William James declared that

to "the poor and unlettered . . . [alcohol stands] in the place of symphony concerts and of literature" (378). Nicholas Warner finds this conceit in American literature, in Harriet Beecher Stowe's *Dred,* for example, in the author's comments on the drinking of the "lowlife drunkard," Cripps: "Why not? He was uncomfortable—gloomy; and every one, under such circumstances, naturally inclines towards *some* source of consolation. He who is intellectual reads and studies; he who is industrious flies to business; he who is none of these—what has he but his whiskey" (134, 249).

42. This was particularly common, of course, in connection with writers of drink poetry: In dedicatory verses to Alexander Brome, both W. Paullet and "C. W." declare that a reader may enjoy the pleasures of wine simply by reading Brome's poetry:

Or else we
May read thy book, and tipple Poetry;
And sing the prayses of the nobler Vine.
(59)

Justin McCarthy said of Omar: "I drank the red wine of Omar from the enchanted chalice of FitzGerald and gloried as joyously as old Omar himself in the intoxication" (Yohannan 191).

8. CARNIVAL, CREATIVITY, AND THE SUBLIMATION OF DRUNKENNESS

1. "In certain moods," Denis Donoghue writes, "I could be persuaded that dialogism is merely a footnote to Nietzsche's Dionysianism" (115).

2. Bakhtin 273; Rutland 131–32; LaCapra 296.

3. Lucian suggested that drinking during carnival was obligatory—"Demetrius the Platonic was reported to Ptolemy Dionysus for a water drinker, and for the only man who had declined to put on female attire at the Dionysia"—and in the "Saturnalia" Cronos also declares that "during my week the serious is barred; no business allowed. Drinking and being drunk, noise and games and dice, appointing of kings and feasting of slaves, singing naked, clapping of tremulous hands, an occasional ducking of corked faces in icy water,—such are the functions over which I preside" (4.7, 108).

4. In the following quotation, drink is slowly squeezed out of carnival: "For several decades after 1750 then the wakes were holidays—great days of high spirits, sport, folly and release. There was eating and drinking on a great scale. A nineteenth-century observer recalled that 'a crowd of persons round a drunken man lying insensible on the streets during the afternoon was not uncommon'" (Reid 127).

5. "To drink wine is to eat," Roland Barthes wrote, thinking along the same lines. "The taste of good wine (the *straight* taste of wine) is inseparable from food" (1977, 96).

6. From time to time, however, statements that reflect this suppression and diversion appear in the commentary: "Rabelais loved his glass of *piot*—there is little reason for believing that the draughts of wine are *always* allegories of higher things"; and "drinking for its opiate effect, obviously very important in Rabelais, is not dealt with

here" (Screech 1979:11; Masters 42). On the other hand, it must be acknowledged that Rabelais collaborates in a sublimated understanding of his work. His fiction mixes creatural celebration and an incompatible allegorization of the body. Alice Fiola Berry explains this disjuncture as a dialectic or dialogue: "Bacchus is always opposed by another voice which praises seriousness over joy, silence over words, and which urges us to ignore Bacchic appearances in favor of high and serious truths lurking beneath the grotesque surface. . . . The Bacchic voice scorns the symbolic and ridicules the allegories with which commentators have 'caulked' (*calfreté*) the works of writers whom Alcofribas admires, and he warns the reader not to emulate them. . . . There is, in general, a tone of Bacchic *raillerie* running throughout the Apollonian argument even in its most empathic moments, undermining it and equalizing its force" (88–90). Nevertheless, Rabelais makes prose wet. Hazlitt, for example, only wrote about a page on Rabelais, but it is saturated with drink: "He is intoxicated with gaiety, mad with folly. His animal spirits drown him in a flood of mirth; his blood courses up and down his veins like wine. His thirst of enjoyment is as great as his thirst of drink: his appetite for good things of all sorts is unsatisfied, and there is a never-ending supply. *Discourse is dry;* so they moisten their words in their cups, and relish their dry jests with plenty of Botargos and dried neats'-tongues. . . . The flagons are set a-running, their tongues wag at the same time, and their mirth flows as a river" (132).

7. Another major force in Bakhtin's pantheon is Hugo. According to Bakhtin, Hugo knew what Rabelais was about when he stated that "Rabelais has placed in a barrel the world which Dante thrust into hell" (126).

8. The purest image of carnival in the New World would be the game that climaxes Graham Greene's *Our Man in Havana,* a game of checkers played with liquor bottles from Wormold's collection. Wormold "unfolded the draughts board. Then he arranged on the board twenty-four miniature bottles of whiskey: twelve Bourbon confronted twelve Scotch. 'What is this, Mr. Wormold?' 'An idea of Dr. Hasselbacher's. I thought we might have one game to his memory. When you take a piece you drink it'" (215).

Works Cited

Abrams, Meyer Howard. 1934. *The Milk of Paradise.* Cambridge, MA: Harvard University Press.

———. 1955. Review of *Coleridge, Opium, and "Kubla Khan,"* by Elisabeth Schneider. *Modern Language Notes* 70(3): 216–19.

Achilles Tatius. 1969. *Achilles Tatius,* ed. S. Gaselee. Cambridge, MA: Harvard University Press.

Ackermann, Elfriede Marie. 1944. "*Das Schlaraffenland* in German Literature and Folksong." PhD diss., University of Chicago.

Addison, William. 1953. *English Fairs and Markets.* London: Batsford.

Ade, George. 1911. *Verses and Jingles.* Indianapolis: Bobbs-Merrill.

Ainsworth, Harrison William. 1976. *Auriol: or, The Elixir of Life.* New York: Arno.

Alford, C. Fred. 1992. *The Psychoanalytic Theory of Greek Tragedy.* New Haven, CT: Yale University Press.

Allen, Don Cameron. 1970. *Mysteriously Meant: The Rediscovery of Pagan Symbolism and Allegorical Interpretation in the Renaissance.* Baltimore, MD: Johns Hopkins University Press.

Alley, Ronald. 1964. *Francis Bacon.* New York: Viking.

Allsop, Kenneth. 1969. "The Technicolor Wasteland." *Encounter* 32(3): 64–71.

Amis, Kingsley. 1972. *On Drink.* London: Cape.

Anderson, Daniel E. 1993. *The Masks of Dionysos: A Commentary on Plato's Symposium.* Albany: State University of New York Press.

Andrews, Tamra. 2000. *Nectar and Ambrosia: An Encyclopedia of Food in World Mythology.* Santa Barbara, CA: ABC-CLIO.

Anselment, Raymond A. 1984. "Alexander Brome and the Search for the 'Safe Estate.'" *Renaissance and Reformation* 8(1): 39–51.

Antreasian, Garo Z. 1952. "Utrillo." *Bulletin of the John Herron Art Institute* 39 (April): 15–17.

Apollodorus. 1975. *The Library of Greek Mythology.* Lawrence, KS: Coronado.

Apuleius. 1951. *The Golden Ass,* trans. Robert Graves. New York: Farrar, Straus and Giroux.

Arberry, A. J. 1947. *Fifty Poems of Hafiz.* Cambridge: University Press.

———. 1948. *Immortal Rose: An Anthology of Persian Lyrics.* London: Luzac.

———. 1958. *Classical Persian Literature.* London: Allen and Unwin.

———. 1971. *Aspects of Islamic Civilization.* Ann Arbor: University of Michigan Press.

Arbman, Ernst. 1963–70. *Ecstasy, or Religious Trance in the Experience of the Ecstatics and from the Psychological Point of View.* Stockholm: Bok för Laget.

Aristophanes. 1912. *The Eleven Comedies.* London: Athenian Society.

Aristotle. 1927. *The Works of Aristotle Translated into English,* vol. 7, ed. W. D. Ross. Oxford: Clarendon.

Athenaeus of Naucratis. 1927–41. *The Deipnosophists.* Cambridge, MA: Harvard University Press.

Atherton, Gertrude. 1908. *The Gorgeous Isle.* New York: Doubleday, Page.

Ausonius. 1967. *Ausonius,* vol. 2. Cambridge, MA: Harvard University Press.

Bacon, Helen H. 1959. "Socrates Crowned." *Virginia Quarterly Review* 35(3): 415–30.

Baeumer, Max. 1976. "Nietzsche and the Tradition of the Dionysian." In *Studies in Nietzsche and the Classical Tradition,* ed. James C. O'Flaherty, Timothy F. Sellner, and Robert M. Helm, 165–89. Chapel Hill: University of North Carolina Press.

Bagley, F. R. C. 1966–67. "Omar Khayyam and Fitzgerald." *Durham University Journal,* n.s., 28(2): 81–93.

Bailey, Anthony. 1997. *Standing in the Sun.* London: Sinclair-Stevenson.

Baines, Barbara J. 1980. "Kyd's Silenus Box and the Limits of Perception." *Journal of Medieval and Renaissance Studies* 10(1): 41–51.

Bakhtin, Mikhail. 1968. *Rabelais and His World.* Cambridge, MA: MIT.

Balakian, Anna. 1974. "Breton and Drugs." *Yale French Studies* 50: 96–107.

Baldwin, James. 1998. "Sonny's Blues." In *Early Novels and Stories,* 831–64. New York: Library of the Americas.

Balzac, Honoré de. 1971. *The Works,* 18 vols. Freeport, NY: Books for Libraries.

Bandera, Cesário. 1975. "Literature and Desire: Poetic Frenzy and the Love Potion." *Mosaic* 8(2): 33–52.

Bann, Stephen. 1989. *The True Vine: On Visual Representation and the Western Tradition.* New York: Cambridge University Press.

Barber, C. L. 1959. *Shakespeare's Festive Comedy: A Study of Dramatic Form and Its Relation to Social Custom.* Princeton, NJ: Princeton University Press.

Baring-Gould, Rev. Sabine. 1987. *Curious Myths of the Middle Ages.* New York: Crescent.

Barnard, Mary. 1963. "The God in the Flowerpot." *American Scholar* 32(4): 578–86.

Barrows, Susanna. 1991. Introduction to *Drinking: Behavior and Belief in Modern History,* ed. Susanna Barrows and Robin Room, 1–25. Berkeley: University of California Press.

Barry, Philip. 1939. *The Philadelphia Story.* New York: Coward-McCann.

Barthes, Roland. 1972. *Mythologies.* New York: Hill and Wang.

————. 1977. *Roland Barthes*. London: Macmillan.

Bartlett, Phyllis. 1951. *Poems in Process*. New York: Oxford University Press.

Baudelaire, Charles. 1986. *My Heart Laid Bare and Other Prose Writings*. London: Soho Book.

Beegel, Susan F. 1984. "Hemingway Gastronomique: A Guide to Food and Drink in *A Moveable Feast*." *Hemingway Review* 4(1): 14–26.

Bell, Gertrude Lowthian. 1928. *Poems from the Divan of Hafiz*. London: Heinemann.

Bell, Robert E. 1982. *Dictionary of Classical Mythology*. Santa Barbara, CA: ABC-CLIO.

Benjamin, Walter. 1978. *Reflections*. New York: Schocken.

Bentley, C. F. 1972. "The Monster in the Bedroom: Sexual Symbolism in Bram Stoker's *Dracula*." *Literature and Psychology* 22(1): 27–34.

Bergsten, Gunilla. 1969. *Thomas Mann's Doctor Faustus*. Chicago: University of Chicago Press.

Béroul. 1970. *The Romance of Tristan*, trans. Alan S. Fedrick. Harmondsworth, UK: Penguin.

————. 1973. *The Romance of Tristan and Isolt*, trans. Norman B. Spector. Evanston, IL: Northwestern University Press.

Berridge, Virginia, and Griffith Edwards. 1981. *Opium and the People: Opiate Use in Nineteenth-Century England*. New York: St. Martin's.

Berry, Alice Fiola. 1975. "Apollo vs. Bacchus: The Dynamics of Inspiration." *PMLA* 90: 88–95.

Besant, Walter. 1888. *The Inner House*. New York: Harper and Brothers.

Bett, W. R. 1952. *The Infirmities of Genius*. New York: Philosophical Library.

Bevan, Edwyn. 1928. *Sibyls and Seers*. London: Allen and Unwin.

Bicknell, Herman. 1875. *Hafiz of Shiraz*. London: Turner.

Bing, Peter. 1988. *The Well-Read Muse: Present and Past in Callimachus and the Hellenistic Poets*. Göttingen: Vandenhoeck and Ruprecht.

Blake, William. 1982. *The Complete Poetry and Prose,* ed. David V. Erdman. Berkeley: University of California Press.

Blotner, Joseph Leo. 1974. *Faulkner; A Biography*. 2 vols. New York: Random House.

Bold, Alan, ed. 1982. *Drink to Me Only: The Prose (and Cons) of Drinking*. London: Robin Clark.

Bonaparate, Marie. 1949. *The Life and Works of Edgar Allan Poe: A Psycho-Analytic Interpretation*. London: Imago.

Bourboulis, Photeine P. 1964. *Ancient Festivals of "Saturnalia" Type*. Thessaloníki: Hetairea Makedonikon Spoudon.

Bowers, John M. 1990. "Augustine as Addict: Sex and Texts in the *Confessions*." *Exemplaria* 2(2): 403–48.

Bownas, Geoffrey, and Anthony Thwaite. 1964. *The Penguin Book of Japanese Verse*. Baltimore, MD: Penguin.

Boyd, Jenny. 1992. "Talkin' 'Bout My Inspiration." *Musician* 163 (May): 46–62.

Braden, Gordon. 1978. *The Classics and English Renaissance Poetry*. New Haven, CT: Yale University Press.

Braden, William. 1967. *The Private Sea: LSD and the Search for God.* Chicago: Quadrangle.

Bramble, J. C. 1974. *Persius and the Programmatic Satire: A Study in Form and Imagery.* Cambridge: Cambridge University Press.

Brant, Sebastian. 1988. *Ship of Fools.* In *Inspired by Drink,* ed. Joan Digby and John Digby, 216–18. New York: Morrow.

Brathwaite, Richard. 1903. *The Law of Drinking.* New Haven, CT: Tuttle, Morehouse and Taylor.

Brewer, E. Cobham. 1935. *The Reader's Handbook.* Philadelphia: Lippincott.

Brill, A. A. 1931. "Poetry as an Oral Outlet." *Psychoanalytic Review* 18: 357–78.

Brillat-Savarin, Jean Anthelme. 1960. *The Physiology of Taste.* New York: Dover.

Brombert, Victor. 1974. "The Will to Ecstasy: The Example of Baudelaire's 'La Chevelure.'" *Yale French Studies* 50: 55–64.

Brome, Alexander. 1982. *Poems,* vol. 1, ed. Roman R. Dubinski. Toronto: University of Toronto Press.

Bromell, Nicholas. 2000. *Tomorrow Never Knows: Rock and Psychedelics in the 1960s.* Chicago: University of Chicago Press.

Broms, Henri. 1968. *Two Studies in the Relations of Hafiz and the West.* Helsinki: Studia Orientalia.

Brower, Robert H., and Earl Miner. 1961. *Japanese Court Poetry.* Stanford, CA: Stanford University Press.

Brown, J. C. E. 1973. "The Rubaiyyat of Omar Khayyam: A Critical Assessment of Robert Graves' and Omar Ali Shah's Translation." *Iran* 11: 63–74.

Buck-Morss, Susan. 1977. *Origin of Negative Dialectics: Theodor Adorno, Walter Benjamin, and the Frankfurt Institute.* New York: Free Press.

———. 1992. "Aesthetics and Anaesthetics." *October* 62: 3–42.

Bullen, A. H., ed. 1893. *Anacreon.* London: Lawrence and Bullen.

Bürgel, J. Christoph. 1991. "Ambiguity: A Study in the Use of Religious Terminology in the Poetry of Hafiz." In *Intoxication Earthly and Heavenly: Seven Studies on the Poet Hafiz from Shiraz,* ed. Michael Glünz and J. Christoph Bürgel, 7–40. Bern: Lang.

Burgess, Robin. 1994. "Kerouac, Alcohol, and the Beat Movement." In *Beyond the Pleasure Dome: Writing and Addiction from the Romantics,* ed. Sue Vice, 225–30. Sheffield, England: Sheffield Academic Press.

Burke, Kenneth. 1957. *The Philosophy of Literary Form.* New York: Vintage.

Burke, Peter. 1978. *Popular Culture in Early Modern Europe.* New York: New York University Press.

Burkert, Walter. 1987. *Ancient Mystery Cults.* Cambridge, MA: Harvard University Press.

Burnett, Anne Pippin. 1983. *Three Archaic Poets: Archilochus, Alcaeus, Sappho.* Cambridge, MA: Harvard University Press.

Burns, Robert. 1968. *The Poems and Songs of Robert Burns,* vol. 1, ed. James Kinsley. Oxford: Clarendon.

Butler, E. M. 1935. *The Tyranny of Greece over Germany.* New York: Macmillan.

Butler, Marilyn. 1985. "Druids, Bards, and Twice-Born Bacchus." *Keats-Shelley Review* 36: 57–76.

Butte, George. 1989. "What Silenus Knew: Conrad's Uneasy Debt to Nietzsche." *Comparative Literature* 41(2): 155–69.

Byron, George Gordon, Baron. 1980. *Complete Poetical Works,* vol. 1. ed. Jerome McGann. Oxford: Clarendon.

Cafarelli, Leslie. 1990. *Prose in the Age of Poets.* Philadelphia: University of Pennsylvania Press.

Calverley, Charles Stuart. 1901. *The Complete Works.* London: Bell.

Campbell, David A. 1932. *Greek Lyric.* Cambridge, MA: Harvard University Press.

———— 1983. *The Golden Lyre: The Themes of the Greek Lyric Poets.* London: Duckworth.

———— 1988. *Greek Lyric,* vol. 2. Cambridge, MA: Harvard University Press.

Campbell, Matthew. 1994. "Changing Habits: James Joyce and Drunken Catholics." In *Beyond the Pleasure Dome: Writing and Addiction from the Romantics,* ed. Sue Vice, 184–91. Sheffield, England: Sheffield Academic Press.

Camporesi, Piero. 1993. *The Magic Harvest: Food, Folklore, and Society.* Cambridge, UK: Polity.

Carey, Henry. 1930. *The Poems of Henry Carey,* ed. Frederick T. Wood. London: Scholartis.

Carpenter, Thomas H. 1993. "The Beardless Dionysus." In *Masks of Dionysus,* ed. Thomas H. Carpenter and Christopher A. Faraone, 185–206. Ithaca, NY: Cornell University Press.

Castle, Terry. 2000. "The Willa Cather Wars." *London Review of Books* December 14: 15–20.

Cave, George. 1972. *Sufi Poetry.* Rawalpindi: R. C. D. Cultural Association.

Chaucer, Geoffrey. 1933. *The Canterbury Tales,* ed. F. N. Robinson. Boston: Houghton Mifflin.

Cheever, D. W. 1862. "Narcotics." *North American Review* 95: 374–415.

Clark, Katerina, and Michael Holquist. 1984. *Mikhail Bakhtin.* Cambridge, MA: Harvard University Press.

Clark, Walter Houston. 1958. *The Psychology of Religion.* New York: Macmillan.

Clej, Alina. 1995. *A Genealogy of the Modern Self: Thomas De Quincey and the Intoxication of Writing.* Stanford, CA: Stanford University Press.

Clements, Patricia. 1985. *Baudelaire and the English Tradition.* Princeton, NJ: Princeton University Press.

Cockerham, Harry. 1974. "Gautier: From Hallucination to Supernatural Vision." *Yale French Studies* 50: 42–54.

Coleman, Robert, ed. 1977. *Vergil: Eclogues.* Cambridge: Cambridge University Press.

Coleridge, Samuel Taylor. 1975. *Biographia Literaria.* New York: Dutton.

Colford, William Edward. 1942. *Juan Melendez Valdes.* New York: Hispanic Institute.

Commager, Henry Steele. 1962. *The Odes of Horace.* New Haven, CT: Yale University Press.

Congreve, William. 1956. *Complete Plays.* New York: Hill and Wang.

Conrad, Barnaby. 1988. *Absinthe.* San Francisco: Chronicle Books.

Cooke, Michael G. 1974. "De Quincey, Coleridge, and the Formal Uses of Intoxication." *Yale French Studies* 50: 26–41.

Cooper, Arthur D. 1973. *Li Po and Tu Fu.* Harmondsworth, UK: Penguin.

Copjec, Joan. 1991. "Vampires, Breast-Feeding, and Anxiety." *October* 58 (fall): 25–43.

Copley, Frank O. 1981. *Exclusus Amator: A Study in Latin Love Poetry.* Madison, WI: American Philological Association.

Corbin, Alain. 1986. *The Foul and the Fragrant: Odor and the French Social Imagination.* New York: Berg.

Cotton, Charles. 1958. *Cotton,* ed. John Buxton. London: Routledge and Kegan Paul.

Courtwright, David. 2001. *Forces of Habit: Drugs and the Making of the Modern World.* Cambridge, MA: Harvard University Press.

Craft, Christopher. 1984. "'Kiss Me with Those Red Lips': Gender and Inversion in Bram Stoker's *Dracula.*" *Representations* 8 (fall): 107–33.

Craig, Randall. 1985. "Plato's *Symposium* and the Tragicomic Novel." *Studies in the Novel* 17(2): 158–73.

Crashaw, Richard. 1966. *Poems,* ed. L. C. Martin. Oxford: Clarendon.

Crawley, A. E. n.d. "Drinks, Drinking." In *Encyclopedia of Religion and Ethics,* vol. 5, ed. James Hasting. New York: Charles Scribner's Sons.

Crowley, John W. 1994. *The White Logic: Alcoholism and Gender in American Modernist Fiction.* Amherst: University of Massachusetts Press.

Culler, Jonathan. 1983. *Barthes.* London: Fontana Paperbacks.

Curtis, Renée. 1983. "Wagner's *Tristan und Isolde:* The Transformation of a Medieval Legend." *Tristana* 8(2): 3–14.

Daiches, David. 1990. *A Wee Dram: Drinking Scenes from Scottish Literature.* London: Andre Deutsch.

Dakers, Andrew Herbert. 1923. *Robert Burns.* London: Chapman and Hall.

Daly, Robert. 1978. *God's Altar: The World and the Flesh in Puritan Poetry.* Berkeley: University of California Press.

Damrosch, Leopold, Jr. 1982. "Burns, Blake, and the Recovery of Lyric." *Studies in Romanticisim* 21(4): 637–60.

Danielou, Jean. 1961. Introduction to *From Glory to Glory: Texts from Gregory of Nyssa's Mystical Writings.* New York: Charles Scribner's Sons.

Darby, William J., et al. 1977. *Food: The Gift of Osiris,* vol. 2. London: Academic.

Dardis, Tom. 1989. *The Thirsty Muse: Alcohol and the American Writer.* New York: Ticknor and Fields.

———. 1994. "'Oh, Those Awful Pressures!' Faulkner's 'Controlled' Drinking." In *Beyond the Pleasure Dome: Writing and Addiction from the Romantics,* ed. Sue Vice, 192–99. Sheffield: Sheffield Academic Press.

Dashti, Ali. 1971. *In Search of Omar Khayyam.* London: Allen and Unwin.

Davenport-Hines, R. P. T. 1999. *Gothic: Four Hundred Years of Excess, Horror, Evil, and Ruin.* New York: North Point.

Davidson, Edward Hutchins. 1949. *Hawthorne's Last Phase*. New Haven, CT: Yale University Press.

Davidson, H. R. Ellis. 1964. *Gods and Myths of Northern Europe*. Baltimore, MD: Penguin.

Davidson, Judson France. 1915. *The Anacreontea*. London: Dent and Sons.

Davis, Gladys M. N. 1914. *The Asiatic Dionysos*. London: Bell and Sons.

Day, Douglas. 1964. "Of Tragic Joy." *Prairie Schooner* 37(4): 354–62.

De Casseres, Benjamin. 1936. *The Adventures of an Exile*, vol. 2. New York: Blackstone.

Decker, Christopher, ed. 1997. *Edward Fitzgerald, Rubáiyát of Omar Khayyám: A Critical Edition*. Charlottesville: University Press of Virginia.

de Estella, R. P. Diego. 1939. *Meditations on the Love of God*. London: Sheed and Ward.

deFord, Miriam Allen. 1936. "Ernest Dowson." In *British Authors of the Nineteenth Century*, ed. Stanley Kunitz, 197–98. New York: Wilson.

Demetz, Peter. 1958. "The Elm and the Vine." *PMLA* (December): 521–33.

de Nerval, Gérard. 1975. "Hashish." In *The Hashish Club: An Anthology of Drug Literature*. By Peter Haining, 105–14. London: Owen.

de Nicolás, Antonio T. 1989. *St. John of the Cross: Alchemist of the Soul*. New York: Paragon House.

De Quincey, Thomas. 1971. *Confessions of an English Opium Eater*, ed. Alathea Hayter. London: Penguin.

Derrida, Jacques. 1993. "The Rhetoric of Drugs." *Differences* 5(1): 1–25.

Detienne, Marcel. 1989. *Dionysos at Large*. Cambridge, MA: Harvard University Press.

Deutsch, Helene. 1969. *A Psychoanalytic Study of the Myth of Dionysus and Apollo*. New York: International Universities Press.

Devereux, Anthony Q. 1993. *Juan Ponce de Leon, King Ferdinand, and the Fountain of Youth*. Spartanburg, SC: Reprint Company.

Digby, Joan, and John Digby, eds. 1988. *Inspired by Drink*. New York: Morrow.

Diodorus Siculus. 1933–67. *Diodorus of Sicily*. Cambridge, MA: Harvard University Press.

Diogenes Laertius. 1980. *Lives of the Eminent Philosophers*, vol. 1. Cambridge, MA: Harvard University Press.

Dodds, E. R. 1951. *The Greeks and the Irrational*. Berkeley: University of California Press.

Dols, Michael. 1982. *Majnun: The Madman in Medieval Islamic Society*. Oxford: Clarendon.

Donaldson, Scott. 1990. "Writers and Drinking in America." *Sewanee Review* 98: 312–24.

Donoghue, Denis. 1985. "Reading Bakhtin." *Raritan* 5(2): 107–19.

Donohue, Harold. 1993. *The Song of the Swan: Lucretius and the Influence of Callimachus*. New York: University Press of America.

Dorosz, Kristofer. 1976. *Malcolm Lowry's Infernal Paradise*. Uppsala: Uppsala University.

Dostoyevsky, Fyodor. 1946. *The Short Stories*, ed. William Phillips. New York: Dial.

Douglas, Charles. 1941. *Artist Quarter*. London: Faber and Faber.

Dover, K. J. 1968. *Aristophanes' Clouds*. Oxford: Clarendon.

Doyle, Charles Clay. 1974. "An Unhonored English Anacreon: John Birkenhead." *Studies in Philology* 71(2): 192–205.

Draper, John. 1967. "Omar Khayyam and Pre-Islamic Persian Culture." *West Virginia University Philological Papers* 16: 5–16.

Dronke, Peter. 1980. "The Art of the Archpoet: A Reading of 'Lingua Balbus.'" In *The Interpretation of Medieval Lyric Poetry*, ed. W. T. H. Jackson, 22–43. New York: Columbia University Press.

Drower, E. S. 1956. *Water into Wine*. London: Murray.

Drury, Nevill. 1999. *Exploring the Labyrinth: Making Sense of the New Spirituality*. New York: Continuum.

Duerr, Hans Peter. 1985. *Dreamtime: Concerning the Boundary between Wilderness and Civilization*. Oxford: Blackwell.

Duke, Michael S. 1977. *Lu You*. Boston: Twayne.

Dumas, Alexandre. 1956. "The Man Who Lived 4000 Years" (from *The Queen's Necklace*). In *Stories to Remember*, ed. Thomas B. Costain and John Beecroft, 130–53. Garden City, NY: Doubleday.

Dunaway, David King. 1989. *Huxley in Hollywood*. New York: Harper and Row.

Duncan-Jones, Katherine. 1985. "Sidney's Anacreontic." *Review of English Studies*, n.s., 36(142): 226–28.

Dundas, Judith. 1933. *Pencils Rhetorique: Renaissance Poets and the Art of Painting*. Newark: University of Delaware Press.

Dyson, A. E. 1969. "*Edwin Drood*: A Horrible Wonder Apart." *Critical Quarterly* 11(2): 138–58.

Eddy, Richard. 1887. *Alcohol in History*. Mauston, WI: Independent Order of Good Templars.

Eigner, Edwin M. 1966. *Robert Louis Stevenson and Romantic Tradition*. Princeton, NJ: Princeton University Press.

Elfenbein, Andrew. 1999. *Romantic Genius: The Prehistory of a Homosexual Role*. New York: Columbia University Press.

Eliade, Mircea. 1964. *Shamanism*. Princeton, NJ: Princeton University Press.

Eliot, T. S. 1932. *Selected Essays, 1917–32*. New York: Harcourt, Brace and Company.

Elliott, Robert C. 1982. *The Literary Persona*. Chicago: University of Chicago Press.

Ellis, Havelock. "A New Artificial Paradise." In *The Hashish Club: An Anthology of Drug Literature*, by Peter Haining, 176–88. London: Owen.

Ellis, Walter M. 1989. *Alcibiades*. London: Routledge.

Elwell-Sutton, L. P. 1988. "Omar Khayyam." In *Persian Literature*, vol. 2. ed. Ehsan Yarshater, 147–60. Albany, NY: Bibliotheca Persica.

Emboden, William. 1977. "Dionysus as a Shaman and Wine as a Magical Drug." *Journal of Psychedelic Drugs* 9(3): 187–92.

Emerson, Caryl, and Gary Saul Morson. 1987. "Penultimate Words." In *The Current in Criticism*, ed. Clayton Koelb and Virgil Lokke, 43–64. West Lafayette, IN: Purdue University Press.

Emerson, Ralph Waldo. 1981. *Selected Writings*. New York: Random House.

Engel, William E. 1993. "Bacchus's *parousia* and Montaigne's *pharmakon.*" In *Montaigne and the Gods,* ed. Daniel Martin, 185–202. Amherst, MA: Hestia.

Epstein, Arthur D. 1971. "Coleridgean Reconciliation in Euripides' *Bacchae.*" *Centennial Review* 15(2): 162–73.

Epstein, Phillip S. 1967. "A Psychiatrist Looks at Jack and the Beanstalk." In *The Book of Grass,* ed. George Andrews, 177–78. New York: Grove.

Erasmus, Desiderius. 1958. *The Praise of Folly.* Ann Arbor: University of Michigan Press.

———. 1965. *The Colloquies of Erasmus.* Chicago: University of Chicago Press.

Euripides. 1960a. *The Bacchae.* In *Complete Greek Tragedies,* vol. 3, ed. David Grene and Richmond Lattimore, 189–260. Chicago: University of Chicago Press.

———. 1960b. *Cyclops.* In *Complete Greek Tragedies,* vol. 2, ed. David Grene and Richard Lattimore, 1–42. Chicago: University of Chicago Press.

Evans, Arthur. 1988. *The God of Ecstasy: Sex-Roles and the Madness of Dionysos.* New York: St. Martin's.

Fang Dai. 1994. *Drinking, Thinking, and Writing: Ruan Ji and the Culture of His Era.* PhD diss., University of Michigan.

Faraone, Christopher A. 1992. "Sex and Power: Male-Targeting Aphrodisiacs in the Greek Magical Tradition." *Helios* 19(1–2): 92–103.

———. 1993. Introduction to *Masks of Dionysus,* ed. Thomas H. Carpenter and Christopher A. Faraone, 1–12. Ithaca, NY: Cornell University Press.

Farber, David R. 1994. *The Age of Great Dreams: America in the 1960s.* New York: Hill and Wang.

Farnell, Lewis Richard. 1977. *The Cults of the Greek States,* vol. 5. New Rochelle, NY: Caratzas Brothers.

Fausset, Hugh. 1929. *Tennyson.* London: Cape.

Fedrick, Alan. 1967. "The Love Potion in the French Prose *Tristan.*" *Romance Philology* 21(1): 23–34.

Feeley-Harnik, Gillian. 1981. *The Lord's Table: Eucharist and Passover in Early Christianity.* Philadelphia: University of Pennsylvania Press.

Fehl, Philipp. 1974. "The Worship of Bacchus and Venus in Bellini's and Titian's Bacchanals for Alfonso d'Este." *Studies in the History of Art* 6: 37–95.

Felltham, Owen. 1631. *Resolves.* London: Seile.

Ferguson, John. 1970. *Socrates: A Source Book.* Toronto: Macmillan.

Ferris, Paul. 1999. *Dylan Thomas.* London: Dent.

Festa-McCormick, Diana. 1980. "The Myth of the *Poètes Maudits.*" In *Pre-Text/Text/Context,* ed. Robert L. Mitchell, 199–216. Columbus: Ohio State University Press.

Field, Eugene. 1924. *Poems.* New York: Scribner's Sons.

Fifield, William. 1976. *Modigliani.* New York: Morrow.

Fisher, N. R. E. 1988. "Drink, *Hybris,* and the Promotion of Harmony in Sparta." In *Classical Sparta: Techniques behind Her Success,* ed. Anton Powell, 26–50. Norman: University of Oklahoma Press.

Fite, Warner. 1934. *The Platonic Legend.* London: Scribner's Sons.

Fitzgibbon, Constantine. 1965. *Life of Dylan Thomas*. London: Dent.

Flaumenhaft, Mera. 1994. "Looking Together in Athens: Euripides' *Bacchae* and the Festival of Dionysus." In *The Civic Spectacle: Essays on Drama and Community,* ed. Mera Flaumenhaft, 57–84. Lanham, MD: Rowman and Littlefield.

Foerster, Werner. 1974. *Gnosis*. Oxford: Clarendon.

F. M. de Fontenelle, Bernard. 1917. *Dialogues,* trans. Ezra Pound. London: Egoist.

Forseth, Roger. 1985. "'Alcoholite on the Altar': Sinclair Lewis, Drink, and the Literary Imagination." *Modern Fiction Studies* 31(3): 581–607.

———. 1986. "Sinclair Lewis, Drink, and the Literary Imagination." In *Sinclair Lewis at 100,* 11–26. St. Cloud, MN: St. Cloud State University.

Fortunescu, Irina. 1973. *Utrillo*. London: Abbey Library.

Franklin, James C. 1978. *Mystical Transformations: The Imagery of Liquids in the Work of Mechthild von Magdeburg*. Rutherford, NJ: Fairleigh Dickinson University Press.

Freeman, Barbara. 1986. "Irigaray at the *Symposium:* Speaking Otherwise." *Oxford Literary Review* 8(1–2): 170–77.

Freud, Sigmund. 1961. *Civilization and Its Discontents*. New York: Norton.

Frye, Northrop. 1968. *Anatomy of Criticism*. New York: Atheneum.

Fulgentius. 1971. *Fulgentius the Mythographer,* trans. Leslie George Whitbread. Columbus: Ohio State University Press.

Furst, Peter T., ed. 1972. *Flesh of the Gods: The Ritual Use of Hallucinogens*. New York: Praeger.

———. 1976. *Hallucinogens and Culture*. San Francisco: Chandler and Sharp.

Gallagher, Catherine. 1995. "Raymond Williams and Cultural Studies." In *Cultural Materialism: On Raymond Williams,* ed. Christopher Prendergast, 307–19. Minneapolis: University of Minnesota Press.

Gallagher, Catherine, and Stephen Greenblatt. 2000. "Counterhistory and the Anecdote." In *Practicing New Historicism,* 49–74. Chicago: University of Chicago Press.

Gallup, Donald C. 1998. *Eugene O'Neill and His Eleven-Play Cycle*. New Haven, CT: Yale University Press.

Garvey, Sheila Hickey. 1985. "Recreating a Myth: *The Iceman Cometh* in Washington, 1985." *Eugene O'Neill Newsletter* 9(3): 17–23.

Gasperetti, David. 1993. "The Carnivalesque Spirit of the Eighteenth-Century Russian Novel." *Russian Review* 52 (April): 166–83.

Gautier, Théophile. 1900. *Complete Works,* vol. 12. London: Athenaeum.

Gayre, Robert. 1986. *Brewing Mead*. Boulder, CO: Brewers Publications.

Geduld, Harry M. 1983. *The Definitive Dr. Jekyll and Mr. Hyde Companion*. New York: Garland.

Gellrich, Michelle. 1995. "Interpreting Greek Tragedy." In *History, Tragedy, Theory: Dialogues on Athenian Drama,* ed. Barbara Goff, 38–58. Austin: University of Texas Press.

Ghiselin, Brewster. 1952. *The Creative Process*. New York: New American Library.

Giangrande, Giuseppe. 1968. "Sympotic Literature and Epigram." In *L'Epigramme grecque,* 93–174. Geneva: Fondation Hardt pour l'étude de l'antiqité classique.

Gilmore, Thomas. 1987. *Equivocal Spirits: Alcoholism and Drinking in Twentieth-Century Literature.* Chapel Hill: University of North Carolina Press.

———. 1992. "Missed Opportunities." *Dionysos* 4(1): 19–26.

Gilson, Etienne. 1940. *The Mystical Theology of Saint Bernard.* London: Sheed and Ward.

Godwin, William. 1972. *St. Leon.* New York: Arno.

Goethe, Johann Wolfgang von. 1964. *Goethe,* ed. David Luke. Baltimore, MD: Penguin.

———. 1902. *Works,* ed. Nathan Haskell Dole. New York: Robertson, Ashford and Bentley.

Goodenough, Erwin Ramsdell. 1953–68. *Jewish Symbols in the Greco-Roman Period,* vol. 6. New York: Pantheon.

Goodman, Alice. 1985. "Falstaff and Socrates." *English* 34(149): 97–112.

Goodwin, Donald. 1970. "The Alcoholism of F. Scott Fitzgerald." *JAMA* 212(1): 86–90.

———. 1988. *Alcohol and the Writer.* New York: Andrews and McMeel.

———. 1993. "Alcohol as Muse." *Dionysos* 5(1): 3–11.

Gorer, Geoffrey. 1936. *Bali and Angkor.* Boston: Little, Brown.

Graña, Cesar. 1990. *On Bohemia: The Code of the Self-Exiled.* London: Transaction.

Grant, Marcus. 1981. "Drinking and Creativity." *British Journal on Alcohol and Alcoholism* 16: 88–93.

Grant, Michael. 1980. *Greek and Latin Authors.* New York: Wilson.

Graves, Robert. 1955. *The Greek Myths,* vol 1. Baltimore, MD: Penguin.

Greek Anthology. 1916–83. 5 vols. Cambridge, MA: Harvard University Press.

Greene, Graham. 1958. *Our Man in Havana.* New York: Viking.

Griffin, Julian. 1967. *E. T. A. Hoffmann's Kreisleriana: A Translation and Study.* Bachelor of Music thesis, Converse College.

Grimal, Pierre. 1986. *Dictionary of Classical Mythology.* New York: Blackwell.

Grube, G. M. A. 1941. *The Drama of Euripides.* London: Methuen.

Grushkin, Paul D. 1987. *The Art of Rock: Posters from Presley to Punk.* New York: Abbeville.

Hafiz. 1952. *Thirty Poems,* trans. Peter Avery and John Heath-Stubbs. London: Murray.

Haining, Peter. 1975. *The Hashish Club: An Anthology of Drug Literature.* London: Owen.

Hakim Bey. 1993. *O Tribe That Loves Boys: The Poetry of Abu Nuwas.* Amsterdam: Entimos.

Hall, Donald. 1978. *Remembering Poets.* New York: Harper and Row.

Harb, F. 1990. "Wine Poetry (khamriyyat)." In *Abbasid Belles-Lettres,* ed. Julia Ashtiany et al., 219–34. New York: Cambridge University Press.

Harding, Geoffrey. 1988. *Opiate Addiction, Morality, and Medicine.* New York: St. Martin's.

Hardwick, Elizabeth. 1947. "Fiction Chronicle." *Partisan Review* 14 (March–April): 196–200.

Harrington, Alan. 1972. *Psychopaths.* New York: Simon and Schuster.

Harrison, Jane Ellen. 1975. *Prolegomena to the Study of Greek Religion.* New York: Arno.

Hart, Pierre R. 1978. *G. R. Derzhavin: A Poet's Progress.* Columbus, OH: Slavica.

Hatfield, Henry. 1974. *Clashing Myths in German Literature: From Heine to Rilke.* Cambridge, MA: Harvard University Press.

Hawthorne, Nathaniel. 1962–94. *Centenary Edition of the Works,* 23 vols., ed. William Charvat, Roy Harvey Pearce, and Claude M. Simpson. Columbus: Ohio State University Press.

Hayman, Ronald. 1977. *Artaud and After.* Oxford: Oxford University Press.

Hayter, Alathea. 1968. *Opium and the Romantic Imagination.* Berkeley: University of California Press.

———. 1980. "'The Laudanum Bottle Loomed Large': Opium in the English Literary World in the Nineteenth Century." *Ariel* 11(4): 37–51.

Hazlitt, William. 1889. *Selections from His Writings.* London: Warne.

Heath, Stephen. 1986. "Psychopathia Sexualis: Stevenson's *Strange Case.*" *Critical Quarterly* 28(1–2): 93–108.

Hedreen, Guy Michael. 1992. *Silens in Attic Black-Figure Vase-Painting.* Ann Arbor: University of Michigan Press.

Hemingway, Ernest. 1954. "Hills Like White Elephants." In *The Short Stories,* 273–78. New York: Scribner's.

Henrichs, Albert. 1978. "Greek Maenadism from Olympias to Messalina." *Harvard Studies in Classical Philology* 82: 121–60.

———. 1979. "Greek and Roman Glimpses of Dionysos." In *Dionysos and His Circle: Ancient through Modern,* ed. Caroline Houser, 1–11. Cambridge, MA: Fogg Art Museum.

———. 1980–82. "Changing Dionysiac Identities." In *Jewish and Christian Self-Definition,* ed. E. P. Sanders, 137–60. Philadelphia: Fortress.

———. 1984a. "Loss of Self, Suffering, Violence: The Modern View of Dionysus from Nietzsche to Girard." *Harvard Studies in Classical Philology* 88: 205–40.

———. 1984b. "Male Intruders among the Maenads: The So-Called Male Celebrant." In *Mnemai: Classical Studies in Memory of Karl K. Hulley,* ed. Harold D. Evjen, 69–92. Chico, CA: Scholar's Press.

Hepworth, James. 1956. "Dionysian Elements in the Works of Thomas Mann." PhD diss., University of Utah.

Herbert, Christopher. 1974. "De Quincey and Dickens." *Victorian Studies* 17(3): 247–63.

Herbert, George. 1967. *Works,* ed. F. E. Hutchinson. Oxford: Clarendon.

Herd, Denise. 1991. "'The Paradox of Temperance': Blacks and the Alcohol Question in Nineteenth-Century America." In *Drinking: Behavior and Belief in Modern History,* ed. Susanna Barrows and Robin Room, 354–75. Berkeley: University of California Press.

Herrick, Robert. 1956. *Poetical Works,* ed. L. Martin. Oxford: Clarendon.

Hershman, D. Jablow. 1988. *The Key to Genius.* Buffalo, NY: Prometheus.

Hesiod. 1908. *The Poems and Fragments,* ed. A. W. Mair. Oxford: Clarendon.

Hill, Art. 1974. "The Alcoholic on Alcoholism." *Canadian Literature* 62: 33–48.

Hill, Reginald. 1999. *Arms and the Women*. New York: Delacorte.

Hinden, Michael. 1990. *A Long Day's Journey into Night*. Boston: Twayne.

Hinton, David. 1993. *Selected Poems of T'ao Ch'ien*. Port Townsend, WA: Copper Canyon.

Hobbes, Thomas. 1968. *Leviathan*. London: Penguin.

Hoffman, R. J. 1989. "Ritual License and the Cult of Dionysus." *Athenaeum* (Pavia) 67: 91–116.

Hoffmann, E. T. A. 1963. *Devil's Elixir*. London: Calder.

Holden, Constance. 1987. "Creativity and the Troubled Mind." *Psychology Today* (April): 9–10.

Horace. 1911. *Complete Works of Horace*. London: Dent.

Horkheimer, Max, and Theodor Adorno. 1995. *Dialectic of Enlightenment*. New York: Continuum.

Houser, Caroline. 1979. *Dionysos and His Circle: Ancient through Modern*. Cambridge, MA: Harvard University, Fogg Art Museum.

Housman, A. E. 1988. *Collected Poems and Selected Prose*. London: Penguin.

Howes, Marjorie. 1988. "The Mediation of the Feminine: Bisexuality, Homoerotic Desire, and Self-Expression in Bram Stoker's *Dracula*." *Texas Studies in Language and Literature* 30(1): 104–19.

Hubbard, M. 1975. "The Capture of Silenus." *Proceedings of the Cambridge Philological Society*, n.s., no. 21: 53–62.

Hubbard, Thomas K. 1991. *The Mask of Comedy: Aristophanes and the Intertextual Parabasis*. Ithaca, NY: Cornell University Press.

Hughes, Jim. 1999. *Altered States: Creativity under the Influence*. New York: Watson-Guptill.

Hughes, Pennethorne. 1965. *Witchcraft*. Baltimore, MD: Penguin.

Hugo, Victor. 1985. *Notre-Dame de Paris*. In *Oeuvres Complète*. Paris: Laffont.

Hunt, Leigh. 1865. "Anacreon." In *The Seer; or, Common-places Refreshed*. London: Roberts Bros.

———. 1923. *The Poetical Works*, ed. H. Milford. London: Oxford University Press.

Hutchison, William G. 1904. *Songs of the Vine*. London: Bullen.

Huxley, Aldous. 1954. *The Doors of Perception*. New York: Harper.

———. 1956. *Heaven or Hell*. New York: Harper.

———. 1977. *Moksha: Aldous Huxley's Classic Writings on Psychedelics and the Visionary Experience*, ed. Michael Horowitz and Cynthia Palmer. New York: Stonehill.

Hyland, Drew A. 1995. *Finitude and Transcendence in the Platonic Dialogues*. Albany: State University of New York Press.

Illich, Ivan. 1993. *In the Vineyard of the Text: A Commentary to Hugh's Didascalicon*. Chicago: University of Chicago Press.

Ingrams, W. H. 1923. *Abu Nuwas in Life and Legend*. Mauritius: M. Gaud and Cie.

Irving, Washington. 1978. "Rip Van Winkle." In *The Sketch Book of Geoffrey Crayon, Gent.*, ed. Haskell Springer, 28–42. Boston: Twayne.

Irving, William Henry. 1928. *John Gay's London*. Cambridge, MA: Harvard University Press.

Isaacs, Neil D., and Jack E. Reese. 1974. "Dithyramb and Paean in *A Midsummer Night's Dream*." *English Studies* 55(4): 351–57.

Isernhagen, Wolfgang. 1994. "Acid against Established Realities." In *50 Years of LSD*, ed. A. Pletscher and D. Ladewig, 121–34. New York: Parthenon.

Jaffe, Audrey. 1990. "Detecting the Beggar: Arthur Conan Doyle, Henry Mayhew, and 'The Man with the Twisted Lip.'" *Representations* 31 (summer): 96–117.

James, Henry. 1970. "Robert Louis Stevenson." In *Partial Portraits*. Ann Arbor: University of Michigan Press.

James, William. 1902. *Varieties of Religious Experience*. New York: Modern Library.

Jamison, Kay R, 1993. *Touched with Fire: Manic Depressive Illness and the Artistic Temperament*. New York: Free Press.

Janson, H. W. 1952. *Apes and Ape Lore in the Middle Ages and the Renaissance*. London: Warburg Institute.

Jaspers, Karl. 1977. *Strindberg and Van Gogh*. Tucson: University of Arizona Press.

Jastrow, Morris. 1913. "Wine in the Pentateuchal Codes." *Journal of the American Oriental Society* 33: 180–92.

Jeanneret, Michel. 1991. *A Feast of Words: Banquets and Table Talk in the Renaissance*. Chicago: University of Chicago Press.

Jennings, Lee B. 1981. "The Role of Alcohol in Hoffmann's Mythic Tales." In *Fairy Tales as Ways of Knowing*, ed. Michael M. Metzger and Katharina Mommsen, 182–94. Bern: Peter Lang.

Jonassen, Frederick B. 1991. "The Inn, the Cathedral, and the Pilgrimage of *The Canterbury Tales*." In *Rebels and Rivals: The Contestive Spirit in The Canterbury Tales*, ed. Susanna Greer Fein, David Raybin, and Peter C. Braeger, 1–36. Kalamazoo, MI: Medieval Institute.

Jonson, Ben. 1975. *Poems,* ed. Ian Donaldson. London: Oxford University Press.

Judd, Elizabeth. 1980. "Hallucinogens and the Origin of Language." *Sociolinguistics Newsletter* 11(2): 7–12.

Jung, C. G. 1953. *Psychology and Alchemy*. New York: Pantheon.

———. 1988. *Nietzsche's Zarathustra,* vol. 2. Princeton, NJ: Princeton University Press.

Juniper, William. 1933. *The True Drunkard's Delight*. London: Unicorn.

Kaiser, Walter. 1963. *Praisers of Folly*. Cambridge, MA: Harvard University Press.

Karmel, Pepe, ed. 1999. *Jackson Pollock: Interviews, Articles, and Reviews*. New York: Museum of Modern Art.

Kazin, Alfred. 1976. "'The Giant Killer': Drink and the American Writer." *Commentary* 61(3): 44–50.

Keats, John. 1973. *The Complete Poems,* ed. John Barnard. London: Penguin.

[Kenko]. 1967. *Essays in Idleness: The Tsurezuregusa of Kenko,* trans. Donald Keene. New York: Columbia University Press.

Kerenyi, Carl. 1976. *Dionysus: Archetypal Image of Indestructible Life*. Princeton, NJ: Princeton University Press.

Kershner, R. B. 1989. *Joyce, Bakhtin, and Popular Literature*. Chapel Hill: University of North Carolina Press.

Kinser, Samuel. 1986. "Presentation and Representation: Carnival at Nuremberg, 1450–1550." *Representations* 13: 1–41.

Kitson, Peter J., ed. 1996. *Coleridge, Keats, and Shelley*. London: Macmillan.

Koch, Robert A. 1978. *The Illustrated Bartsch*, vol. 15, *Early German Masters*. New York: Abaris.

Koken, John M. 1960. *Here's to It!* New York: Barnes.

Koski-Jännes, Anja. 1985. "Alcohol and Literary Creativity: The Finnish Experience." *Journal of Creative Behavior* 19(2): 120–36.

Kott, Jan. 1965. *Shakespeare Our Contemporary*. London: Methuen.

———. 1973. *The Eating of the Gods: An Interpretation of Greek Tragedy*. New York: Random House.

Kristeva, Julia. 1973. "The Ruin of a Poetics." In *Russian Formalism*, ed. Stephen Bann and John E. Bowlt, 102–21. New York: Barnes.

Kunzle, David. 1973–90. *The Early Comic Strip: Narrative Strips and Picture Stories in the European Broadsheet from c. 1450 to 1825*. Berkeley: University of California Press.

———. 1990. *The History of the Comic Strip*, vol. 2. Berkeley: University of California Press.

LaCapra, Dominick. 1983. *Rethinking Intellectual History: Texts, Contexts, Language*. Ithaca, NY: Cornell University Press.

Lachmann, Renate. 1988–89. "Bakhtin and Carnival." *Cultural Critique* 11: 115–54.

Lajer-Burcharth, Ewa. 1985. "Modernity and the Condition of Disguise: Manet's 'Absinthe-Drinker.'" *Art Journal* 45(1): 18–25.

Landor, Walter Savage. 1927–36. *Complete Works*. London: Chapman and Hall.

Laporte, Dominique. 2000. *The History of Shit*, trans. Rodolphe el-Khoury and Nadia Benabid. Cambridge, MA: MIT Press.

Laski, Marghanita. 1987. *Ecstasy*. Bloomington: Indiana University Press.

Leary, Timothy. 1982. *Changing My Mind, among Others*. Englewood Cliffs, NJ: Prentice-Hall.

Lebel, Jean-Jacques. 1967. "Theory and Practice." In *New Writers IV*, 13–49. London: Calder and Boyars.

Lee, Martin A. 1985. *Acid Dreams*. New York: Grove.

Legouis, Émile. 1926. "The Bacchic Element in Shakespeare's Plays." *Proceedings of the British Academy* 24: 115–32.

Leonard, Linda Schierse. 1989. *Witness to the Fire: Creativity and the Veil of Addiction*. New York: Random House.

Le Roy Ladurie, Emmanuel. 1979. *Carnival in Romans*. New York: Braziller.

Lesky, Albin. 1966. *A History of Greek Literature*. London: Methuen.

Levarie, Janet. 1973. "Renaissance Anacreontics." *Comparative Literature* 25(3): 221–39.

Levinson, Ronald B. 1953. *In Defense of Plato*. Cambridge, MA: Harvard University Press.

Lewis, I. M. 1971. *Ecstatic Religion: An Anthropological Study of Spirit Possession and Shamanism*. Harmondsworth, UK: Penguin.

———. 1988. "Shamanism." In *The Study of Religion, Traditional and New Religions*, ed. Peter Clarke and Stewart Sutherland, 67–77. London: Routledge.

Lewy, Hans. 1929. *Sobria ebrietas: Untersuchunger zur Geschichte der antiken Mystik.* Gliessen: A. Töpelmann.

Lightfoot, William E. 1972. "Charlie Parker: A Contemporary Folk Hero." *Keystone Folklore Quarterly* 17 (Summer): 49–54.

Lilienfeld, Jane. 1999. *Reading Alcoholisms: Theorizing Character and Narrative in Selected Novels of Thomas Hardy, James Joyce, and Virginia Woolf.* New York: St. Martin's.

Lind, L. R. 1957. *Latin Poetry in Verse Translation.* Boston: Houghton Mifflin.

Lindsay, Jack. 1934. *Medieval Latin Poets.* London: Elkin Mathews and Marrot.

Lipton, Lawrence. 1959. *The Holy Barbarians.* New York: Messner.

Lissarrague, François. 1990. *The Aesthetics of the Greek Banquet: Images of Wine and Ritual.* Princeton, NJ: Princeton University Press.

————. 1993. "On the Wildness of Satyrs." In *Masks of Dionysus,* ed. Thomas H. Carpenter and Christopher A. Faraone, 207–20. Ithaca, NY: Cornell University Press.

Lodge, David. 1990. *After Bakhtin.* New York: Routledge.

Lomberg, Jon. 1983. "The Tripping Eye." In *Psychedelic Reflections,* ed. Lester Grinspoon and James B. Bakalar, 82–90. New York: Human Sciences.

Lombroso, Cesare. 1981. *Man of Genius.* New York: Scribner's Sons.

London, Jack. 1913. *John Barleycorn.* New York: Grosset and Dunlap.

Loomis, Roger Sherman. 1975. *Arthurian Legends in Medieval Art.* Millwood, NY: Kraus Reprint.

Louth, Andrew. 1981. *The Origins of the Christian Mystical Tradition.* Oxford: Clarendon.

Lovelace, Richard. 1987. *Selected Poems,* ed. Gerald Hammond. Manchester: Carcanet.

Lowes, John Livingston. 1936. *The Road to Xanadu.* Boston: Houghton Mifflin.

Lucas, F. L. 1948. *The Decline and Fall of the Romantic Ideal.* Cambridge: University Press.

Luce, Louise Fiber. 1978. "Alchemy and the Artist in Balzac's 'Gambara.'" *Centerpoint* 3(1): 67–74.

Lucia, Salvatore Pablo, ed. 1963. *Alcohol and Civilization.* New York: McGraw-Hill.

Lucian of Samosata. 1905. *The Works . . . ,* 4 vols. Oxford: Clarendon.

Ludwig, Arnold M. 1995. *The Price of Greatness: Resolving the Creativity and Madness Controversy.* New York: Guilford.

Lundquist, James. 1973. *Sinclair Lewis.* New York: Ungar.

Lutz, H. F. 1922. *Viticulture and Brewing in the Ancient Orient.* New York: Stechart.

Lyly, John. 1902. *The Complete Works,* ed. R. Warwick Bond III. Oxford: Clarendon.

Lynch, John Patrick. 1986. "The Ancient Symposium as an Institution." *Classical Bulletin,* no. 4: 1–15.

Lyons, John D. 1974. "Artaud: Intoxication and Its Double." *Yale French Studies* 50: 120–29.

Lyu, Claire. 1994. "'High' Poetics: Baudelaire's *Le Poeme du hachisch.*" *MLN* 109(4): 698–740.

MacLaine, Alan Hugh. 1965. *Robert Fergusson.* New York: Twayne.

Maffesoli, Michel. 1993. *The Shadow of Dionysus: A Contribution to the Sociology of the Orgy.* Albany: State University of New York Press.

Magennis, Hugh. 1986a. "The Exegesis of Inebriation: Treading Carefully in Old English." *English Language Notes* 23(3): 3–6.

———. 1986b. "Water-Wine Miracles in Anglo-Saxon Saints' Lives." *English Language Notes* 23(3): 7–9.

———. 1999. *Anglo-Saxon Appetites: Food and Drink and Their Consumption in Old English and Related Literatures.* Dublin: Four Courts.

Malcolm, Andrew. 1972. *The Pursuit of Intoxication.* New York: Washington Square.

Mangan, James. 1975. "An Extraordinary Adventure in the Shades." In *The Hashish Club: An Anthology of Drug Literature,* ed. Peter Haining, 54–67. London: Owen.

Manlove, Colin. 1988. "'Closer Than an Eye': The Interconnection of Stevenson's *Dr. Jekyll and Mr. Hyde.*" *Studies in Scottish Literature* 23: 87–103.

Marchant, W. T. 1968. *In Praise of Ale; or Songs, Ballads, Epigrams, and Anecdotes Relating to Beer, Malt, and Hops.* London: Redway, 1888. Reissued by Singing Tree Press.

Marcovich, Miroslav. 1978. "Xenophanes on Drinking-Parties and Olympic Games." *Illinois Classical Studies* 3: 4–42.

Markus, Julia. 1995. *Dared and Done: The Marriage of Elizabeth Barrett Browning and Robert Browning.* New York: Knopf.

Marrus, Michael R. 1974. "Social Drinking in the *Belle Epoque.*" *Journal of Social History* 7(2): 115–41.

Marshall, Roderick. 1989. *Falstaff, the Archetypal Myth.* Shaftesbury, UK: Element.

Martin, Hubert. 1972. *Alcaeus.* New York: Twayne.

Mason, Tom. 1990. "Abraham Cowley and the Wisdom of Anacreon." *Cambridge Quarterly* 19(2): 103–37.

Masters, Robert E. L., and Jean Houston. 1968. *Psychedelic Art.* New York: Grove.

Matthews, John. 1981. *The Grail: Quest for the Eternal.* London: Thames and Hudson.

Maynard, Theodore. 1919. *A Tankard of Ale: An Anthology of Drinking Songs.* London: Macdonald.

McCarthy, John A. 1979. *Christoph Martin Wieland.* New York: Twayne.

McDonagh, Josephine. 1992. "Opium and the Imperial Imagination." In *Reviewing Romanticism,* ed. Philip W. Martin and Robin Jarvis, 116–33. New York: St. Martin's.

McGinn, Bernard. 1992. *The Foundations of Mysticism,* vol. 1. New York: Crossroads.

McGinty, Park. 1978. *Interpretation and Dionysos: Method in the Study of a God.* The Hague: Mouton.

McKenna, Terence. 1991. *The Archaic Revival, Speculations on Psychedelic Mushrooms, the Amazon, Virtual Reality, UFOs, Evolution, Shamanism, the Rebirth of the Goddess, and the End of History.* San Francisco: HarperSanFrancisco.

McNally, Sheila. 1984. "The Maenad in Early Greek Art." In *Women in the Ancient World: The Arethusa Papers*, ed. John Peradotto and J. P. Sullivan, 107–42. Albany: State University of New York Press.

McNutt, Joni G. 1993. *In Praise of Wine.* Santa Barbara, CA: Capra.

McVicker, Cecil Don. 1968. "Poe and 'Anacreon': A Classical Influence on 'The Raven.'" *Poe Studies* 1(1): 1–2.

Meisami, Julie Scott. 1991. "The Ghazal as Fiction." In *Intoxication Earthly and Heavenly:*

Seven Studies on the Poet Hafiz from Shiraz, ed. Michael Glünz and J. Christoph
  Bürgel, 88–103. Bern: Lang.
Meredith, George. 1956. "An Essay on Comedy." In *Comedy,* ed. Wylie Sypher. Gar-
  den City, NY: Doubleday.
Metzner, Ralph. 1968. *Ecstatic Adventure.* New York: Macmillan.
Mickel, Emanuel J., Jr. 1969. *The Artificial Paradises in French Literature.* Chapel Hill:
  University of North Carolina Press.
Mierau, Maurice A. 1986. "Carnival and Jeremiad: Mailer's *The Armies of the Night.*"
  Canadian Review of American Studies 17(3): 317–26.
Miles, Barry. 1998. *Jack Kerouac: King of the Beats.* New York: Holt.
Miller, Jon. 1998. "'Heaven's Good Cheer': Puritan Drinking in the Meditations of
  Edward Taylor." *Dionysos* 8(2): 30–44.
Miller, Richard. 1977. *Bohemia: The Protoculture Then and Now.* Chicago: Nelson-
  Hall.
Milligan, Barry. 1995. *Pleasures and Pains: Opium and the Orient in Nineteenth-Century
  English Culture.* Charlottesville: University Press of Virginia.
Million, Cary. 1997. "Collecting, Codifying and Commodifying Art: Several Senses
  of Psychedelic Posters." PhD diss., Temple University.
Milton, John. 1968. *Poems,* ed. John Carey and Alastair Fowler. London: Longmans.
Miner, Earl. 1971. *The Cavalier Mode from Jonson to Cotton.* Princeton, NJ: Princeton
  University Press.
Miola, Robert S. 1980. "Spenser's Anacreontics: A Mythological Metaphor." *Studies in
  Philology* 77(1): 50–66.
Moore, Thomas. 1929. *The Poetical Works,* ed. A. D. Godley. London: Oxford Uni-
  versity Press.
Morgan, Michael L. 1990. *Platonic Piety: Philosophy and Ritual in Fourth-Century
  Athens.* New Haven, CT: Yale University Press.
Morison, Samuel Eliot. 1974. *The European Discovery of America: The Southern Voy-
  ages, A. D. 1492–1616.* New York: Oxford University Press.
Mornin, Edwin. 1979. "Drinking in Joseph Roth's Novels and Tales." *International
  Fiction Review* 6(1): 80–84.
Morson, Gary Saul, and Caryl Emerson. 1990. *Mikhail Bakhtin: Creation of a Poetics.*
  Stanford, CA: Stanford University Press.
Mulroy, David. 1992. *Early Greek Lyric Poetry.* Ann Arbor: University of Michigan
  Press.
Murray, Gilbert. 1933. *Aristophanes, a Study.* Oxford: Clarendon.
Murray, Oswyn. 1983. "The Greek Symposion in History." In *Tria Corda: Scritti in
  onore di Arnaldo Momigliano,* ed. E. Gabba, 257–72. Como, Italy: Edizioni New
  Press.
———. 1990. "The Affair of the Mysteries: Democracy and the Drinking Group." In
  Sympotica: A Symposium on the Symposion, 149–61. Oxford: Clarendon.
Myers, Alan. 1988. *An Age Ago: A Selection of Nineteenth-Century Russian Poetry.* New
  York: Farrar, Straus, Giroux.

Nabokov, Vladimir. 1980. *Lectures on Literature,* ed. Fredson Bowers. New York: Harcourt Brace Jovanovich.

Nashe, Thomas. 1910. *Complete Works,* vol. 1, ed. Ronald B. McKerrow. London: Sidgwick and Jackson.

Navia, Luis E. 1985. *Socrates, The Man and His Philosophy.* Lanham, MD: University Press of America.

Neumann, Harry. 1965. "Diotima's Concept of Love." *American Journal of Philology* 81(341): 33–59.

Nevinson, Henry Woodd. 1923. *Changes and Chances.* New York: Harcourt, Brace.

Newlove, Donald. 1981. *Those Drinking Days.* New York: Horizon.

Nietzsche, Friedrich. 1993. *The Birth of Tragedy.* London: Penguin.

Nikolchina, Miglena. 1993. "Feminine Erotic and Paternal Legacy: Revisiting Plato's *Symposium.*" *Paragraph* 16(3): 239–60.

Nock, Arthur Darby. 1972. *Essays on Religion and the Ancient World.* Cambridge, MA: Harvard University Press.

Nonnus of Panopolis. 1940. *Dionysiaca,* vol. 1. Cambridge, MA: Harvard University Press.

Norlander, Torsten. 1997. *Alcohol and the Creative Process.* Göteborg, Sweden: Göteborg University, Department of Psychology.

North, Julian. 1994. "Opium and the Romantic Imagination." In *Beyond the Pleasure Dome: Writing and Addiction from the Romantics,* ed. Sue Vice, 109–17. Sheffield: Sheffield Academic Press.

Norwood, Gilbert. 1954. "The *Bacchae* and Its Riddle." *Essays on Euripidean Drama,* 52–73. Berkeley: University of California Press.

Nussbaum, Martha. 1990. Introduction to *The Bacchae of Euripides,* trans. C. K. Williams, vii–xliv. New York: Farrar, Straus, Giroux.

Nye, Andrea. 1994. "Irigaray and Diotima at Plato's Symposium." In *Feminist Interpetations of Plato,* ed. Nancy Tuana, 197–215. University Park: Pennsylvania State University Press.

Oates, Joyce Carol. 1988. "Jekyll/Hyde." *Hudson Review* 40(4): 603–8.

O'Bell, Leslie. 1984. "The Spirit of Derzavin's Anacreontic Verse." *Die Welt der Slaven* 29(1): 62–87.

O'Brien, John. 1995. *Anacreon Redivivus.* Ann Arbor: University of Michigan Press.

O'Brien, John M. 1980. "Alexander and Dionysus: The Invisible Enemy." *Annals of Scholarship* 1: 83–105.

———. 1992. "Dionysus." *Dionysos* 4(1): 3–13.

O'Brien-Moore, Ainsworth. 1924. *Madness in Ancient Literature.* Weimar: R. Wagner Sohn.

O'Connor, Ulick. 1991. *Biographers and the Art of Biography.* Dublin: Wolfhound.

O'Flaherty, Wendy Doniger. 1980. "Dionysus and Siva: Parallel Patterns in Two Pairs of Myths." *History of Religions* 20(1–2): 81–112.

Oldenburg, Ray. 1993. "Augmenting the Bar Studies." *Social History of Alcohol Review* 28–29: 30–38.

Oldham, John. 1987. *Poems,* ed. Harold Brooks. Oxford: Clarendon.

Origen. 1957. *The Song of Songs: Commentary and Homilies,* trans. R. P. Lawson. Westminster, MD: Newman.

———. 1989. *Commentary on the Gospel according to John: Books 1–10.* Washington, DC: Catholic University of America Press.

Orman, John M. 1984. *The Politics of Rock Music.* Chicago: Nelson-Hall.

Ortega y Gasset, José. 1972. "Three Bacchanalian Pictures 1911." In *Velazquez, Goya, and the Dehumanization of Art.* London: Studio Vista.

Osborne, Robin. 1985. "The Erection and Mutilation of the Hermai." *Proceedings of the Cambridge Philological Society,* n.s. 31: 47–73.

Otto, Walter F. 1965. *Dionysus: Myth and Cult.* Bloomington: Indiana University Press.

Ovid. 1958. *Metamorphosis,* trans. Horace Gregory. New York: Viking.

———. 1990. *The Love Poems,* trans. A. D. Melville. Oxford: Oxford University Press.

Pachori, Satya S. 1974–75. "Shelley's 'Indian Serenade': Hafiz and Sir William Jones." *Osmania Journal of English Studies* 11(1): 11–25.

Padel, Ruth. 1995. *Whom Gods Destroy: Elements of Greek and Tragic Madness.* Princeton, NJ: Princeton University Press.

Panter, Barry et al. 1995. *Creativity and Madness.* Burbank, CA: Aimed.

Patch, Howard Rollin. 1970. *The Other World, according to Descriptions in Medieval Literature.* New York: Octagon.

Payne, John, trans. 1907. *Flowers of France: The Renaissance Period: From Ronsard to Sainte-Amant.* London: Villon Society.

Paz, Octavio. 1973. *Alternating Currents.* New York: Viking.

Peirce, Sarah. 1988. "Visual Language and Concepts of Cult on the 'Lenaia Vases.'" *Classical Antiquity* 17(1): 59–95.

Peppiatt, Michael. 1996. *Francis Bacon: Anatomy of an Enigma.* London: Weidenfeld and Nicolson.

———. 1999. "Francis Bacon at Work." In *Francis Bacon: A Retrospective,* 25–37. New York: Abrams.

Petrarch, Francesco. 1992. *Letters of Old Age,* vol. 2. Baltimore, MD: Johns Hopkins University Press.

Petronius. 1959. *The Satyricon,* trans. William Arrowsmith. New York: Meridian.

Pettinger, Peter. 1998. *Bill Evans: How My Heart Sings.* New Haven, CT: Yale University Press.

Phillips, Margaret Mann. 1964. *The "Adages of Erasmus."* Cambridge: Cambridge University Press.

Philostratus, Flavius. 1931. *Imagines.* London: Heinemann.

Plato. 1951. *The Symposium,* trans. Walter Hamilton. London: Penguin.

———. 1961. *The Collected Dialogues,* ed. Edith Hamilton and Huntington Cairns. Princeton, NJ: Princeton University Press.

Plimpton, George, ed. 1984. *Writers at Work: Paris Review Interviews,* 6th ser. New York: Viking.

Plochmann, George Kimball. 1971. "Supporting Themes in the *Symposium.*" In *Essays in Ancient Greek Philosophy,* ed. John P. Anton and George L. Kustas, 328–44. Albany: State University of New York Press.

Plutarch. 1970. *De Iside et Osiride,* ed. J. Gwyn Griffiths. Cardiff: University of Wales Press.

———. 1961. *The Table-Talk.* In *Moralia,* vol. 9. Cambridge, MA: Harvard University Press.

Poe, Edgar Allan. 1902. *Complete Works,* 17 vols., ed. James A. Harrison. New York: Crowell.

Pollock, Walter Herries. 1879. *Lectures on French Poets.* London: C. K. Paul.

Pope, Alexander. 1903. *The Complete Poetical Works.* Boston: Houghton Mifflin.

Porter, Cole. 1992. *Complete Lyrics,* ed. Robert Kimball. New York: Da Capo.

Porter, Roy. 1993. "Consumption: Disease of the Consumer Society?" In *Consumption and the World of Goods,* ed. John Brewer and Roy Porter, 58–81. London: Routledge.

Possiedi, Paolo. 1992. "Anacreon as an Emblem in Leopardi's 'Praise of the Birds.'" In *Giacomo Leopardi: Estetica e poesia,* ed. Emilio Speciale, 101–17. Ravenna: Longo Editore.

Press, John. 1955. *The Fire and the Fountain.* New York: Oxford University Press.

Priestley, Brian. 1984. *Charlie Parker.* New York: Hippocrene.

Prior, Matthew. 1959. *Literary Works,* ed. H. Bunker Wright and Monroe K. Spears. Oxford: Clarendon.

Proehl, Geoffrey S. 1997. *Coming Home Again: American Family Drama and the Return of the Prodigal.* Madison, NJ: Fairleigh Dickinson University Press.

Quaife, G. R. 1987. *Godly Zeal and Furious Rage: The Witch in Early Modern Europe.* New York: St. Martin's.

Rabelais. 1957. *Gargantua and Pantagruel,* trans. J. M. Cohen. Harmondsworth, UK: Penguin.

Raben, Joseph. 1983. "Shelley the Dionysian." In *Shelley Revalued,* ed. Kelvin Everest. Totowa, NJ: Barnes and Noble Books.

Rang, Florens Christian. 1983. *Historische Psychologie des Karnevals,* ed. Ludwig Jäger. Berlin: Brinkmann und Bose.

Raphael, Matthew J. 2000. *Bill W. and Mr. Wilson.* Amherst: University of Massachusetts Press.

Raymond, Irving Woodworth. 1927. *The Teaching of the Early Church on the Use of Wine and Strong Drink.* New York: Columbia University Press.

Reckford, Kenneth J. 1987. *Aristophanes' Old-and-New Comedy,* vol. 1. Chapel Hill: University of North Carolina Press.

Rector, Monica. 1984. "The Code and Message of Carnival: '*Escolas-de-Samba.*'" In *Carnival!* ed. Thomas Sebeok, 37–165. Berlin: Mouton.

Reichel-Dolmatoff, G. 1987. *Shamanism and Art of the Eastern Tukanoan Indians.* Leiden: Brill.

Reid, Douglas A. 1982. "Interpreting the Festival Calendar: Wakes and Fairs as Carnivals." In *Popular Culture and Custom in Nineteenth-Century England,* ed. Robert D. Storch, 125–53. New York: St. Martin's.

Reischuck, Albert W. 1991. *Amadeo Modigliani: Art and Life*. MA thesis, Kent State University.

Relihan, Joel C. 1992. "Rethinking the History of the Literary Symposium." *Illinois Classical Studies* 17(2): 213–44.

Revard, Stella. 1991. "Cowley's *Anacreontiques* and the Translation of the Greek Anacreontea." In *Acta Conventus Neo-Latini Torontonensis: Proceedings of the Seventh International Congress of Neo-Latin Studies,* ed. Alexander Dalzell et al., 594–99. Binghamton, NY: Medieval and Renaissance Texts and Studies.

Riche, Barnabe. 1618. *The Irish Hubbub*. London: Marriot.

Rickels, Laurence A. 1988. *Aberrations of Mourning: Writing on German Crypts*. Detroit: Wayne State University Press.

Ripinsky-Naxon, Michael. 1993. *The Nature of Shamanism*. Albany: State University of New York Press.

Riu, Xavier. 1999. *Dionysism and Comedy*. Lanham, MD: Rowman and Littlefield.

Robertson, John W. 1970. *Edgar A. Poe, A Study*. New York: Haskell House.

Robinson, K. E. 1980. "The Disenchanted Restoration Lyric." *Durham University Journal* 73(1): 67–73.

Romero, Christiane Zehl. 1979. "M. G. Lewis' *The Monk* and E. T. A. Hoffmann's *Die Elixiere des Teufels*—Two Versions of the Gothic." *Neophilologus* 63: 574–82.

Ronell, Avital. 1992. *Crack Wars*. Lincoln: University of Nebraska Press.

Rorabaugh, W. J. 1979. *The Alcoholic Republic: An American Tradition*. New York: Oxford University Press.

Rose, June. 1991. *Modigliani, the Pure Bohemian*. New York: St. Martin's.

Rosen, Stanley. 1968. *Plato's Symposium*. New Haven, CT: Yale University Press.

Rosenmeyer, Patricia A. 1992. *The Poetics of Imitation: Anacreon and the Anacreontic Tradition*. Cambridge: Cambridge University Press.

Rosenmeyer, Thomas G. 1968. "Tragedy and Religion: *The Bacchae*." In *Euripides,* ed. Erich Segal, 150–70. Englewood Cliffs, NJ: Prentice-Hall.

Rothenberg, Albert. 1990. *Creativity and Madness*. Baltimore, MD: Johns Hopkins University Press.

Ruck, Carl A. P. 1986. "The Wild and the Cultivated: Wine in Euripides' *Bacchae*." In *Persephone's Quest: Ethnogens and the Origins of Religion,* ed. R. Gordon Wasson, 179–224. New Haven, CT: Yale University Press.

Rudgley, Richard. 1994. *Essential Substances: A Cultural History of Intoxicants in Society*. New York: Kodansha International.

Runia, David T. 1993. *Philo in Early Christian Literature*. Minneapolis: Fortress.

Russell, D. A., and M. Winterbottom, eds. 1972. *Ancient Literary Criticism*. Oxford: Clarendon.

Rutland, Barry. 1990. "Bakhtinian Categories and the Discourse of Postmodernism." In *Mikhail Bakhtin and the Epistemology of Discourse,* ed. Clive Thomson, 123–36. Amsterdam: Rodopi.

Rypka, Jan. 1968. *A History of Iranian Literature*. Dordrecht, Holland: D. Reidel.

Sachs, Hans. 1990. *Nine Carnival Plays,* ed. Randall W. Listerman. Ottawa: Dovehouse Editions.

Said, Edward. 1979. *Orientalism.* New York: Vintage.

Saintsbury, George. 1895. *Miscellaneous Essays.* London: n.p.

Sale, William. 1977. *Existentialism and Euripides: Sickness, Tragedy, and Divinity in the Medea, the Hippolytus, and the Bacchae.* Berwick, Australia: Aureal.

Sandblom, Philip. 1995. *Creativity and Disease.* New York: Marion Boyars.

Scaliger, J. C. 1905. *Select Translations from Scaliger's Poetics,* ed. Frederick Morgan Padelford. New York: Holt.

Schenker, Daniel. 1981. "Fugitive Articulation: An Introduction to *The Rubáiyát of Omar Khayyám.*" *Victorian Poetry* 19(1): 49–64.

Schimmel, Annemarie. 1980. *The Triumphal Sun: A Study of the Works of Jalaloddin Rumi.* London: East-West.

———. 1986. "Hafiz and His Contemporaries." In *The Cambridge History of Iran,* vol. 6, ed. Peter Jackson, 929–47. London: Cambridge University Press.

Schivelbusch, Wolfgang. 1992. *Tastes of Paradise: A Social History of Spices, Stimulants, and Intoxicants.* New York: Pantheon.

Screech, M. A. 1979. *Rabelais.* Ithaca, NY: Cornell University Press.

———. 1980a. *Ecstasy and the Praise of Folly.* London: Duckworth.

———. 1980b. "The Winged Bacchus (Pausanias, Rabelais, and Later Emblematists)." *Journal of the Warburg and Courtauld Institutes* 43: 259–61.

Scuderi, Antonio. 1996. "Cain and Abel, the Drunk and the Angel: Dario Fo and God." *Veltro: Revista della Civiltà Italiana* 40(3–4): 284–88.

Sedgwick, Eve Kosofsky. 1990. *Epistemology of the Closet.* Berkeley: University of California Press.

———. 1993. *Tendencies.* Durham, NC: Duke University Press.

Segal, Charles. 1982. *Dionysiac Poetics and Euripides' Bacchae.* Princeton, NJ: Princeton University Press.

Sells, Michael. 1996. "Bewildered Tongue: The Semantics of Mystical Union in Islam." In *Mystical Union in Judaism, Christianity, and Islam,* ed. Moshe Idel and Bernard McGinn, 87–124. New York: Continuum.

Seneca. 1929. *Seneca in Ten Volumes,* vol. 2. Cambridge, MA: Harvard University Press.

———. 1932. *Seneca's Letters to Lucilius,* vol. 2, trans. E. Phillips Barker. Oxford: Clarendon.

Seward, Desmond. 1979. *Monks and Wine.* New York: Crown.

Seymour, Richard. 1981. "Chemical Muse." *Street Pharmacologist* 5(6): 5–7, 14–17.

Seznac, Jean. 1953. *Survival of the Pagan Gods.* New York: Pantheon.

Shakespeare, William. 1969. *Complete Works,* ed. W. J. Craig. London: Oxford University Press.

Shapiro, Gary. 1990. "Translating, Repeating, Naming: Foucault, Derrida, and *The Genealogy of Morals.*" In *Nietzsche as Postmodernist,* ed. Clayton Koelb, 39–56. Albany: State University of New York Press.

Shapiro, Harold. 1988. *Waiting for the Man: The Story of Drugs and Popular Music.* New York: Morrow.

Sharpe, James. 1996. *Instruments of Darkness: Witchcraft in England, 1550–1750.* London: Hamilton.

Shaw, George Bernard. 1948. Preface to *The Miraculous Birth of Language,* by Richard Albert Wilson. New York: Philosophical Library.

Sheaffer, Louis. 1968. *O'Neill, Son and Playwright.* New York: Paragon House.

Shelley, Mary. 1990. "The Mortal Immortal: A Tale." In *The Mary Shelley Reader,* ed. Betty T. Bennett and Charles E. Robinson, 314–26. New York: Oxford University Press.

Shelley, Percy Bysshe. 1951. *Selected Poetry and Prose,* ed. Kenneth Neil Cameron. New York: Holt, Rinehart and Winston.

Sheridan, Richard Brinsley. 1957. *Six Plays.* New York: Hill and Wang.

Sherratt, Andrew. 1991. "Sacred and Profane Substances: The Ritual Use of Narcotics in Later Neolithic Europe." In *Sacred and Profane,* ed. Paul Garwood et al., 50–64. Oxford: Oxford University Committee for Archaeology.

Shilin, Tan. 1992. *The Complete Works of Tao YuanMing.* Hong Kong: Joint Publishing (H.K.).

Showalter, Elaine. 1986. "Syphilis, Sexuality, and the Fiction of the Fin de Siècle." In *Sex, Politics, and Science in the Nineteenth-Century Novel,* ed. Ruth Bernard Yeazell, 88–115. Baltimore, MD: Johns Hopkins University Press.

Sider, David. 1980. "Plato's Symposium as a Dionysian Festival." *Quaderni urbinati di cultura classica* 33: 41–56.

Sidky, H. 1997. *Witchcraft, Lycanthropy, Drugs, and Disease: An Anthropological Study of the European Witch-Hunts.* New York: Lang.

Sidney, Sir Philip. 1951. "An Apologie for Poetrie." In *The Great Critics,* ed. James Harry Smith and Edd Winfield Parks, 190–232. New York: Norton.

Silver, Isidore. 1961. *Ronsard and the Hellenic Renaissance in France.* St. Louis, MO: Washington University.

Simon, Andre. 1948. *Drink.* London: Burke.

———. 1964. *Wine in Shakespeare's Days and Shakespeare's Plays.* London: Curwen.

Sinclair, Andrew. 2000. *Dylan the Bard: A Life of Dylan Thomas.* New York: Dunne.

Sinclair, Upton. 1956. *The Cup of Fury.* Great Neck, New York: Channel.

Siskin, Clifford. 1988. *The Historicity of Romantic Discourse.* New York: Oxford University Press.

Slocombe, George. 1969. *Rebels of Art.* Port Washington, NY: Kennikat.

Smith, Anne, ed. 1978. *The Art of Malcolm Lowry.* New York: Barnes and Noble.

Smith, J. B. 1991. "Grinding Old People Young: A Continental Theme in Irish and English Tradition." *Ulster Folklife* 37: 62–70.

Smith, Margaret. 1928. *Rabi'a the Mystic.* Cambridge: Cambridge University Press.

Smith, Michael Harold. 1975. *The Measureless Caverns: Coleridge's "Kubla Khan" and the Critics.* PhD diss., Pennsylvania State University.

Smith, Sir William. 1967. *Dictionary of Greek and Roman Biography and Mythology*. 3 vols. New York: AMS.

Snyder, Gary. 1980. *The Real Work: Interview and Talks*. New York: New Directions.

Solomon, David, ed. 1964. *LSD, the Consciousness-Expanding Drug*. New York: Putnam's Sons.

———. 1966. *The Marijuana Papers*. Indianapolis: Bobbs-Merrill.

Sophocles. 1946. *The Searching Satyrs*, trans. Roger Lancelyn Green. Leicester, UK: Ward.

Sournia, Jean-Charles. 1990. *A History of Alcoholism*. Oxford: Blackwell.

———. 1994. "Alcoholism, Gambling and Creativity." In *Beyond the Pleasure Dome: Writing and Addiction from the Romantics*, ed. Sue Vice, 58–61. Sheffield, England: Sheffield Academic Press.

Southern, John. 1938. *Pandora*. New York: Columbia University Press.

Spenser, Edmund. 1999. *The Shorter Poems*, ed. Richard A. McCabe. New York: Penguin.

Spilka, Mark. 1960. "The Necessary Stylist." *Modern Fiction Studies* 6(4): 283–97.

Stallybrass, Peter, and Allon White. 1986. *The Politics and Poetics of Transgression*. Ithaca, NY: Cornell University Press.

Stam, Robert. 1989. *Subversive Pleasures: Bakhtin, Cultural Criticism, and Film*. Baltimore, MD: Johns Hopkins University Press.

Stanislawski, Dan. 1975. "Dionysus Westward: Early Religions and the Economic Geography of Wine." *Geographical Review* 65(4): 427–44.

Steadman, John M. 1965. "Tantalus and the Dead Sea Apples." *JEGP* 64(1): 35–40.

Steele, Richard. 1899. *Tatler*, ed. George A. Aitken. London: Duckworth.

Steiner, Deborah. 1986. *The Crown of Song: Metaphor in Pindar*. New York: Oxford University Press.

Stephens, John. 1972. "The Mead of Poetry." *Neophilologus* 56(3): 259–68.

Sterling, William Hilton. 1970. *The Wedding at Cana in Western Art of the 14th, 15th, 16th Centuries*. 2 vols. PhD diss., University of Iowa.

Stevens, Jay. 1987. *Storming Heaven: LSD and the American Dream*. New York: Atlantic Monthly Press.

Stevenson, Robert Louis. 1979. *The Strange Case of Dr. Jekyll and Mr. Hyde*. Harmondsworth, UK: Penguin.

Stewart, Marilyn. 1984. "Carnival and *Don Quixote*: The Folk Tradition of Comedy." In *The Terrain of Comedy*, ed. Louise Cowan, 143–62. Dallas: Dallas Institute of Humanities and Culture.

Stock, R. D. 1989. *The Flutes of Dionysus: Daemonic Enthrallment in Literature*. Lincoln: University of Nebraska Press.

Stoker, Bram. 1983. *Dracula*. Oxford: Oxford University Press.

Stravinsky, Igor. 1962. *Chroniques de ma Vie*. Paris: Éditions Denoël.

Streit, Clarence K. 1946. *Hafiz in Quatrains: A Transfusion Presenting the Spirit of the Persian Poet*. New York: Abramson.

Strich, Fritz. 1949. *Goethe and World Literature*. London: Routledge and Kegan Paul.

Sullivan, John Michael. 1981. *Women, Wine, and Song: Three Minor Genres of Seventeenth-Century British Poetry*. PhD diss., University of Minnesota.

Sullivan, J. W. N. 1960. *Beethoven: His Spiritual Development*. New York: Vintage.

Suther, Marshall. 1965. *Visions of Xanadu*. New York: Columbia University Press.

Sutton, Dana Ferrin. 1974. "Sophocles' Dionysicus." *Eos* 62: 205–26.

Suzuki, Daisetz T. 1959. *Zen and Japanese Culture*. New York: Pantheon.

Swarzenski, Hanns. 1951. "The Battle between Carnival and Lent." *Bulletin of the Museum of Fine Arts* (Boston) 49, no. 275: 2–11.

Symonds, John Addington. 1966. *Wine, Women, and Song: Medieval Latin Students' Songs*. New York: Cooper Square.

Symons, Arthur. 1929. *Studies in Strange Souls*. London: Sawyer.

Taylor, Anya. 1991. "Coleridge and Alcohol." *Texas Studies in Language and Literature* 33(3): 355–72.

———. 1999. *Bacchus and Romantic England: Writers and Drink, 1780–1830*. New York: St. Martin's.

Taylor, Bayard. 1854. "The Vision of Hashish." *Knickerbocker Magazine* (April): 402–8.

———. 1855. *Poems of the Orient*. Boston: Ticknor and Fields.

Taylor, Edward. 1960. *Poems*, ed. Donald E. Stanford. New Haven, CT: Yale University Press.

Teçusan, Manuela. 1990. "*Logos Sympotikos:* Patterns of the Irrational in Philosophical Drinking: Plato outside the *Symposium*." In *Sympotica: A Symposium on the Symposium,* ed. Oswyn Murray, 238–62. Oxford: Clarendon.

Tek Chand. 1974. *Gin or Genius*. Bombay: Bharatiya Vidya Bhavan.

Thomas, D. M. 1981. *Comedy, Criticism, and Cosmic Despair: Changing Views of the Drunkard in the Victorian Novel*. PhD diss., Indiana University.

Thomas, Keith. 1971. *Religion and the Decline of Magic*. London: Weidenfeld and Nicolson.

Thompson, E. P. 1966. *The Making of the English Working Class*. New York: Vintage.

Thormahlen, Marianne. 1993. *Rochester*. New York: Cambridge University Press.

Tibullus. 1972. *Poems*, trans. Philip Dunlop. Harmondsworth, UK: Penguin.

Tigerstedt, E. N. 1970. "*Furor Poeticus:* Poetic Inspiration in Greek Literature before Democritus and Plato." *Journal of the History of Ideas* 31(2): 163–78.

Toal, M. F., ed. 1959. *The Sunday Sermons of the Great Fathers*. Chicago: Regnery.

Tolstoy, Leo. 1998. "Why Do Men Stupefy Themselves." In *Readings on Fyodor Dostoyevsky,* ed. Tamara Johnson, 63–66. San Diego, CA: Greenhaven.

Toussaint-Samat, Maguelonne. 1992. *A History of Food*. Oxford: Blackwell Reference.

Tremlett, George. 1992. *Dylan Thomas*. New York: St. Martin's.

Trevelyan, Humphrey. 1941. *Goethe and the Greeks*. Cambridge: University Press.

Trilling, Lionel. 1965. *Beyond Culture*. New York: Harcourt Brace Jovanovich.

———. 1978. *The Opposing Self*. New York: Harcourt Brace Jovanovich.

Tucker, Susie I. 1972. *Enthusiasm*. Cambridge: Cambridge University Press.

Tyler, Parker. 1989. "Dragtime and Drugtime, or, Film a la Warhol." In *Andy Warhol: Film Factory,* ed. Michael O'Pray, 94–103. London: BFI.

Utrillo's White Period. n.d. Los Angeles: Dalzell Hatfield Galleries.

Vaughan, Henry. 1965. *The Complete Poetry,* ed. French Fogle. New York: New York University Press.

Veeder, William, and Gordon Hirsch. 1988. *Dr. Jekyll and Mr. Hyde after One Hundred Years.* Chicago: University of Chicago Press.

Verdeyen, Paul. 1994. *Ruusbroec and His Mysticism.* Collegeville, MN: Liturgical.

Vernant, Jean-Pierre, and Pierre Vidal-Naquet. 1988. *Myth and Tragedy in Ancient Greece.* New York: Zone.

Verrall, A. W. 1910. *The Bacchants of Euripides.* Cambridge: Cambridge University Press.

Vice, Sue. 1992. "The *Volcano* of a Postmodern Lowry." In *Swinging the Maelstrom: New Perspectives on Malcolm Lowry,* ed. Sherrill Grace, 136–48. Montreal: McGill-Queen's University Press.

von Strassburg, Gottfried. 1967. *Tristan.* Harmondsworth, UK: Penguin.

Waddell, Helen. 1927. *The Wandering Scholars.* Boston: Houghton Mifflin.

———. 1929. *Mediaeval Latin Lyrics.* London: Constable.

Wakefield, Dan. 1992. *New York in the Fifties.* Boston: Houghton Mifflin/Seymour Lawrence.

———. 1994. "Hamill: A Drinking Life: A Memoir." *Nation,* February 7: 166–68.

Walker, John. 1956. *Bellini and Titian at Ferrara: A Study of Styles and Tastes.* London: Phaidon.

Waller, Edmund. 1968. *Poems,* ed. G. Thorn Drury. New York: Greenwood.

Warde, Newell E. 1978. *Johann Peter Uz and German Anacreontism: The Emancipation of the Aesthetic.* Frankfurt: P. Lang.

Warner, Nicholas. 1997. *Spirits of America: Intoxication in Nineteenth-Century American Literature.* Norman: University of Oklahoma Press.

Waterfield, Robin. 1994. Introduction to *Plato's Symposium,* xi–xl. New York: Oxford University Press.

Watson, Rowland. 1951. *Merry Gentlemen, A Bacchanalian Scrapbook.* London: T. W. Laurie.

Weales, Gerald. 1969. "Eugene O'Neill, *The Iceman Cometh.*" In *Landmarks of American Writing,* ed. Hennig Cohen, 353–67. New York: Basic.

Weinberg, Florence. 1972. *The Wine and the Will: Rabelais's Bacchic Christianity.* Detroit: Wayne State University Press.

Weintraub, Stanley. 1980. "Medicine and the Biographer's Art." In *Medicine and Literature,* ed. Enid Rhodes Peschel, 128–39. New York: N. Watson Academic.

Wensinck, A. J. 1969. *Mystic Treatises by Isaac of Ninevah.* Wiesbaden: Dr. Martin Sändig oHG.

Werner, Alfred. 1974. "The Lonely World of Maurice Utrillo." *Modern Artist* 38 (fall): 40–45.

West, James. 1998. *William Styron, a Life.* New York: Random House.

Whelan, Brent. 1988. "Counter-culture and the Postmodern. *Cultural Critique* (winter): 63–86.

Wiedemann, Erik. 1976. "Songs of the Viper." *Musik and Froskning* 2: 116–30.

Wilde, Oscar. 1948. "The Decay of Lying." In *The Eighteen-Nineties,* ed. Martin Secker, 525–54. London: Richards Press.

Wilder, Thornton. 1977. *The Alcestiad.* New York: Harper and Row.

Wilkins, John. 2000. *The Boastful Chef: The Discourse of Food in Ancient Greek Comedy.* Oxford: Oxford University Press.

Williams, Clyde V. 1969. *Taverners, Tapsters, and Topers: A Study of Drinking and Drunkenness in the Literature of the English Renaissance,* vol. 1. PhD diss., Louisiana State University.

Williams, George Walton. 1963. *Image and Symbol in the Sacred Poetry of Richard Crashaw.* Columbia: University of South Carolina Press.

Williams, J. D. Lewis, and T. A. Dowson. 1988. "The Signs of All Times: Entoptic Phenomena in Upper Palaeolithic Art." *Current Anthropology* 29(2): 201–46.

Wilson, Edmund. 1941. "Philoctetes: The Wound and the Bow." In *The Wound and the Bow,* 272–95. Cambridge, MA: Houghton Mifflin.

Wilson, Elizabeth. 2000. *Bohemians: The Glamorous Outcasts.* New Brunswick, NJ: Rutgers University Press.

Wilson, Jean. 1987. "'Eine Genre kopieren': Convention and Conversion in Hofmannsthal's *Der Schwierige*." *Seminar* 23(3): 227–35.

Wilson, Ross. 1969. "The Dictionary and Drink." In *The New Rambler,* 24–43. London: Johnson Society.

Wimsatt, William K., Jr., and Cleanth Brooks. 1957. *Literary Criticism: A Short History.* New York: Vintage.

Winandy, André. 1974. "Rabelais's Barrel." *Yale French Studies* 50: 8–25.

Wind, Edgar. 1967. *Pagan Mysteries in the Renaissance.* Harmondsworth, UK: Penguin.

Winick, Charles. 1959. "The Use of Drugs by Jazz Musicians." *Social Problems* 7: 240–53.

———. 1961. "How High the Moon: Jazz and Drugs." *Antioch Review* 21(1): 53–68.

Winnington-Ingram, R. P. 1969. *Euripides and Dionysus: An Interpretation of the Bacchae.* Amsterdam: Hakkert.

Wolfson, Harry Austryn. 1962. *Philo.* Cambridge, MA: Harvard University Press.

Woodruff, Paul. 1998. Introduction to *Euripides' Bacchae,* ix–xlii. Indianapolis: Hackett.

Wordsworth, William. 1974. *Prose Works,* ed. W. J. B. Owen and Jane Worthington Smyser. Oxford: Clarendon.

Wright, Thomas. 1875. *A History of Caricature and Grotesque in Literature and Art.* London: Chatto.

———. 1968. *The Latin Poems Commonly Attributed to Walter Mapes.* New York: Johnson Reprint.

Xenophon. 1996. *The Shorter Socratic Writings,* ed. Robert C. Bartlett. Ithaca, NY: Cornell University Press.

Yohannan, John D. 1977. *Persian Poetry in England and America.* Delmar, NY: Caravan.

Youngquist, Paul. 1999. "Rehabilitating Coleridge: Poetry, Philosophy, Excess." *ELH* 66: 885–909.

Zabus, Chantal. 1998. "The Yoruba Bacchae." In *(Un)Writing Empire,* ed. Theo D'Haen, 203–28. Amsterdam: Rodapi.

Zaehner, R. C. 1957. *Mysticism, Sacred and Profane.* London: Oxford University Press.

Zola, Émile. 1970. *L'Assommoir.* London: Penguin.

Publication History

An earlier version of chapter 2 appeared in *Texas Studies in Literature and Language* 42, no. 3 (2000): 314–45. Copyright 2000 by the University of Texas Press. All rights reserved.

An earlier version of chapter 8 appeared in *Mosaic* 30, no. 2 (1997): 1–18. Reprinted with permission of *Mosaic*.

Excerpts from "Wine Poetry (khamriyyat)," by F. Harb, are from *Abbasid Belles-Lettres*, ed. Julia Ashtiany et al. (New York: Cambridge University Press, 1990), 219–34. Reprinted with permission of Cambridge University Press.

Excerpt from *Alceus*, by Hubert Martin (New York: Twayne, 1972). Copyright 1972 Twayne Publishers. Reprinted with permission of The Gale Group.

Excerpt from *Three Archaic Poets: Archilochus, Alcaeus, Sappho,* by Anne Pippin Burnett (Cambridge, MA: Harvard University Press, 1983). Reprinted with permission of Duckworth Publishers.

Excerpt from translation of Anacreon by Patricia A. Rosenmeyer is from *The Poetics of Imitation: Anacreon and the Anacreontic Tradition* (Cambridge: Cambridge University Press, 1992). Reprinted with permission of Cambridge University Press.

Citation of Archilochus is from *The Well-Read Muse: Present and Past in Callimachus and the Hellenistic Poets,* by Peter Bing (Göttingen: Vandenhoeck and Ruprecht, 1988).

Excerpts from Euripides, "The Bacchae," from *Complete Greek Tragedies*, vol. 3, ed. David Grene and Richmond Lattimore (Chicago: University of Chicago Press). Reprinted with permission of University of Chicago Press.

Excerpts from Hafiz, *Thirty Poems,* trans. Peter Avery and John Heath-Stubbs (London: Murray, 1952), 54. Reprinted with permission of John Murray (Publishers) Ltd.

Excerpt from Robert H. Bower and Earl Miner, *Japanese Court Poetry* (Stanford, CA: Stanford University Press, 1961). Reprinted with permission of Stanford University Press.

Index

Hayter, Alathea, 58, 133, 181, 183, 184
Hazlitt, William, 120, 186
Heath, Robert, 25
Hedreen, Guy, 167
Heine, Heinrich, 110
Hemingway, Ernest, xvii, 99, 113, 115, 121, 127–28, 181
Hendrix, Jimi, 115
Henrichs, Albert, 6, 40–41, 89, 109
Henry, O., 177
Heraclitus, 39, 175
Herbert, George, 4, 91
Herd, Denise, 72
Herodotus, 141
Herrick, Robert, vii, 9, 14, 23, 103, 158, 163, 181
Hesiod, 105, 158
Hicks, George, 171
Hill, Reginald, 110
history, xviii, xx; cultural history, xvi
Hobbes, Thomas, 73
Hoffmann, E. T. A., 68, 108, 116–17, 135, 180
Hogarth, William, xv
Hogg, James, 107
Hölderlin, Friedrich, 110
Hollar, Wenzel (Wenceslaus), 93
Hollywood film, xv, 72, 171
Homer, 40, 102, 105, 126, 156, 160, 164
homosexuality, 107, 155, 159, 169
Hopkins, Gerard Manley, 11, 72, 75
Horace, 18, 21, 24, 27, 102, 106, 109, 115, 117, 125, 126, 157, 177, 181
Horkheimer, Max, xviii
Houser, Caroline, 90
Housman, A. E., 22, 34, 101
Houston, Jean, 174
Howe, Julia Ward, 116
Hugo, Victor, 144, 186
humanism, 7, 79
Hunt, Leigh, 24, 163
Husserl, Edmund, xviii
Huxley, Aldous, 77, 84–86, 115

Huysmans, J.-K. (Joris-Karl), 106
Hyginus, 165

Icarius, 157
Illich, Ivan, 77
Image, Selwyn, 178
Ingoldsby Legends, The , 91
inspiration, artistic, xx, 99–138, 178
intoxication: duality, xiv, 4, 45; euphoria, 17, 19–27, 67, 73, 142–43, 160, 161; pain of, xiv; spiritual, xx, 78–97, 99, 101, 172
Irving, Washington, 68, 150–51
Isaac Bishop of Ninevah, 171, 172
Isernhagen, Wolfgang, 112

James, Henry, 170
James, William, 3, 58, 77, 78, 84–85, 184
Jamshid, 156–58
Jarry, Alfred, 109
Jeanneret, Michel, 19
Jesus Christ, 37, 89–90, 175
John Barleycorn, 158
John Chrysostom, Saint, 95, 171
John of the Cross, Saint, 78, 81, 171, 172
Johnson, Lionel, 125, 178
Johnson, Samuel, 32, 142, 181
Jonson, Ben, 13, 103, 117, 137
Jordan, Thomas, 162
Joyce, James, 112
Judd, Elizabeth, 156
Jung, Carl, 86, 91, 112, 146
Juniper, William, 90
Juvenal, 42

Karoli, Christa, 96
Kast, Erik, 85
Keats, John, 15, 20, 34
Kekulé, August, 177
Kenko, 161
Kerouac, Jack, 182, 184
Kersten, Hermann, 168
Kesey, Ken, 85, 114, 124, 184

Marty Roth taught in the English department at the University of Minnesota for thirty-seven years and is now an independent scholar. Among his publications are *Comedy and America: The Lost World of Washington Irving* and *Foul and Fair Play: Reading Genre in Classic Detective Fiction*.